★ ★ ★ ★ ★

"This compelling account of Lincoln and Douglass's friendship is the story of America itself and it shows how intertwined race is with our history. Kilmeade understands that if we don't acknowledge our complex past, we'll never be the country we dream of being."
—**BRAD MELTZER,** coauthor of *The Lincoln Conspiracy*

"Accessible, accurate, inspiring, and timely."
—**VICTOR DAVIS HANSON,** senior fellow at the Hoover Institution and author of *The Dying Citizen*

"*The President and the Freedom Fighter* should be in every home, school, and library in our country."
—**JOHN CRIBB,** author of *Old Abe*

"Brian Kilmeade is a master!"
—**TIM GREEN,** author of *Football Genius* and *Unstoppable*

"To the immense benefit of the nation, two giants of America's story are beautifully captured in this highly readable account of how their extraordinary lives intertwined. A must read to understand today's highly complex discussions of race and social justice."
—**ADMIRAL JAMES STAVRIDIS, PHD, U.S. NAVY (RETIRED),** author of *Sailing True North*

NEW YORK TIMES BESTSELLER

# THE PRESIDENT AND THE
# FREEDOM FIGHTER

# THE
# PRESIDENT
## AND THE
# FREEDOM
# FIGHTER

ABRAHAM LINCOLN,
FREDERICK DOUGLASS,
*and* THEIR BATTLE *to* SAVE
AMERICA'S SOUL

## BRIAN KILMEADE

SENTINEL

SENTINEL
An imprint of Penguin Random House LLC
penguinrandomhouse.com

First published in hardcover in the United States by Sentinel,
an imprint of Penguin Random House LLC, in 2021.

This paperback edition with a new afterword and updated epilogue published in 2022.

Most Sentinel books are available at a discount when purchased in quantity for sales promotions or corporate use. Special editions, which include personalized covers, excerpts, and corporate imprints, can be created when purchased in large quantities. For more information, please call (212) 572-2232 or e-mail specialmarkets@penguinrandomhouse.com. Your local bookstore can also assist with discounted bulk purchases using the Penguin Random House corporate Business-to-Business program. For assistance in locating a participating retailer, e-mail B2B@penguinrandomhouse.com.

Owing to limitations of space, image credits may be found on pages 299–301.

ISBN 9780525540588 (trade paperback)

Library of Congress Cataloging-in-Publication Data

Names: Kilmeade, Brian, author.
Title: The president and the freedom fighter : Abraham Lincoln, Frederick Douglass,
and their battle to save America's soul / Brian Kilmeade.
Identifiers: LCCN 2021024463 (print) | LCCN 2021024464 (ebook) |
ISBN 9780525540571 (hardcover) | ISBN 9780525540601 (ebook)
Subjects: LCSH: Lincoln, Abraham, 1809–1865—Friends and associates. |
Douglass, Frederick, 1818–1895—Friends and associates. | Slavery—Law and legislation—United
States—History. | Slaves—Emancipation—United States. | Presidents—United States—Biography. |
Abolitionists—United States—Biography. | United States—Politics and government—1849–1877. |
United States—History—1849–1877.
Classification: LCC E457.2 .K49 2021 (print) | LCC E457.2 (ebook) | DDC 973.7092—dc23
LC record available at https://lccn.loc.gov/2021024463
LC ebook record available at https://lccn.loc.gov/2021024464

Printed in the United States of America
1st Printing

BOOK DESIGN BY MEIGHAN CAVANAUGH

*For all the teachers who have dedicated their careers to showing young learners that America is a truly exceptional nation— not because we are perfect, but because we try to be.*

Liberty has been won. The battle for
Equality is still pending.

# CONTENTS

———◆———

# PREAMBLE

We hold these truths to be self-evident, that all men are
created equal, that they are endowed by their Creator with
certain unalienable Rights, that among these are Life, Liberty and the pursuit of Happiness.

—DECLARATION OF INDEPENDENCE, JULY 4, 1776

I n an early draft of the Declaration of Independence, Thomas
Jefferson called slavery "a cruel war against human nature itself."[1]
James Madison argued that "it would be wrong to admit in the
Constitution the idea that there could be property in men."[2] Benjamin
Franklin, a former slaveholder, described slavery as "an atrocious de-
basement of human nature."[3] But in the early days of the republic, slav-
ery remained legal, the law of the land.

The Founders recognized that slavery, which was still practiced on
every continent, threatened the new nation's foundation. But the men
who possessed the genius to launch a country that changed the world
could not agree upon a way to end the institution of human bondage.
The closest they came was to acknowledge, as Jefferson confided sadly

to a friend, "We have the wolf by the ear, and we can neither hold him, nor safely let him go."

Every generation since—including our own—has grappled with this legacy of racial inequity, bequeathed by our political parents. In 1861, that inheritance threatened to destroy the United States in a bloody civil war. No longer was it possible to ignore the question of whether the Declaration's ideals of "Life, Liberty and the pursuit of Happiness" applied to all people. But how could a practice that was so much a part of the nation's way of life be abolished? And could the United States survive the abolition?

The job of guiding the nation to a fairer future fell to two remarkable Americans, an unexpected pair. One was White, born impoverished on a frontier farm, the other Black, a child of slavery who had risked his life escaping to freedom in the North. Without fancy pedigrees, neither had had an easy path to influence. No one would have expected them to become friends—or to change the country. But Abraham Lincoln and Frederick Douglass believed in their nation's greatness and were determined to make the grand democratic experiment live up to its ideals. Sharing little more than the conviction that slavery was evil, the two men's paths converged, and they would ultimately succeed where the Founders fell short.

This is their story.

# THE PRESIDENT AND THE
# FREEDOM FIGHTER

# ONE

# FROM THE BOTTOM UP

I do not remember to have ever met a slave who could tell of his birthday.

—FREDERICK DOUGLASS, 1845

Abraham Lincoln had a problem. His flatboat, carried by the rush of spring waters, had run aground atop a mill dam in the Sangamon River. The square bow of the eighty-foot-long boat hung over the dam, cantilevered like a diving board. Meanwhile, the stern was sinking lower and lower as it took on water. If Lincoln didn't think of something quickly, the vessel might break apart.

The young man had built the boat with a plan in mind. Along with his cousin, he would take on cargo, travel down the river from central Illinois to New Orleans, and there dismantle the boat, selling both its timber and the cargo on behalf of a man willing to underwrite the venture. Together, he and his cousin had cut down trees for lumber upstream from where they were now marooned. They had built the boat and loaded it with dried pork, corn, and live hogs. All had seemed well when they set off only hours before, but now, on April 19, 1831, far from his intended destination, Lincoln had to do something to save his boat and his cargo.

As goods slid slowly astern in the tilting craft, Lincoln went into action. Removing his boots, hat, and coat, he improvised. First, he and his two-man crew shifted most of the goods to the nearby shore. Next, while he hurriedly bored a large hole with a hand drill, his team began rolling the remaining cargo of heavy barrels forward, thereby shifting the boat's center of gravity.

The strategy worked: As the flatboat's bow began to tilt downward, water poured out the hole. As the boat got lighter, it rose in the water. After plugging the hole, Lincoln and his men, helped by the spring currents, managed to ease the box-like craft clear of the dam.

The crowd of villagers that had gathered to observe the spectacle of a sinking boat was astonished. No one had seen anything like it. But then they had also never met Abraham Lincoln, just two months beyond his twenty-second birthday. At first sight, he was unmistakably a country bumpkin, dressed in ill-fitting clothes that exaggerated his six-foot, four-inch height, with long arms and exposed ankles sticking out of too-short shirts and homespun trousers. He made, said one observer, "a rather Singular grotesque appearance." But the young man who saved the boat possessed a loose-limbed grace that disguised both unexpected strength and a driving ambition to make something of himself. Weighing over two hundred pounds, he could lift great weights and throw a cannonball farther than anyone around.[1] He ran and jumped with the best of his peers.

To the people he met, the young man's appearance quickly became secondary. "When I first [saw] him," reported one New Salemite, "i thought him a Green horn. His Appearance was very od [but] after all this bad Apperance I Soon found [him] to be a very intelligent young man."[2] Lincoln surprised people, who found he was not an illiterate rube but a man with a lively wit and keen intelligence.

He impressed not only that day's onlookers but also the owner of the flatboat. After completing the trip to New Orleans, Lincoln returned to New Salem to accept the man's offer to clerk at a new general store. He would sell foodstuffs, cloth, hardware, tobacco, gunpowder, boots, whiskey, and other goods to the people of New Salem and the local farmers who visited the little market town to sell their grains.

Like "a piece of floating driftwood," as Lincoln later described himself, he accidentally lodged at New Salem.[3] He would establish a new and happy life there, a world apart from his childhood in the backwoods.

# "THE SHORT AND SIMPLE ANNALS OF THE POOR"*

Before striking out on his own, as Abraham Lincoln himself would tell the story, he had been under the thumb of his hard-luck father.

Born during the Revolution, Thomas Lincoln was still a boy when his family, following in the footsteps of distant cousin Daniel Boone, left the Shenandoah Valley for the territory known as Kentucky. Barely two years later, in 1786, Thomas's father, Abraham, died when planting corn in a field, shot by a roving Native American war party. His entire estate went to the eldest son, leaving the youngest, Thomas, destitute, "a wandering laboring boy [who] grew up literally without education."[4]

Thomas Lincoln eventually saved enough money to buy a farm in Hardin County and, in 1806 took Nancy Hanks as his wife. The following year they became parents, with the birth of daughter Sarah. Three

---

* When asked about his childhood, Lincoln explained that his early years weren't worth a close look. His first two decades could be summed up, he said, as "The short and simple annals of the poor," quoting a 1750 poem by Thomas Gray, "Elegy Written in a Country Churchyard."

years later, the little family expanded again with the arrival of a son, Abraham, born on February 12, 1809, and named for his grandfather.

Unfortunately for baby Abraham, the Lincoln family's stability was short-lived. Before he turned two, poor soils forced the family to abandon their first log cabin for more fertile ground a few miles away. Just five years later, after a title dispute over land ownership, the Lincolns started yet again, this time moving across the Ohio River to a crude, dirt-floored home in Indiana. The family lived a life of long days of work, brutally cold winter nights, and next to no comforts.

Then life got even tougher. Nancy Lincoln fell ill with milk sickness, poisoned by milk from a cow that had eaten snakeroot while grazing in the forest. After a week of watching his mother suffer acute intestinal pains and persistent vomiting, Abraham Lincoln was left motherless at age nine.

Fourteen months later, Thomas Lincoln remarried. The arrival of widow Sarah Bush Lincoln was a bright spot in the boy's hardscrabble childhood. "Mama," as Abraham called his stepmother, brought three children with her. As she blended two families into one, Sarah became the boy's "best friend in the world."[5]

He would never express such affection for his father; the son would remember Thomas Lincoln as a taskmaster. At age eight, Lincoln later said, his father "[put] an axe put into his hands . . . and [until] his twenty-third year, he was almost constantly handling that most useful instrument."[6] Virtually all the work on the farm was handwork, the tools crude, and the chores many, with livestock to care for, fields to plant, wood to cut and split, and gardens to tend. Abraham attended school only at the rare times when there wasn't other work to be done, and Thomas always seemed to have more tasks for his growing son. By law, boys at that time were effectively indentured servants obliged to work for their fathers until they came of age, and Thomas took full advantage. He hired Abraham out to other farmers and kept the wages his son earned. Even when Abraham hired himself out as a boatman in his late teens, the wages he earned belonged to his father.

Thomas was known to beat Abraham, and he kept him at work on the farm so much that the boy got less than one full year of formal schooling in his entire childhood, never attending classes after he turned fifteen. But Abraham would not be held back. Few as they were, his school days inspired in him an intense love of learning. He was eager for knowledge, looking for it wherever he could. "He must understand Every thing—even to the smallest thing—Minutely and Exactly," Sarah would remember years later. "He would then repeat it over to himself & again—sometimes in one form and then in another & when it was fixed in his mind to suit him he . . . never lost that fact or his understanding of it."[7]

Thomas Lincoln could barely scratch out his own name, and Sarah could neither read nor write. But Abraham was a fast learner who mastered reading despite his irregular visits to the schoolroom. He found a new world in books and was desperate to read all he could. Although books were rare in rural Indiana, Sarah had brought some of her late husband's from Kentucky and encouraged Abraham to read them. He read her family Bible and John Bunyan's *Pilgrim's Progress*, and he reread *Aesop's Fables* so often he could recite the moral stories from memory. Daniel Defoe's novel *Robinson Crusoe* and biographies of Benjamin Franklin and George Washington were other favorites. According to a cousin who lived with the Lincolns, Abe (some called him that, though he preferred his full first name) was a "Constant and voracious reader."[8]

Thomas had no patience for a son who "fool[ed] hisself with eddication."[9] Nonetheless, Abraham read widely and began traveling downriver, his imagination filling with thoughts of the day when he could leave behind both his father and the hard and monotonous labor of frontier farming.

Finally, in February 1830, Abraham turned twenty-one. The next month he served his father one last time, helping the Lincolns make another move, this time to Illinois. Abe led an ox team on the long trek. He helped build a log cabin "at the junction of the timber-land and prairie." He aided in planting a corn crop and split enough rails to fence ten acres of ground.[10] But that would be the last growing season for Abe Lincoln. Now, at last an adult, he left the farm behind and set out looking for a life of his own.

# BORN TO SLAVERY

Abraham Lincoln's father permitted him few school days. The child given the birth name Frederick Augustus Washington Bailey got none at all.

Born on a farm on Maryland's Eastern Shore, he never knew the exact date of his birth. He spent his early childhood in the care of his grandmother after his mother was hired out to another farm miles away. Although she managed a few nighttime visits, Harriet Bailey was just a vague memory to the son who had no recollection of ever seeing her in daylight.

The child knew nothing of his father beyond the rumor that the White man who impregnated his mother might have been her enslaver, Aaron Anthony, a man he feared and hated. He once watched Anthony whip an aunt "till she was literally covered with blood." The very young boy would carry the harsh recollection forever, a "horrible exhibition," a "terrible spectacle," and a glimpse of "the blood-stained gate, the entrance to the hell of slavery."[11]

At age six, Fred Bailey was relocated by his owner to a grand, eighteenth-century mansion house on the Wye River. Put to work in the house, he was a playmate and companion to twelve-year-old Daniel, youngest son of Edward Lloyd V, a former governor of Maryland.

Young "Mas' Daniel" took a liking to his boy, acting as his protector. He shared bread with him, too, when the usual fare for the plantation's Black inhabitants was a daily portion of boiled cornmeal mush. Daniel's kindness led Fred to observe many years later that, "The equality of nature is strongly asserted in childhood . . . *Color* makes no difference with a child."[12]

In the eyes of no one else, however, were the boys anything like equal. On school days Daniel disappeared into the plantation's schoolroom, a place where no Black face was welcome. Still, the enslaved child benefited from the tutoring Daniel received. The Lloyds spoke correct English, a very different language from the broken, half-African dialect spoken on the plantation. The precocious Bailey, who stowed everything he heard in his prodigious memory, was left curious, hungry to know more.

In March 1826, at age eight, he was sent to the next stop in his enslavement. With no close family ties to sever, he left behind only the "hardship, whipping and nakedness" of the plantation.[13] Fred Bailey stepped aboard the sloop *Sally Lloyd*, headed for Baltimore and servitude in the home of his owner's brother. After years spent wearing nothing more than a crude linen shirt that hung to his knees, he wore his first pair of trousers, an outfit better suited for the city that would be his home. On its overnight sail, the vessel and its cargo of sheep crossed the Chesapeake Bay; to a farm boy who had always lived upriver, it seemed an unfathomably large expanse of water. When the city came into sight, young Fred was equally amazed by the tall church spires and five-story buildings. The *Sally Lloyd* entered a harbor full of three-masted seagoing vessels, warehouses, and steamships belonging to merchants in what had become one of the country's busiest ports.

A crewman escorted the eight-year-old to Aliceanna Street, an easy walk from the harbor, and the home of an aspiring shipbuilder named Hugh Auld. Auld and his wife, Sophia, met him at the door, together with their son, Thomas. "Little Tommy" was told the new arrival was to be "his Freddy." The dark-skinned boy would be caring for the younger White one.

Little did Freddy Bailey know that he was about to get the unexpected gift of the ABCs, the instrument that would permit him to elevate himself to one of the great men of the century.

# A HUNGER FOR KNOWLEDGE

The city differed in a thousand ways from the rural life Freddy had lived. On Baltimore's paved streets, the noise was constant, but there were fewer of the "country cruelties" he had known on the plantation. In his new home, he slept on a mattress of straw, his first bed after the cold, damp dirt floors on which he had always slept. He wore clean clothes and ate better than ever before. But the kindness of Sophia Auld was the biggest shock of all.

As wholly owned property, he previously "had been treated as a *pig* on the plantation." But Miss Sopha, as he called his new mistress, "made me something like [Tommy's] half-brother in her affections."[14] A regular churchgoer, Mrs. Auld continually surprised him. Part of the explanation was that she had not grown up in a slaveholding family. Not having been hardened to the barbarity of owning other people, she didn't expect the cowering servility demanded by the previous White adults Freddy had known. Miss Sopha actively encouraged him to look her in the eye, and he "scarcely knew how to behave towards her."[15]

Though his primary job was to keep Tommy out of harm's way, he also ran errands for Mistress Auld. Moving freely on the streets of Baltimore, he explored a city where a minority of Whites were slaveholders and a majority of the Black inhabitants were freemen. As a "city slave," he had become, in comparison to his status on the plantation, "almost a free citizen."[16] That wasn't quite true, of course; in the night he could hear his less fortunate brothers and sisters being walked to the docks in chains. But looking back later, he described how important was his arrival in a cosmopolitan city of eighty thousand people. "Going to live at Baltimore," he would write at age twenty-five, "laid the foundation, and opened the gateway."[17]

The revelation that truly changed his life occurred in the Auld household. Listening to Miss Sopha read the Bible aloud, Freddy began to recognize that words had power. When he asked if he, too, might learn to read, she agreed without hesitation. An apt pupil, he quickly mastered the alphabet. Teacher and student moved on to sounding out simple words of three and four letters. Taking pride in his progress, Mrs. Auld told her husband how well Freddy was doing, confiding that she hoped he might one day be able to read the Bible.

Hugh Auld was flabbergasted. He was appalled that his wife didn't understand that teaching the Black child "the A B C" was irresponsible, unwise, and unlawful. She was violating the basic code of slaveholding society, which demanded total compliance on the part of the enslaved. Slavery and education were incompatible, he told her; tutoring Freddy was an invitation for him to violate Auld's property rights. "He should know nothing but to obey his master—to do as he is told to do."[18]

The reading lessons ended abruptly, and Miss Sopha hardened her heart toward the boy she had previously treated with affection. Yet her reaction proved less significant than the bright light of understanding that Auld's words lit in the mind of Fred Bailey.

Although directed at his wife, Auld's rebukes had been a revelation to the wary nine-year-old, who had stood by, watching and listening, as Hugh chastised Sophia. He saw for the first time a fundamental truth about slavery. "Learning would do him no good," Auld had said, "but probably a great deal of harm—making him disconsolate and unhappy. . . . If you learn him now to read, he'll want to know how to write; and, this accomplished, he'll be running away with himself."[19]

In the coming years the enslaved child, by then a man, would quote Auld's words often. They had sparked the crucial understanding that reading and knowledge were the keys to his freedom. Young as he was, Freddy saw that ignorance was a weapon in the hands of the slaveholder, one that was far more dangerous than the whip.

Mistress Auld no longer tutored him, but Hugh Auld's words inspired a new determination to learn. Seeking instruction elsewhere, Fred deciphered words on signs. He bartered for reading lessons with little White boys he befriended when doing errands in the town. In return for biscuits he pocketed at the Auld home, these "hungry little urchins" gave him "the more valuable bread of knowledge."[20]

Tommy grew up and Fred, no longer charged with child-minding duties, spent his days performing small tasks in the shipyard of Auld & Harrison. As Hugh Auld had predicted, Fred taught himself to write, laboriously copying the letters that ships' carpenters incised on beams. He worked secretly at night with a dog-eared Webster's speller. He filled in the blanks in forgotten copybooks from Tommy's early schooling.

Nothing the boy learned would mean more to him than the word *abolition*. When he first heard Auld and other slaveholders speak the term *abolitionist*, Freddy observed that they spat out the syllables with anger, disgust, and even fear. The term's meaning was unknown to him, but he heard other variations, such as *abolition movement* and *abolitionism*.

The child did not yet know the idea of abolition had a growing currency among the educated, especially in the North. While national politicians had argued for decades about a gradual end to slavery by various means, including colonization, in which the enslaved would be resettled in Africa, an outspoken Boston printer and newspaperman named William Lloyd Garrison had founded, in 1831, an anti-slavery newspaper called

*The Liberator.* In its pages he advocated for the immediate, unconditional, and total abolition of slavery. He believed the entire Constitution itself was a corrupt pro-slavery document, and some years later he would burn a copy of the founding document in public, proclaiming it "a Covenant with Death: an Agreement with Hell."[21] As a member of Congress, former president John Quincy Adams had begun talking about slavery as a matter of national conscience. Although not as radical in his beliefs as Garrison, Adams wondered aloud "whether a population spread over an immense territory, consisting of one great division all freemen, and another of master and slaves, could exist permanently together as members of one community or not."[22]

In the idea of abolition, Freddy saw hope for his future—a future that he decided would be a relentless quest for freedom.

TWO

# A FIGHTING CHANCE

I knew Mr. L well . . . he was a great man long years since. . . .
[I] Knew he was a Rising man.

—ELIZABETH EDWARDS

A fter returning from New Orleans in July 1831, Abraham Lincoln settled in New Salem, Illinois. The river town was no metropolis; just two years before it had been an uninhabited ridge overlooking the Sangamon River. Now, with a gristmill and sawmill at the river's edge, New Salem had grown into a village much larger than any community Lincoln had ever called home, with a population of more than a hundred men, women, and children.

Its founders had wanted their frontier settlement to become the market town for the surrounding rural hamlets and farms. That had happened, and the village's streets were already lined with houses and shops for a blacksmith, cooper, hatmaker, and other tradesmen, along with two general stores, a tavern, and two doctor's offices. This seemed the perfect place for Lincoln, a young man with little experience in the wider world but great aspirations. He spent his days at his employer's store behind the counter, his nights sleeping in a cot in the attic above.

The townspeople immediately took to the young clerk, who had a gift for telling stories and entertaining an audience. They were impressed with the size and strength of this stranger, but that also meant that Lincoln would meet with an unexpected test after one of his admirers bragged that the tall and sinewy young man "could outrun, whip, or throw down any man in Sangamon country." Word of the boast reached Jack Armstrong, a local man who headed a pack of neighborhood rowdies, and he responded by challenging Lincoln to a fight, as he did whenever a new neighbor with a reputation for strength came to town.[1] As the town schoolteacher, Mentor Graham, explained, taking on the local bully "was an ordeal through which all Comers had to pass."[2]

Lincoln felt he had no choice but to accept the challenge, but only if he could dictate the terms. Young as he was, Lincoln was also savvy. He knew from experience that not all frontier fighting was the same. Word traveled around town; this would be a public event, and Lincoln, wanting to avoid a violent, anything-goes brawl, in which eye gouging and ear biting were accepted tactics, let it be known he wouldn't be "tussled & scuffled."[3] He insisted his rite of initiation must be less animal attack and more a test of skill and strength. A wrestling match was agreed upon.

Wrestling had rules, and a match typically started with an "Indian hug," in which the wrestlers wrapped their arms around each other's torso. What followed would involve practiced holds and other maneuvers, with the goal being to throw the opponent, not pin him.

On the appointed day a crowd of local men gathered to watch the spectacle. People said Jack Armstrong was the best fighter in Sangamon County, "a man in the prime of life, square built, muscular and strong as an ox."[4] But this match might be a fight worth watching, as Lincoln was an experienced wrestler. His height and strength suited him to the sport, and his intelligence was an added asset. As one of his New Salem neighbors put it, Lincoln was "a scientific wrestler."[5]

Lincoln's employer at the store put ten dollars on his young clerk. His bet was matched by a tavern keeper who favored Jack Armstrong. Men of lesser means bet knives and whiskey on the outcome. The fight would take place in front of the store where a relaxed Lincoln, according to one witness, stood with his back against the wall waiting for the fight to begin, "seaming undaunted and fearless."[6]

Once the fight was under way, neither man gained a clear early advantage. "They wrestled for a long time," recalled one New Salem man, "withough either being able to throw the other."[7] Armstrong was accustomed to winning, both by thrashing his opponents and taking their money in wagers, but he soon realized that this new man in town wasn't about to give up—and that Lincoln might even beat him.

Deciding that winning was more important than the agreed-upon rules, Armstrong broke his hold and dove for Lincoln's legs. But Lincoln countered with a rapid maneuver of his own. As twelve-year-old Robert Rutledge reported, "Mr. Lincoln seized him by the throat and thrust him at arms length from him."[8]

Suddenly, the match was at an impasse. Although everyone had seen Armstrong commit a foul, his supporters, caught up in the overheated moment, were ready to jump in to defend their champion. The match could have degenerated into a big brawl, with neighbors taking on neighbors. But Lincoln didn't let that happen.

"Jack, let's quit," he said to his opponent. "I can't throw you—you can't throw me."[9]

To Lincoln, the outcome of a wrestling match was much less important than gaining friends in a town where he wanted very much to fit in. He gave the other man an out and Armstrong agreed to call the match a draw. They left the bettors to argue about what exactly had happened,

*An illustration from an early twentieth-century children's biography depicting Lincoln's wresting match with Jack Armstrong.*

launching a debate that continues to this day since the many accounts of the fight—from friends of both men, bystanders, and others—agree on little. One thing is clear, however: A tough fight ended with the two men sharing a bond of mutual respect and friendship that would last their lifetimes.

As his authorized biographers put it many years later, Lincoln gained something important in the eyes of New Salem. "He became from that moment, in a certain sense, a personage, with a name and standing of his own."[10] The farmer boy from nowhere was now a known and respected man.

## LIKABLE LINCOLN

Lincoln stood out in New Salem. In the words of Dr. Jason Duncan, a Vermont native who practiced medicine in New Salem, the young man had "intelligence far beyond the generality of youth of his age and opportunities."[11] Unlike many in the two-saloon town where whiskey drinking was a dawn-to-dark pastime, Lincoln never drank alcohol. Yet he wore his smarts and sobriety lightly, and his customers liked him.

Lincoln's boss soon rewarded his young clerk by giving him the added responsibility of managing the town's gristmill. The young man was moving up the ranks of the town, but he had something on his mind beyond promotions: more education. Whenever and wherever he could, he read. He read in bed. He read sitting astride a log by a stream. One friend spotted him reading in the woods, lying on the ground with his legs extended upward along a tree trunk. He read while walking, so absorbed in his text that he would sometimes stop, oblivious to anything but the words on the page, before continuing on, never having lifted his gaze. Neighbors lent him books from their libraries, and Lincoln began to memorize long passages from Shakespeare (*Macbeth* became his particular favorite). He talked poetry with the town blacksmith and committed to memory poems by Robert Burns, which he then recited in a proper Scots dialect.

If he was to rise in society, Lincoln decided, he needed to talk like he was somebody. He recognized his own unpolished way of speaking was different from the speech of his more educated customers, and he set his mind to learning proper English. He asked around and borrowed a grammar book, which he memorized. As he taught himself how to speak correctly—to use plural verbs with plural nouns and such niceties as when to use the word *shall*—he also made it his business to learn how to speak effectively since he would need to persuade people to believe not only in him but in his ideas. During his first winter in New Salem, he spent many, many hours studying and "practicing polemics" from a little volume called *The Columbian Orator*.

*The Columbian Orator* offered advice on how to use cadence, emphasis, pauses, demeanor, and even gesticulations to enhance oral expression. But the bulk of the book consisted of writings by George Washington, Napoleon, Ben Franklin, Cicero, Socrates, and dozens of other historic figures remembered for their speeches. Lincoln copied the ones he liked most into his copybook word for word. Some he could recite verbatim. He absorbed the structure, syntax, and sentiment of the great men's words. The man managing the gristmill was clearly hungry for something bigger.

Lincoln remained in New Salem for almost six years, during which he struggled to make a living. The store failed as New Salem's growth slowed and Lincoln's employer demonstrated his true colors—he was, observed schoolteacher Graham, "an unsteady . . . rattle brained man, wild & unprovidential."[12]

Lincoln's sudden unemployment provided him an opportunity. In the spring of 1832, Lincoln tried soldiering, signing up for the local militia when a conflict with a local Sauk chief named Black Hawk prompted the Illinois governor to gather a fighting force. To his great satisfaction, Lincoln was elected captain of his volunteer company, which consisted largely of men he knew from New Salem. After three months' service, he returned from the little conflict in northern Illinois, remembered as the Black Hawk War. His only bloody battles, he later joked, were with mosquitoes.

Lincoln would spend the next few months picking up enough odd jobs in and around New Salem to sustain himself, but the ambitious lad wasn't looking for just a job. He was looking for a calling. With his local popularity running high, he decided to try his hand at politics, and that autumn he took his first step; at the urging of his neighbors, he ran for the Illinois General Assembly. In his first public speech, he made plain the simplicity of his motives:

> I am young and unknown to many of you; I was born and have
> ever remained in the most humble walks of life. I have no

wealthy or popular relations or friends to recommend me. My case is thrown exclusively upon the independent voters of the county, and if elected, they will have conferred a favour upon me for which I shall be unremitting in my labours to compensate. But if the good people in their wisdom shall see fit to keep me in the background, I have been too familiar with disappointments to be very much chagrined.[13]

Lincoln's early political priorities were equally simple. Adopting the thinking of Henry Clay, leader of the national Whig Party, he ran on a platform of improving roads and waterways—improvements that would mean a lot to the voters of rural Illinois. He promised to make education a priority, too. Every man, he insisted, should "receive at least, a moderate education."[14] No other boys would have to fight for an education the way he had if he could help it.

Due most likely to a lack of name recognition in the outlying districts, Lincoln lost the election. In his home precinct, though, he won 277 of the 300 votes. Those who did know him clearly saw that he was "a rising man."[15]

Seemingly unfazed by his political defeat, Lincoln bided his time—and got to know more people. He and a partner opened a store of their own. In 1833, Lincoln was appointed the village postmaster. He pored over newspapers that arrived from near and far, reading out his favorite bits to his customers. The townspeople saw him as a reliable source of news and opinions. His stockpile of off-color stories didn't hurt.

When that store failed, too, Lincoln was left with heavy debts, and his postmaster's salary wasn't even sufficient to pay his room and board. The county surveyor offered him work, and Lincoln taught himself metes and bounds from a book. His good reputation continued to grow. "When any dispute arose among the Settlers," one neighbor remembered, "Mr. Lincolns Compass and chain always settled the matter satisfactorily."[16] The work also got him into the surrounding countryside, enlarging his circle of acquaintances. But he aimed higher than surveying, setting his sights on becoming a lawyer.

Even as a teenager in Indiana, he had attended lawsuits conducted before the local justice, and in New Salem he added law books to his reading list, among them Blackstone's *Commentaries*, a basic work on British common law. Using forms that he found in one reference work, he drafted deeds, wills, and contracts for friends and neighbors, "never charging one cent for his trouble."[17]

In a village with no lawyers, it was inevitable that the talkative and competent young man would be asked to act the advocate. In his first trial, he was charged with defending the honor of a young woman in a case brought against a suitor who had refused to marry her. With no formal training, Lincoln drew upon common sense in his pleading. Dressed in the workaday clothing of a surveyor, he made a strong case that the girl deserved damages. His surveying assistant was in attendance and told the story.

"[Lincoln] made a comparison [and] cald the young man a white dress, the young lady a glass bottle," the man recalled. "He said you could soil the dress, it cold be made to look well again, but strik a blow at the bottle and it was gon."[18] In his debut at the plaintiff's table, Lincoln with his plainspoken argument won the day. His client was awarded a hundred dollars in damages.

In August 1836, he won something else. He ran again for a seat in the Illinois legislature, this time running what he called "a hand-shaking campaign" to make sure he won over voters outside New Salem.[19] The strategy worked, and his victory catapulted the twenty-seven-year-old to his first elective office.

Looking to leave behind his country-boy appearance, Lincoln bought himself a new suit—it was part of his personal reinvention—before boarding a four-horse stage bound for the state capital. Though larger than New Salem, Vandalia was a modest place, with a population of less than a thousand, its capitol building a dilapidated brick structure of just two stories. When he took his seat as a member of the legislature, the novice politician said little, listened intently, and attended faithfully. He saw these first sessions as part of his education. "He was reserved in manner," a friend reported, but "but learned much."[20]

In 1830s Illinois, few people lost any sleep over the evils of slavery. Lincoln's constituents were almost all White and unworried about the state's small number of enslaved people. Of greater concern were the eastern abolitionists whom they feared as radicals. Lincoln, like most of his neighbors, was of Southern birth. Unlike them, Lincoln was gravely uncomfortable with slavery, due, in part, to his upbringing. Lincoln's father, he recalled, had wanted to leave Kentucky "partly on account of slavery," having often heard the practice condemned from the pulpit of their church.[21] When a resolution to condemn abolitionist societies was raised before the General Assembly during his first term, Lincoln spoke up, going further than many would have, saying on the record that "the institution of slavery is founded on both injustice and bad policy."[22] On the other hand, he also accepted that Congress lacked the power to interfere with slavery in individual states, and many years would be required before he became a friend to abolitionism.

In those days, his law studies, not abolition, were Lincoln's top priority. He'd begun to suspect he'd need to have the power and social status a lawyer had if he was to be a successful legislator. A fellow lawmaker and friend from his militia days, John Todd Stuart, pushed Lincoln to pursue his law studies in earnest, and with more borrowed books—this time from his friend's firm, Stuart & Drummond, in nearby Springfield—Lincoln spent every available minute between legislative sessions studying the law. Although he "studied with nobody" (Lincoln's words), he passed the exams with ease, and on September 9, 1836, he was awarded a license to practice law.[23]

As one friend observed, "[Lincoln's] ambition was a little engine that knew no rest."[24] Now, as a lawyer and legislator—he would serve eight years in the Illinois House of Representatives—he had a way to harness it.

# THE TURNING POINT

During the summer of 1834, while Abraham Lincoln was glad-handing neighbors and winning votes with his easy manner and lighthearted stories, Fred Bailey made a dangerous choice.

Bailey was back in the fields after spending eight years in Baltimore. As an enslaved person, he was considered little different than a slaveholder's horses, sheep, and other chattels; the bondsman had no say in what he did or where he went. Ordered back to Maryland's Eastern Shore, Bailey had no choice but to go. Making matters even worse, he was lent out for a year to a farmer who was intent upon erasing all memory of the looser discipline of Bailey's city days. At almost seventeen, he now labored for Edward Covey, a man reputed to be "a first rate hand at breaking young negroes."[25]

On Covey's farm, enslaved workers rose before first light and worked until dark and beyond, even on the coldest and hottest days. Bailey was awkward and unfamiliar with his new tasks in the fields. "The work was simple . . . yet to one entirely unused to such work, it came very hard."[26] He was subjected to brutal whippings for his failures, and in every way was "made to drink the bitterest dregs of slavery."[27]

He tilled fields that lay beside the waters of the Chesapeake Bay, his life a misery. But as he glimpsed the boats sailing by, he could not help but sense intimations of freedom in the schooners carrying their passengers to destinations forbidden to the enslaved. More than once he thought to himself, "One hundred miles straight north, and I am free!"

Bailey could not resign himself to a life in bondage—"It cannot be that I shall live and die a slave"—but Covey did everything he could to break him.[28]

One scorching August day, Fred Bailey collapsed while harvesting wheat. Felled by sunstroke, he crawled to a nearby fence seeking shelter from the sun. When Covey found him, he kicked Bailey savagely and ordered him to rise. Though the seventeen-year-old managed to stand, he collapsed again. The slave breaker then delivered a blow to his head with a hickory club, gashing open a large wound.

With blood oozing from his skull, Bailey managed to make his way into the woods. Eluding pursuit, he stumbled for miles until he reached his home farm hours later. He told his enslaver that Covey aimed to kill him, and at first, Auld seemed affected by the story. Soon, however, as the boy recalled the events in his autobiography years later, Captain Auld "became cold as iron." This was a transformation that Bailey was coming to understand: As he watched, the man's "humanity fell before the systematic tyranny of slavery." After a few minutes of pacing, apparently arguing with his own conscience, Auld decided to take Covey's side. "My dizziness was laziness," Douglass later reported the slaveholder told him, "and Covey did right to flog me."[29] Auld let Bailey stay overnight on his home farm, but ordered him to return to Covey before first light the next day.

Bailey managed to avoid facing the slave breaker until Monday morning. He was in the hayloft working before sunrise when Covey quietly snuck into the barn. As Bailey came down the ladder, Covey emerged from the shadows to grab him from below, attempting to bind his legs with a long rope, prepared to give him a beating. Instinctively, Fred jumped free. In the instant that he crashed to the stable floor, he understood that he was less afraid for his life than he was for the death of his freedom. This time, he resolved, he would not submit and take his whipping like an animal with no will of its own. He would defend himself.

He seized Covey by the throat and, holding him in an iron grip, rose to his feet. The two men grappled, but Fred carefully parried the blows sent his way, making no attempt to injure Covey. But the farmer, shocked that Bailey was actually fighting back, demanded, "Are you going to resist, you scoundrel?"

"*Yes, sir,*" was Bailey's polite reply, his gaze eye to eye with Covey's.

Covey called for help. When another bondsman came to Covey's aid, Fred incapacitated him with a wicked kick to the ribs. The fight continued, one man against the other.

Covey attempted to drag his opponent to the stable door, but Fred floored him. They fought on. For almost two hours the confrontation continued, and with the sun up and its rays lighting the barnyard, Covey finally realized this was a fight he could not win. Both men were exhausted, and Covey, who was "huffing and puffing at a great rate," brought the contest to a close.[30]

"Go to work," he ordered, adding, "I would not have whipped you half so much as I have had you not resisted."

In truth, Fred Bailey realized, Covey had drawn no blood. Nor would he summon the constable, despite the fact that Bailey had raised his hand to a White man, a crime that would ordinarily be punished by a beating at the whipping post in the town square—or worse. He would pay no penalty because the man's cherished reputation as a slave breaker would have suffered if word of his failure to discipline Bailey got out.

Not once during Bailey's four remaining months in his service would Covey again lay so much as a finger on him, but Bailey gained something much greater than a reprieve from whippings. By risking everything, he shifted the balance of power. His unlikely victory, he later said, was "the turning point in my '*life as a slave.*'" Until their fight, Covey had been on the verge of breaking his spirit. But resistance had "rekindled in my breast the smouldering embers of liberty; it brought up my Baltimore dreams, and revived a sense of my own manhood. I was a

THE PRESIDENT AND THE FREEDOM FIGHTER

changed being after that fight. I was *nothing* before; I WAS A MAN NOW. It . . . inspired me with a renewed determination to be A FREEMAN."³¹

# HOPE AND FAILURE

Like Abraham Lincoln, Frederick Bailey owned a well-thumbed copy of *The Columbian Orator.* He had purchased it at age thirteen, for a precious fifty cents, from a bookshop on Baltimore's Thames Street. He brought the "gem of a book" from the city to the country, and as the child in bondage had grown into a man, *The Columbian Orator* had been more than an introduction to public speaking.³²

The book aimed to educate young White minds to the principles of freedom and the responsibilities of citizenship, but its editor had been strongly opposed to slavery. Bailey found himself drawn again and again to the text of an imaginary dialogue, in which a slaveholder berates an enslaved man, calling him an "ungrateful rascal" for attempting to escape. "You have been comfortably fed and lodged, not over-worked," insists the angry enslaver, "and attended with the most humane care when you were sick." Why would he want to run away?

The response is a deeper question, one that rejects the logic of slavery. "What have you done, what can you do for me that will compensate for the liberty that you have taken away?"

But, the slaveholder counters, the enslaved man had been "fairly purchased." Again, the response is a question: "Did I give my consent . . . when I was treacherously kidnapped in my own country . . . put in chains [and] brought hither . . . like a beast in the market[?]" A slave is not a beast, he insists. "Look at these limbs; are they not those of a man?"

In the end, the debate is resolved in favor of the bondsman when, recognizing that his argument for enslavement has been demolished, the slaveholder relents and acknowledges the other man's humanity, granting him freedom.[33]

The dialogue wasn't a transcript of a real moment; it never happened. Yet for a Black man with a growing passion for words and ideas, as well as deep desire for freedom, the dialogue had the power of revelation. "Slaveholders," Bailey thought, "are only a band of successful robbers, who left their homes and went into Africa for the purpose of stealing and reducing my people to slavery."[34] *The Columbian Orator* showed him how words and reason might sway minds, and the dialogue dovetailed with his own experience. Above all, it embodied a most deep-seated hope: "I could not help feeling that the day might come, when the well-directed answers made by the slave to the master, in this instance, would find their counterpart in myself."[35] Freedom seemed closer, perhaps even possible, as he committed the dialogue to memory.

When his year of service to Edward Covey had ended, Bailey was sent to work on a neighboring farm on the Eastern Shore. He found William Freeland wasn't the brutal taskmaster Covey was, and the possibility of freedom seemed constantly in his thoughts. Freeland's more permissive rules also meant that Bailey was able to quietly run a Sabbath school.

On Sundays, behind a barn or at the home of a freeman, he tutored as many as forty students in the rudiments of reading and writing. Bailey brought his Webster's spelling book and, as a teacher standing before his first flock, he began to find his voice, to shape his arguments, to gain confidence in the power of his words. Most of his pupils kept mum about their learning and their charismatic instructor.

Bailey also plotted an escape. He and five others planned to steal a canoe, paddle north on the Chesapeake, and follow the North Star to freedom. They chose a date—Easter eve 1836—and he laboriously forged traveling papers. The plan might have worked, but one of the coconspirators betrayed them. Just hours before their planned departure, Bailey and the others were rounded up and thrown in jail. The rest were released after a week, but, identified by his jailers as the mastermind, Bailey spent another week within the walls of the stone prison, worried that he might be handed over to slave traders and "sold south" to the much harder labor of a cotton or sugar plantation, "beyond the remotest hope of emancipation."[36]

To his surprise, however, he was sent back to Baltimore, once again to serve Hugh Auld. There Frederick Bailey would work in the shipyards, and within the relative freedom of the city, he would make a better plan.

# ESCAPING TO FREEDOM

In Baltimore, Fred Bailey no longer did errands. He now stood six-one, his solid frame well muscled from his years of toil in the fields. Although he learned the caulker's trade in the shipyards, his wages were not his to keep, despite helping to construct some of the fleetest ships on the sea, the schooners called Baltimore clippers. The unfairness of having to hand over his pay to a slaveholder for doing the same job done by White workers on the same docks fed his simmering desire to be his own man.

He made fast friends among the city's free Black population. His appetite for words led him to become an active member of a debating club, the East Baltimore Mental Improvement Society. And there he met and fell in love with Anna Murray. Five years older than Fred, Anna was a free woman of color.

Like him, she had been born on the Eastern Shore; unlike his, her parents had gained their freedom from servitude. She had come to Baltimore at age seventeen to make a place for herself and had worked as a

*Although her parents had been enslaved, Anna Murray was free when she met Frederick Bailey, and she played an essential role in helping him escape bondage.*

maid for the postmaster. Despite being illiterate, she could read music and taught Fred to play the violin; soon they were playing duets. She lived in rooms of her own and would underwrite the adventure that was about to unfold, selling one of her two featherbeds and drawing upon her savings.[37]

His months under Hugh Auld's control had darker moments, too. Four White apprentices in one shipyard had attacked Bailey; when a blow with a handspike to the back of his head sent him to the ground, one of them delivered a vicious kick with his boot, nearly blinding Bailey in one eye. Dozens of White men watching the fight had urged his assailants on with cries of "kill him—kill him . . . knock his brains out—he struck a white person!"[38] As he recovered from his wounds, he was more resolved than ever to escape bondage, but the final spur would be a bitter quarrel with Auld, after the slaveholder abruptly withdrew hard-earned privileges.

Over a period of weeks, Fred and Anna meticulously planned his departure to a new life. When the day came—September 3, 1838—Douglass stood alone on the platform, since the plan called for Anna to follow later. Waiting for the Philadelphia, Wilmington and Baltimore train, he wore a red shirt, loosely tied black cravat, and wide-brimmed canvas hat of a sailor, and he carried free papers lent him by a man retired from the sea in case he was stopped by officials or slave catchers and ordered to produce proof he was free. Although Stanley was both darker and much older than he, Bailey planned to bluster his way to the North with Stanley's "sailor's protection," a document emblazoned with an American eagle.[39]

The timing was important, and to avoid suspicion, only when the train was ready to depart did a friend arrive with Bailey's baggage; then, with the train already in motion, Bailey jumped aboard. For his fellow passengers, this was just another day, but this particular Monday felt like it just might be the most important day of Bailey's life.

With the journey underway, his sailor suit and the eagle did their job: The train conductor let him pass. At Havre de Grace, Maryland, the fugitive took a ferry across the Susquehanna and boarded a second train, this one bound for Wilmington, Delaware. Again, his papers passed muster. A steamboat ride to Philadelphia would follow, and he hoped to catch a train from there to New York. But first he had to get out of slave country. Until then, any man could call his bluff, looking to collect the substantial reward for turning in a young and healthy runaway whose market value was perhaps a thousand dollars.

For hours, he had to keep his composure and suppress his rising panic. "The heart of no fox or deer, with hungry hounds on his trail, in full chase, could have beaten more anxiously or noisily than did mine," he later wrote, "from the time I left Baltimore till I reached Philadelphia."[40]

Three times on the journey he encountered men who could have sent him home in chains. When a free Black man he knew seemed to be asking him too many questions, Bailey managed to slip away. When he spied a ship's captain on whose ship he had worked the previous week, Bailey's fear peaked again, but the man failed to recognize him.

The closest call came when a German blacksmith he knew well looked directly and intently in his direction. But the White man proved to be an unlikely ally after Bailey thought he saw a spark of recognition in the man's eye. "I really believe he knew me," he remembered later, but this would prove to be the escapee's lucky day. Despite the fact that Bailey wore an obvious disguise, "[the blacksmith] had no heart to betray me. At any rate he saw me escaping and held his peace."[41]

Frederick Bailey made it to New York at 1:00 A.M. the next day. Good fortune had ridden with him, along with his tattered copy of *The Columbian Orator*. At first he wandered the streets, knowing no one, feeling untethered: "I was free from slavery," he later remembered, "but I was free from home as well."[42] After a night spent sleeping among the barrels on a wharf, he found shelter in the home of an abolitionist named David Ruggles, the editor of *Mirror of Liberty*, the nation's first Black-owned and -operated magazine. He managed to get word of his safe arrival to Anna, and she made haste to New York, where they were married, on September 15, in Ruggles's parlor.

Anna was not the only one to change her name. The couple decided to begin their new lives together in New Bedford, Massachusetts, where Fred hoped to put his shipyard skills to use. They made their way to the Massachusetts port, planning to settle into the town's well-established Black community. "To preserve a sense of my identity," he later wrote, he retained the name Frederick, but because in the eyes of the law he remained someone's property, he needed to take steps to keep slave catchers off his trail. He became thereafter to his fellow citizens in New Bedford and to posterity Frederick Douglass.

# THREE

## SELF-MADE MEN

He was the insurgent slave, taking hold of the right
of speech, and charging on his tyrants the bondage
of his race.

—NATHANIEL ROGERS

rederick Douglass soon discovered that prejudice was alive
and thriving in the North. White workers in the New Bedford, Massachusetts, shipyards refused to work side by side
with Black laborers. Yet, for a man still reveling in his newfound freedom, the setback seemed almost unimportant. Douglass was starting
a new life, with a new wife, and "no work [was] too hard—none too
dirty."[1] He reveled in being a free man.

Douglass felt safe in a town of many Quakers, with their strong anti-
slavery tradition, along with more than a thousand Black faces, three-
quarters of whom were free men, the remainder fellow fugitives. He
found work when, seeing a pile of coal in front of a minister's manse, he
knocked at the back door and asked if he could move the gritty fuel to
its storage in the cellar. After he made short work of the job, the lady of

the house gave him two silver half-dollars. A new sensation rolled over him as he held the coins in his palm: He was now "not only a freeman but a free-working man." No slaveholder would be taking this pay. "*It was mine* [and] *my hands were my own*."²

Within a year, Anna and Frederick welcomed their first child, daughter Rosetta, then a son, Lewis, born in the autumn of 1840. Douglass tended to his growing family and performed whatever menial work he could get, from cutting wood and sweeping chimneys to loading ships and pumping the bellows at a foundry. This last job suited him best. With almost no spare time to improve his mind, he could nail a newspaper to a post near his bellows and read as he worked. Sometimes the publication he studied was William Lloyd Garrison's *Liberator*, to which Douglass now subscribed. He took in the abolitionist's words hungrily. As he absorbed Garrison's compelling arguments, he felt his "heart burning at every true utterance against the slave system."³

He looked for a house of worship and, after having been ordered to the balcony at a Methodist church because they were Black, the Douglasses joined the African Methodist Episcopal Zion Church, a small church on Second Street near the docks. There Frederick took an active role, first as sexton and Sunday school teacher, then from the pulpit. Word of the tall, handsome man's powerful sermonizing soon spread beyond Zion's Black congregation. The fugitive, once happily anonymous in the obscurity of a busy whaling port, would soon take a fateful trip to Nantucket Island, where he would begin to speak to a much larger public.

## A NEW DESTINY

When the sloop *Telegraph* steamed out of New Bedford harbor on Tuesday, August 10, 1841, the passengers included Frederick and Anna Douglass. Forbidden to go below—Whites only, the ship's notorious captain decreed—the couple and three dozen other abolitionists, both White and Black, rode in solidarity, exposed to a mix of sun, wind, and rain on the upper deck. After a sixty-mile sail, they arrived on Nantucket Island for a three-day convention of abolitionists.

In the three years since his arrival in New England, Douglass had taken no holiday, often working in the foundry "all night as well as all day."[4] He needed a rest but also wished to attend the events at the Nantucket Atheneum, together with other like-minded opponents of slavery, one of whom had invited him to come along. In particular, he looked forward to hearing William Lloyd Garrison, editor of *The Liberator* and founder of the Massachusetts Anti-Slavery Society, the organization sponsoring the convention.

Garrison was largely self-educated, having grown up in poverty in Newburyport, Massachusetts, after his alcoholic father abandoned the family. He went to work as an apprentice printer at age thirteen and quickly mastered both writing and setting type; as publisher of *The Liberator*, he now composed his editorials as he typeset them, never putting pen to paper. Garrison's voracious reading over the years had led him to

*A late-in-life photo of William Lloyd Garrison, founder and editor of* The Liberator, *and Frederick Douglass's first mentor.*

take a moral stand in favor of racial equality. At first a supporter of colonization, he had rejected the gradual approach to freeing the enslaved, becoming an abolitionist true believer.

Despite a slightly owlish appearance, the bald and bespectacled thirty-five-year-old was fearless, accustomed to the fact that his ideas upset people. He faced down outbursts of violence at his public appearances and ignored regular threats on his life. He was a pacifist, stressed nonviolence, and believed that membership in the society should include women. He rejected alliances with any political party, firm in his belief that the U.S. Constitution was a pro-slavery document. To cautious people, including many who opposed slavery, he was a dangerous radical.

Douglass idolized this White man, who had the perfect certainty of one who knew he was right. Garrison had promised in the first issue of *The Liberator*, "I will be as harsh as Truth, and as uncompromising as Justice. . . . Tell a man whose house is on fire to give a moderate alarm; tell him to moderately rescue his wife from the hands of a ravisher; tell the mother to gradually extricate her babe from the fire into which it has fallen—but urge me not to use moderation. . . . I am in earnest—I will not equivocate—I will not excuse—I will not retreat a single inch—and I will be heard."[5]

More than a thousand people attended the Nantucket convention, many of them off-islanders. The Atheneum's hall was full for the Wednesday evening meeting when Garrison introduced a resolution condemning the complicity of people in the North who "act[ed] as the body-guard of slavery."[6] He invited discussion from the floor.

As Douglass later remembered, "I felt strongly moved to speak."[7] A local Quaker had already urged him to do so, but Douglass hesitated. He had stood in front of audiences in churches and meetings before, but he had never addressed a largely White audience. "The truth was, I felt myself a slave, and the idea of speaking to white people weighed me down." But he rose and, with all eyes on him, moved to the platform.[8]

At first, he stammered. He felt his limbs trembling and apologized for his ignorance, intimidated by the large crowd. Of the countless speeches he delivered over the years, this would be "the only one I ever made," he said later, "of which I do not remember a single connected sentence."[9] He spoke extemporaneously, with no notes before him. As he recounted his life story, he felt his tension ease.

The audience was captivated. Before them stood a runaway slave who, even at that moment, remained the legal property of a White man in Maryland. He was young—just twenty-three—and if his speech was grammatically imperfect, he was obviously highly intelligent. He exhibited a sharp wit as well as an unexpected eloquence. He drew his listeners in, a man speaking not only for himself but for millions of others. To him, slavery was no abstraction. Frederick Douglass, formerly Frederick Bailey, did not have to imagine life in bondage.

"Flinty hearts were pierced," said one listener, "and cold ones melted."[10] His audience listened in a surprised silence, and when Douglass finished, Garrison took back the podium. He was as stunned as everyone else at what they'd just witnessed. Still absorbing the experience they'd shared, Garrison realized, "I never hated slavery so intensely as at that moment."[11]

He asked the audience, "Have we been listening to a thing, a piece of property, or a man?" He spoke to a hall full of Garrisonians, already converts to the anti-slavery cause. Would they allow this "self-emancipated young man" to be returned to slavery?

"NO!" was the thunderous and unanimous response.[12]

Would they welcome him as brother man in their state? In response they shouted, Yes, yes, yes, they would.

Douglass's performance and his powerful story planted an idea in Garrison's mind. He offered Douglass a job, complete with a contract and a salary. As a paid lecturer, Garrison proposed, Douglass would travel the speaking circuit. The cause had other Black speakers, but

*The strikingly handsome Frederick Douglass looks intently at the camera in this daguerreotype image, taken about 1841.*

none had been enslaved and none had Douglass's rhetorical gifts. His task would be to open people's minds to the humanity of those in bondage, to galvanize audiences far and wide just as he had that evening in Nantucket. He would be a living embodiment of why abolition was a moral imperative, necessary to mankind.

On hearing the proposal, however, Frederick Douglass again hesitated. He wondered aloud, Garrison reported, whether "he was not adequate to the performance of so great a task."[13] Douglass also worried a new notoriety might lead to his discovery and that he would be risking recapture and a return to slavery. But he also felt an undeniable calling, understanding this work could help lead to freedom for others still bound by the knots of servitude.

By the time he and Anna Douglass boarded the *Telegraph* to return to New Bedford the next day, Frederick Douglass had truly embraced his calling. No longer would he depend upon his calloused hands to put bread on the table before his family. With the guidance of the fatherly

William Lloyd Garrison, Douglass's mind and words, his gifts of self-expression, and his harrowing personal story would take him to a new destiny.

# LINCOLN, LEGISLATOR AND LAWYER

During Douglass's New Bedford days, Lincoln, too, relocated, when the state of Illinois, in 1839, removed its capital to Springfield, a rapidly growing town of some 2,500 people near the center of the state. The young legislator found a room over a general store, which he shared with the proprietor, Joshua Speed, who soon became a trusted friend and confidant, and joined the law practice of his friend John Stuart.

Lincoln's personality and persistence, his hard work and goodwill, and his association with the well-liked Stuart gained him acceptance among his Springfield neighbors. It didn't hurt that as a first-term legislator in the Illinois General Assembly, Lincoln had cast a vote in favor of making Springfield the new state capital. He soon was appointed a Springfield trustee, which cemented his local influence, but most of his income came not from public offices but his law practice. Since the court sat in Springfield for a total of just four weeks a year, for two months at a time Lincoln traveled the Eighth Circuit, which encompassed most of central Illinois. He rode an aging and tired horse called Old Tom from one county seat to another, seeking business. This likable man gained a reputation far and wide for his integrity and fairness.

His confidence growing, Lincoln began to think in national terms. He was outraged by outbreaks of violence in Louisiana, where a band of vigilantes lynched alleged gamblers, and in Mississippi, where a mixed-race man accused of murder was burned to death. Another clash closer to home, in Alton, Indiana, made national news when the editor of an abolitionist paper, Elijah P. Lovejoy, was shotgunned by a pro-slavery rabble, his printing press broken up and thrown into the Mississippi. To Lincoln, these mob executions were ominous, and he delivered a speech on the subject at Springfield's Lyceum.

Mob justice was just wrong, he argued, and would "subvert our national freedom." He preached *a reverence for the constitution and laws*. He embraced neither slavery nor abolitionism; for him, the guiding principle was "reason, cold calculating, unimpassioned reason."[14]

Lincoln played an official role in the national election of 1840 after he was selected as a presidential elector for the Whig Party in Illinois. He was already well known for speeches he gave while running for his legislative seat and his gift for skewering his opposition to the great amusement of the crowd. He traveled across the state in 1840 on behalf of the party's nominee, aging general William Henry Harrison, victor at the Battle of Tippecanoe during the War of 1812, almost thirty years earlier. As Lincoln campaigned for Harrison in Illinois, his chief opponent was another rising Illinois politician, Stephen Douglas, who stumped for the incumbent, Democrat Martin Van Buren.

Lincoln and Douglas repeatedly faced off at campaign events, previewing their later rivalry when they would oppose one another in the U.S. Senate race in 1858. Douglas, a hard-driving young Democrat who stood a foot shorter than Lincoln, could fill a room with his booming voice, large head, bushy eyebrows, and ever-present cigar. Nonetheless, Lincoln's man, Harrison, would win the presidency—and Lincoln got his first write-up in national press when the *National Intelligencer*, the principal newspaper in Washington, D.C., quoted a speech he gave praising Harrison.

A life-changing new passion arrived in Lincoln's life when he met another Harrison supporter, twenty-year-old Mary Todd, at a Christmas party in December 1839. His law partner's cousin, Mary was pretty, pert, and so passionate about politics that a relation had called her a "violent little Whig" when she was just fourteen.[15] Mary had ambitions,

*These images of Mr. and Mrs. Abraham Lincoln were taken prior to their move to Washington in 1847, after he won the right to represent Illinois's Seventh District in the House of Representatives; this is the earliest known photograph of the then-obscure frontier lawyer.*

too, joking that she planned to marry a man who would become president.

Though both were born in Kentucky, their upbringings could hardly have been more different. The fourth of seven children, she grew up in a slaveholding family that occupied a fourteen-room mansion tended by Black "servants." Her hometown, Lexington, was one of the largest cities west of the Allegheny Mountains. When she met the tall and lank Lincoln—she was visiting a married older sister in Springfield—Mary, a decade younger than he, was a pleasantly plump five-foot-two with blue eyes and a reddish tinge to her brown hair. After more than a dozen years of study at a series of academies, she was well educated, well mannered, and entirely at home in civilized society; Lincoln, inexperienced and shy in the presence of women, was bowled over. Despite their differences, a shared love of poetry and politics helped bring them together.

Lincoln's store of memorized poems charmed Mary, while the fact that she actually knew Henry Clay, a friend of her father's and a man Lincoln idolized, added to her attraction.

Their courtship was on-again, off-again, and after asking for her hand, he broke off their engagement because of doubts that he could support and please her. But three years after meeting, Mary and Abraham married on November 4, 1842. Their marriage would have its ups and downs, with Mary adjusting to the demands of housekeeping in a home without servants. Terrified by thunderstorms and plagued by headaches, she could be willful, while Lincoln was by habit remote and was sometimes depressed ("generally," remarked Joshua Speed, who knew him as well as anyone, "he was a very sad man").[16] Nine months after their marriage, on August 1, 1843, their first son, Robert Todd Lincoln, arrived.

With his new commitment to marriage and family, Lincoln left the legislature, investing his full energies in building his law practice. As a general practitioner, he drafted wills and petitions, handling bankruptcies, divorces, estates, and criminal cases. He prepared diligently. Comfortable in front of audiences, he demonstrated great skills as a courtroom litigator. As his reputation grew, he appeared often before the Illinois Supreme Court, compiling an enviable record.

In 1844, he purchased a cottage in Springfield, the only house he would ever own, on the corner of Eighth and Jackson Streets. The same year he formed a new law firm with him as senior partner. He prospered and their marriage thrived, yet neither he nor Mary would be willing to settle for life in Springfield. His larger political aspirations simmered.

——✦——

# FOUR

# ON THE ROAD

We looked up to [Frederick Douglass] almost as we do to
the memory of Abraham Lincoln.

—Congressman George W. Murray

F rederick Douglass's reputation grew by the day. After joining
Garrison's team of lecturers, he traveled to dozens of towns in
Massachusetts, Rhode Island, and New Hampshire, emerging
as more than a spokesman for the abolitionist cause. He was its chief ex-
hibit, a living case history, a "graduate of the peculiar institution," who
literally bore the scars of slavery, as Douglass said, *with my diploma written on my back!*"[1]

He moved audiences with stories from his enslaved past, but his time
traveling also meant new chapters were added to an already eventful
life. During his first autumn on the road, in late September 1841, he was
ordered to move to the "Negro car" at a train station in Lynn, Massachusetts. When his White traveling companions demanded to know
why, the conductor growled at Douglass, "Because you are black."

The situation deteriorated after the conductor summoned a band of railroad enforcers and they assaulted Douglass. He still refused to leave, gripping his seat with all his strength. Moments later the toughs tore the seat free from its floor bolts and ejected it, along with its occupant, from the car. His luggage was next, landing on Douglass, who lay dazed on the platform.[2]

The incident prompted an outcry in the town, with public protests on behalf of Douglass, threats of a railroad boycott, and outraged accounts in the *Lynn Record*. Douglass responded to the community's support by moving to Lynn, which was convenient to Boston and home to many sympathetic Quakers. With the help of the American Anti-Slavery Society, he bought a home in December, and three months later, on March 3, 1842, Anna gave birth to their third child, Frederick Jr.

Yet the man of the house would be there only rarely. He won over audiences at Boston's famed Faneuil Hall and barnstormed across New York State, following the route of the Erie Canal. He spoke to full houses in New York City and Hartford, Connecticut. In 1843 he embarked on a six-month, hundred-meeting tour with lectures and conventions in Vermont, New York, Ohio, Pennsylvania, and Indiana.

Though he impressed his audiences, Douglass and his abolitionist entourage were often unwelcome. They were regularly refused admission to churches and halls and were heckled and pelted with rotten vegetables and racist epithets. But it wasn't until an event in Pendleton, Indiana, that the violence escalated dangerously out of control.

*Abolition* was a fightin' word among Indiana settlers, many of whom had moved there from nearby slaveholding states and held to their Southern sympathies. When Douglass and two colleagues arrived for a two-day meeting, they were warned that a mob planned to disrupt the events. Worried about their house of worship, the trustees at Pendleton's Baptist church, where Douglass and company were scheduled to speak, told the abolitionists they were no longer welcome. They attempted to convene outside on the church steps, but loud jeers and a rainstorm intervened and they adjourned.

The next day being pleasant—it was September 15, 1843—they tried again in a nearby wood, having arranged seats and a makeshift platform. During an opening song, one of the lecturers scheduled to speak, William White, scanned the audience. Among the crowd, which numbered more than a hundred people, the young Harvard graduate spotted perhaps a dozen troublemakers. Though a few more drifted in, they quietly departed when the speeches began, melting into the forest. It seemed like maybe the abolitionists were going to be able to conduct their program without harassment.

"In a few minutes we heard a shout," White later reported. Thirty or more men marched two by two into the clearing; coatless, their sleeves rolled up, they carried bricks, stones, and eggs. Their leader, a coonskin cap on his head, ordered the abolitionists to "be off."

None of the abolitionists budged, but members of the crowd rose to exit. As White pleaded with them to stay, the man in the coonskin cap issued an order.

*"Surround them!"* he yelled.

His mob surged forward, hurling rocks and rotten eggs. The attackers made short work of wrecking the platform, but true to the Garrisonian principle of nonviolence, Douglass stood safely aside. Then, looking around him, he realized he could not catch sight of William White. Fearing White might be in danger, Douglass instinctively grabbed a large stick and entered the fray in search of his friend.

The entrance of the Black man into the melee immediately drew the fury of the mob, and Douglass had to run for his life. A torrent of blows struck him as he fled, one of them smashing his hand. The riot's leader led the pursuit, and a blow to the head knocked Douglass to the ground, where he lay unconscious and defenseless. As the man prepared to strike

*This illustration from his 1881 autobiography* Life and Times of Frederick Douglass, Written by Himself, *portrays Douglass at the moment when, forced to defend himself in Pendleton, Indiana, his commitment to civil disobedience first wavered.*

again, William White appeared and raced into the melee to save his friend.[3] Despite bleeding from a head wound and having had two teeth knocked from his mouth, he threw himself at Douglass's attacker, preventing what might have been a death blow.[4] When the townspeople finally restored peace, the unconscious Douglass was loaded into a wagon and transported to the nearby farm of a Quaker.

Douglass recovered in time to deliver a lecture the following evening, but the beating in the woods changed him. When Garrison had drafted him into the ranks of the abolitionists, Douglass agreed to the importance of nonviolence; as he later wrote, he had been "a No Resistant till I got to fighting with a mob in Pendleton." When he leapt to defend his friend, he defied Garrison's prohibition on fighting back—doing so seemed necessary, even divine, Douglass felt, and on other days, in other places, he would have no choice but to fight again. He had no regrets, admitting "I cannot feel I did wrong." Yet in picking up a cudgel and entering the fray, he opened a tiny crack that would eventually become a yawning schism separating Douglass and Garrison, the two most essential men of abolitionism.[5]

## WRITTEN BY HIMSELF

Douglass's right hand, sorely injured at Pendleton, never recovered its strength and dexterity. Nonetheless, he put that same hand, his writing hand, to work putting his autobiography on paper.

Anna birthed their fourth child, Charles, on October 21, 1844, and with a new baby to help care for, Douglass spent the winter in Lynn. He had something new to prove, too, since people in his audiences had begun to wonder aloud, "How [could] a man, only six years out of bondage, and who had never gone to school a day in life, . . . speak with such eloquence—with such precision of language and power of thought[?]"[6] Douglass answered with his story, this time his whole story.

Over the course of the next six months, seated at a table at the home he shared with his family on Union Street, he wrote out the story of his life as an enslaved person in Talbot County, Maryland, and on the streets of Baltimore. Just as he once found his public voice, knees shaking, speaking to a crowd in Nantucket, he trusted his own truth as he wrote. From the first page, he took the reader on a sometimes hellish journey into his world, one that no White person had known. The title he gave his life story, *Narrative of the Life of Frederick Douglass, an American Slave, Written by Himself*, was itself a rebuttal to his doubters. The book was like no other, its narrative more powerful than any fictional story.

The small volume, consisting of 125 pages plus a preface from William Lloyd Garrison, went on sale in May 1845 for fifty cents. Admiring reviews accumulated, including a gratifying rave in the *Lynn Pioneer*, which called the book "the most thrilling work which the American press ever issued—*and the most important*. If it does not open the eyes of this people, they must be petrified into eternal sleep."[7] By autumn, the book, released by Garrison's Massachusetts Anti-Slavery Society, sold an astonishing 4,500 copies. Editions in English, French, and German were in the works, and before the decade ended, Douglass's *Narrative* sold more than 30,000 copies. In comparison, neither *Walden* by Henry David Thoreau nor Walt Whitman's *Leaves of Grass*, both published in the next decade, would sell more than a few hundred copies in their first year.

Douglass used the written word skillfully, speaking directly to his reader. He was at times sarcastic, at others wistful, but always his words carried an undeniable authenticity. In telling his story he named names:

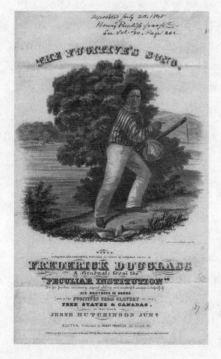

*This song was published in 1845, the same year as* Narrative of the Life of Frederick Douglass. *The sheet music cover stated that the abolitionist song was "respectfully dedicated, in token of confident esteem to Frederick Douglass" and identified him as "a graduate from the peculiar institution."*

His readers met Sophia and Hugh Auld and Edward Covey. Douglass also revealed the name Frederick Augustus Washington Bailey as his own. The fiction of Frederick Douglass fell away, thereby exposing him to the risk that slave catchers would appear at his door. According to a recent Supreme Court decision, a fugitive slave could be legally recaptured despite residence in a free state. Even so, Douglass chose to send a copy of *Narrative* to his owner in Maryland. The Aulds were outraged at their portrayal, and Hugh promised to regain his lost property and "place him in the cotton fields of the South."[8]

By the time those words were written, however, Frederick Douglass was well out of reach, having steamed across the Atlantic for a speaking tour of Ireland, Scotland, and England. The trip would stretch to twenty months, and for Douglass the journey abroad was a revelation. For the first time in his life, no one cared his skin was a different color. Not once while overseas, he reported, did he meet with "a single word, look, or gesture, which gave me the slightest reason to think my color was an offense to anybody."[9] On boarding his ship in Liverpool, however, for the trip home, he was reminded that no man of African ancestry should expect to be treated as the equal of the White man. Despite his prepaid ticket for a first-class cabin, he was refused his berth and exiled to segregated quarters in the steamship's stern.

## THE NORTH STAR

With a little help from new friends, Douglass returned to America a free man. On his behalf a small band of English Quakers had contacted Hugh Auld, asking to buy his freedom. Auld agreed: In return for payment of £150 (in American currency, $710.96), he filed a bill of sale and a deed of manumission at the Baltimore Court House. The documents formally freed "Frederick Bailey, or Douglass, as he calls himself."[10]

When he arrived in Boston on April 20, 1847, Douglass leapt off the ship and caught the first train to Lynn. There, as he reported to one of his English benefactors, "I was met by my two bright-eyed boys, Lewis and Frederick, running and dancing with joy to meet me."[11] He would depart barely a week later on another lecture tour. But those would be his last days as Garrison's headline performer.

While in England, Douglass hatched a new life plan. Now a renowned world figure—one English newspaper called him that "illustrious transatlantic"—Douglass possessed a new confidence in his ability to run his own public life.[12] He hoped to launch an anti-slavery newspaper, believing that, if done well, a Black-run paper "would be a *telling* act against the American doctrine of natural inferiority, and the inveterate prejudice which so universally prevails in [the United States] against the colored race."[13] His admirers abroad had raised $2,174 to underwrite start-up costs, including the purchase of a printing press.

When William Lloyd Garrison got wind of the idea, he dismissed it. "The land is full of the wreck of such experiments," said Garrison. In fact, a handful of earlier Black-operated papers had failed, among them *Freedom's Journal*, *The Elevator*, and *The Colored American*.[14] Garrison insisted that Douglass could better serve the cause by carrying on as abolitionism's most persuasive spokesman, traveling and pleading the cause directly to audiences.

Taken aback by Garrison's objections, Douglass briefly put his plan on hold. But his desire to prove himself soon won out, and by October, Douglass was purchasing type. In November he moved to Rochester, New York, where he rented office space. He became his own man, confident his proposed publication would make him an even more effective advocate for Black Americans.

He chose Rochester deliberately. The western New York location gave him a healthy distance from Garrison and *The Liberator*, with which he would compete for readers and advertisers. Rochester was also a hotbed of abolitionism, for many years a way station on the Underground Railroad. Rochester had a substantial Black community, and Douglass's family would join him there a few months later. The upstate city became home for Anna and Frederick for the next quarter century.

Douglass christened his paper *The North Star*, echoing the advice— *Go north! Follow the North Star!*—that runaways were traditionally given when they ran for freedom. Issue number 1 went on sale on December 3, 1847, and within weeks Douglass's four-page weekly had a mailing list of seven hundred, a number that would eventually rise to an average of three thousand subscribers.

Still hungry to learn, he found his new paper "the best school possible." As its founding editor and writer, he taught himself to be a journalist and master the rules of grammar. "It obliged me to think and read, it taught me to express my thoughts clearly, and was perhaps better than any other course I could have adopted."[15]

*The North Star* gave Douglass a broad public platform. In the first issue he attacked Henry Clay, Abraham Lincoln's idol, a colonization man who, while favoring the return of bondsmen to their "ancestral" home in Africa, remained a slaveholder himself. "Do you think that God will hold you guiltless," demanded Douglass in *The North Star*, "if you die with the blood of these fifty slaves clinging to your garments?"[16] His argument echoed the "Moral Persuasion" central to Garrison's thinking, yet by choosing Clay as a target, Douglass also took a step away from his former benefactor. In the first issue of *The North Star*, Douglass opened a political conversation.

Douglass also worked to educate himself concerning the issues of the day. Among them was the Mexican War, which was drawing to a close. Launched by slaveholder president James Polk, the conflict was, in the eye of abolitionists, a transparent attempt by Southern politicians to extend their influence by adding slave states to the Union. To others, it was simply a way to solidify the recent Texas annexation, though along the way it did upset the balance of power between free and slaveholding states. Douglass saw signs that slavery and politics were inseparable everywhere he looked.

In the summer of 1848, he traveled to nearby Seneca Falls to speak at America's first women's rights convention. He was true to his paper's motto, printed on the masthead, which proclaimed, "Right Is of No Sex—Truth Is of No Color." His was the only Black face in attendance, but Elizabeth Cady Stanton and her friends were his allies, all of them anti-slavery advocates. Theirs was a shared pursuit of equality.

# MR. LINCOLN GOES TO WASHINGTON

As Douglass gained fame, Lincoln the family man and lawyer decided to resume his public life, this time as a U.S. congressman. After her husband won Illinois's Seventh District seat, Mary refused to be left behind in provincial Springfield. On moving into Mrs. Sprigg's boardinghouse on First Street, in December 1847, they were a family of four, including son Robert, now four years old, and toddler Eddie, a year and a half.

Washington, D.C., was a revelation to the Lincolns, a burgeoning city with a population of more than thirty thousand White and ten thousand Black citizens, including roughly two thousand men and women in bondage. Lincoln witnessed the city's racial inequalities in small ways and large. One day at Mrs. Sprigg's, the quiet of the house was interrupted by the arrival of three officers to seize one of her waiters. Guns drawn, they put irons on his wrists and dragged him away while his wife and the Lincolns watched. The man had been using his wages to buy his freedom and had done nothing wrong. But just sixty dollars short of the purchase price, his owner had changed his mind. The police had been sent to return the man to slavery.[17]

Lincoln was gaining a new awareness of the issue that divided the country, with the practice entirely legal in more than a dozen states in a wide swath that encompassed the entire South. Slaveholders, dependent upon free labor, regarded slavery as a fundamental right; a growing number of people in the North, galvanized by abolitionists, thought human bondage a fundamental wrong. But Lincoln, as a first-year congressman, had no illusions about changing the country's course.

He served diligently on committees and missed almost no roll call votes. With the White House and Senate in Democratic hands, his Whig Party wielded little power, but he eyed the campaign of 1848. Looking to gain an advantage over the opposition, Lincoln, in his first major speech, accused President James Polk of provoking the Mexican War. Calling the war a land grab and a transparent attempt to expand slavery, the freshman congressman dismissed Polk as a "bewildered, confounded, and perplexed man."[18] The speech got Lincoln nowhere since it angered constituents back home for his opposition to a war in which many of them fought. As for Polk, he simply ignored the accusations and never so much as uttered Lincoln's name.

In his second session the following winter, Lincoln tried a different approach. Rather than getting into a dispute about the recent past, he looked to pass legislation that would lead to the abolition of slavery in Washington, D.C.

His attitude toward slavery remained a bundle of contradictions. To the man on the street in Illinois, as in the North in general, slavery had little immediate reality. With just 1 percent of the Black population living in the free states, relatively few White citizens interacted with people of color. Most of Lincoln's own experience with the enslaved had been limited to encounters at the Kentucky homes of friends or with the Todd family, where living conditions bore almost no resemblance to the hardships of bondsmen who worked in the cotton fields or on sugarcane plantations.

By nature, Lincoln was against slavery, as his father had been. But as a lawyer and lawmaker, he also believed the Constitution protected the rights of each state to decide its own policy. Although the "peculiar institution," in the words of powerful pro-slavery senator John Calhoun, wasn't a daily presence in his life, Lincoln had gotten disquieting glimpses of slavery's cruelty. Returning from Kentucky a few years earlier, he had shared a long, meandering steamboat ride with a coffle of "ten or a dozen slaves, shackled together with irons." The sight of the poor wretches had stayed with him, the memory of it a "continual torment."[19] In his Washington days, the business of slavery was an inescapable, day-to-day fact of life.

Foreign visitors to the American capital had often remarked upon the hypocrisy of a country that boasted of its individual freedoms when numerous so-called "slave pens" could be seen on the city's streets. Lincoln overlooked one of them from the Capitol. "[It was] a sort of negro-livery stable," he wrote, "where droves of negroes were collected [and] temporarily kept . . . precisely like droves of horses."[20] These human corrals were way stations for the enslaved, many of whom were headed to the deep South from Virginia's played-out tobacco plantations.

In particular, Lincoln found his growing anger directed at slave traders; he called them "a small, odious, and detested class."[21] He also recognized that an ongoing congressional debate concerning the slave trade in the District of Columbia was dividing not only the nation but his party. In response, he drafted a bill he hoped might stand a chance of passage, incorporating elements calculated to appeal to various constituencies. One required "full cash value" be paid to slaveholders as compensation for those they freed. The law would declare all children born of enslaved women after 1850 free at birth. Another clause would require city authorities to arrest and return fugitives who sought safe harbor in Washington. Finally, a referendum would be mandated in the district to approve (or reject) the legislation, since Lincoln believed abolition was a matter for the people, not Congress, to decide.

When he went public with the laboriously negotiated bill, a barrage of angry criticism led former backers to melt away. Lincoln had tried to craft a compromise with enough sweeteners that his congressional brethren on both sides of the slavery argument could hold their noses, ignore what they did not like, and advance the issue, but the strategy failed. Lincoln would never formally introduce the bill and, instead, reaped only insults, even from abolitionists appalled that Lincoln's proposal allowed for apprehending fugitives within the district for return to their slaveholders. John Calhoun also attacked Lincoln—though not by name, calling him only a "member from Illinois"—and denounced the bill, which Calhoun claimed was a threat to life in the South as he knew it and would lead to "the prostration of the white race."[22]

Looking to please everyone, Lincoln satisfied no one. When Congress adjourned in the early morning hours of Sunday, March 4, 1849, his congressional term ended. After wrapping up his affairs, he headed back to Springfield, where, Lincoln noted later, "he went to the practice of the law with greater earnestness than ever before."[23] Like everyone else, he had found the problem of slavery intractable. Dreams of a career in national politics looked to be fading away.

## A NEW MENTOR

As the decade drew to a close, Abraham Lincoln walked away from politics. Meanwhile, Frederick Douglass struggled to keep his paper afloat.

His seed money quickly spent, Douglass mortgaged his new brick home in Rochester to pay his employees. He traveled often to lecture and seek new subscribers, and he looked to his allies for contributions. Among the most important would be a new American friend, an upstate New Yorker named Gerrit Smith, who would contribute more than money. As Garrison's control over his protégé faded, Smith became the single most important influence on Douglass's thinking about how to confront slavery and the slavers.

Smith had introduced himself in a nearly illegible letter that landed on Douglass's desk a few days after the first issue of *The North Star* went on sale. The stranger sent warm greetings and a five-dollar check, good for a two-year subscription. "I welcome you to the State of New York," Douglass read as he deciphered Smith's scrawl. "May you and yours, and your labors of love for your oppressed race, be all greatly blessed of God."[24]

To Douglass's surprise, the envelope also contained a deed for forty acres of land in a place called Timbuctoo. Douglass published the letter in the next issue of *The North Star*, thereby inaugurating a friendship that would be both public and private.

Gerrit Smith was a very rich man, the owner of vast tracts of undeveloped land in upstate New York. His father, Peter, a business partner of America's first multimillionaire, John Jacob Astor, had accumulated more than a million acres of real estate. But Gerrit, despite being raised in a mansion near Syracuse, had seen his share of unhappy moments. On the day after his graduation from Hamilton College in 1818, his mother died; one year later, his wife of seven months passed away unexpectedly. Then the young man abandoned what he called the "laudable pursuit" of literature (he read Greek and Latin and greatly admired the poetry of Lord Byron) when his still-grieving father handed him full responsibility for the massive family estate. It was a task Gerrit had neither asked for nor wanted.[25]

Some years later, Gerrit Smith and his second wife grew interested in issues of social reform. As a budding philanthropist, his favorite charities included the American Temperance Society, which regarded alcohol consumption as a sin that corrupted body, mind, and soul, and the American Colonization Society, an organization devoted to resettling

*Gerrit Smith, the very rich New Yorker who provided land to Black homesteaders and influenced Frederick Douglass's thinking on the merits of the Constitution, pictured here in the 1840s.*

American Blacks in Africa. Over time, Smith's thinking shifted from colonization, never a practical solution in a country with millions of enslaved people, to abolitionism. He proudly boasted he had become an "antislavery fanatic."

Smith's home in Peterboro, New York, became an important stop on the Underground Railroad, and he personally purchased the freedom of dozens of the enslaved. Peterboro was a rarity for its time, a fully integrated town, and on a typical evening in his own dining room Smith shared his table with fashionable visitors of his own social class, "three or four Indians from the neighborhood," and "a sprinkling of negroes from the sunny South, on their way to Canada."[26] But the Timbuctoo community he founded more than a hundred miles away in the Adirondack Mountains was his most remarkable social experiment.

In North Elba, New York, he set out to create a self-sustaining community. In 1846, he designated 120,000 acres for the purpose, giving forty-acre parcels to each of a hoped-for total of three thousand Black New Yorkers, both freemen and fugitives. Smith believed strongly in political action, and his "Smith Grants" would enable the inhabitants of Timbuctoo to gain access to the ballot box by fulfilling New York State's strict property requirement. Black men had to have assets of $250 to vote, though there was no such requirement for White males.

Smith's first letter to Douglass opened the dialogue between the two men, and Douglass soon visited Smith's Peterboro estate. He found that Smith, unlike Garrison, valued discussion and argument. While Garrison brooked no dissent among his followers, Douglass and his new friend often disagreed, both in their in-person conversations and in the pages of *The North Star*, which in the coming years regularly published Smith's responses to Douglass's editorials.

## CONSTITUTIONALLY SPEAKING

Although the two shared a passionate hatred of slavery, they started from fundamentally different positions in thinking about the United States Constitution. Douglass came to the discussion tutored by Garrison to hate the Constitution. The founding document was so flawed, Garrison maintained, that it could only be rejected and reinvented. Though it did not explicitly condone slavery, article 1, section 2 of the Constitution distinguished "free Persons" from "other Persons." Without being called by name, these "other persons"—logically, they could only be the enslaved—were assigned a value for purposes of congressional apportionment of three-fifths that of "free persons." According to Garrison's reading, the Constitution thus enshrined slavery as legal and legitimate, rendering the entire document, in his opinion, corrupt, pro-slavery, and worthless.

Gerrit Smith took a different view. He saw no need to nullify the Constitution. As Lincoln had done, Smith studied Blackstone's *Commentaries*, the foundational work of English law. From its dense pages he extracted the notion of "natural law," which he concluded was incompatible with slavery. Thus, in Smith's interpretation, the Constitution was an aspirational document, a working instrument that could be improved, its flaws fixed. Most significant of all, Smith believed that the Constitution empowered Congress to legislate the abolition of slavery in the Southern states. This had led to a parting of the ways with Garrison, and Smith had founded his own political party, the Liberty Party, in 1840. He had even run for president himself under the Liberty Party banner, but he caused little more than a ripple in the election of 1848, when he got just 2,500 votes out of roughly three million cast. But Douglass found himself drawn to Smith's thinking.

By 1850, Douglass was veering sharply away from Garrison's and toward Smith's interpretation of American law. At first the change was slow, but the passage of the Fugitive Slave Act sped the process.

The Fugitive Slave Act was one of the five laws that made up the Compromise of 1850. Senators Henry Clay and Stephen Douglas had masterminded the Compromise, hoping to unite the representatives of free and slave states and put the slavery debate behind them. One of the laws abolished the slave trade (though not slavery itself) in Washington. Another defined Texas's disputed western and northern boundaries. Other acts established territorial governments in Utah and New Mexico, freshly acquired in the Mexican War along with California, and permitted California to join the Union as a free state. Both sides won something, it seemed. But the fifth law proved incendiary.

The draconian Fugitive Slave Act required federal and local law enforcement officials to arrest and return runaways in all states and territories, including the free states. It specified fines and imprisonment for citizens caught aiding escapees. The Fugitive Slave Act removed runaway cases from Northern courts, stripping away due process. In short, it required Northerners who opposed slavery to betray their principles, in effect to collaborate with the enforcement of slavery.

Some in the North called it the "Kidnapping Act," and for Douglass, this was personal. If the law had been in effect when he escaped a dozen years before, anyone who helped him could have been punished; had he been caught, even in Northern territory, he would have been shackled and returned to bondage. But the passage of the Fugitive Slave Act posed another question, too: If the federal government could enforce slavery, could it not also choose to abolish it?

In May 1851, Douglass, after carefully thinking through his argument, took a public stand against the act at an American Anti-Slavery Society convention meeting in Syracuse. His argument boiled down to this: Consistent with "the noble purposes in its preamble," Douglass believed the Constitution could "be wielded in behalf of emancipation."[27] He wanted not to reject the founding document but to put it to work. In the preamble, its purposes are clearly stated, key among them to "secure the Blessings of Liberty." That was the document's true promise, and in Douglass's reading, it could power abolition. It was an almost complete reversal in his thinking.

When Garrison got wind of Douglass's speech, he was apoplectic. He labeled his protégé an apostate and declared him an avowed enemy; in the years to come, the Garrisonians would do everything they could to undermine Douglass's work. But new ally Gerrit Smith welcomed Douglass to the ranks of political abolitionists and looked for new ways they might work together for the cause. Douglass's change of heart led to the merger of the *Liberty Party Paper*, which Smith backed, and *The North Star*. The first issue of the combined publication, renamed *Frederick Douglass' Paper*, appeared on June 30, 1852. Its motto, suggested by Gerrit Smith, was "All Rights for All."

Douglass, a decade out of slavery, now free of both Hugh Auld and Garrison, had forged his own public identity. During the next decade, he would continue to opine from the columns of his paper about slavery and American politics. He had truly become his own man.

————◆————

# FIVE

# WHERE THERE IS SMOKE

One flash from the heart-supplied intellect of Harriet Beecher Stowe could light a million camp fires in front of the embattled host of slavery, which not all the waters of the Mississippi, mingled as they are with blood, could extinguish.

—FREDERICK DOUGLASS, *My Bondage and My Freedom*, 1855

D ouglass and Lincoln were far from the only people drawn to the thorny problem of slavery. After decades of denial and willful ignorance, new voices in the 1850s brought human bondage to people's attention. Among them was a minister's wife in Maine—she would make millions of people cry—and a senator who would find himself lying in a pool of his own blood on the floor of Congress.

In July 1851, Frederick Douglass received a letter from an early subscriber to *The North Star*. Mrs. H. E. B. Stowe wanted Douglass's help in a writing project of her own, which she described as "a series of sketches" about slavery. The first ones had already appeared in a weekly paper, *The National Era*, but she needed to get direct testimony about plantation life. "I wish to be able to make a picture," she told Douglass, "that shall be graphic & true to nature in its details."[1]

A petite woman who stood less than five feet tall, Harriet Beecher Stowe would write a very big book. She reworked her serial sketches into the novel *Uncle Tom's Cabin; or, Life Among the Lowly*. Published in 1852, it found an immense audience, selling more rapidly than any book in the nation's history, three hundred thousand copies in 1852 alone. The next decade would see some two million copies printed in the United States and several times that worldwide.

In reaction to the Fugitive Slave Act, Frederick Douglass had ratcheted up his rhetoric. "I am a peace man," he proclaimed before issuing a stern warning to those who favored slavery and, in particular, slave catchers. He could imagine fugitives and their protectors fighting back.

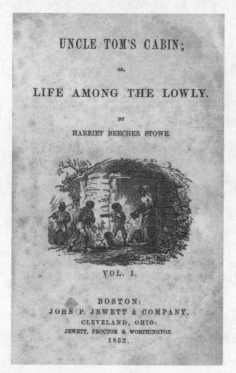

*The title sheet from an early edition of Mrs. Stowe's moving novel.*

"I believe that two or three dead slaveholders," said Douglass, "will make this law a dead letter."[2] But Mrs. Stowe's emotionalism in response to the same legislation impacted the slavery debate beyond Douglass's angry words.

Mrs. Stowe wanted her readers see slavery with "new eyes."[3] In a sentimental manner, she told the story of her title character. Though saintly and kind to everyone, Tom was beaten to death by slaveholder Simon Legree and his overseers. A fugitive named Eliza met a better fate when she escaped slavery, her son Harry clutched to her bosom, by leaping onto an ice floe that carried her across the Ohio River. Readers of the melodrama also met the mischievous Topsy, a badly abused enslaved woman, and Cassy, who, having seen two of her children sold, killed her third child.

Stowe could tell a story, and the humanity of her Black characters

*Harriet Beecher Stowe in a photograph taken shortly after the publication of* Uncle Tom's Cabin.

shone through on every page; their hardships and the perils they experienced left readers in tears. To millions of White people who knew few or no Blacks, the book offered a larger revelation: The enslaved were people, too. They had human voices, feelings, and hopes.

Douglass and Stowe would not meet until early 1853, when she invited him to visit her. The two did not see eye to eye on all matters, since several fugitives at the close of *Uncle Tom's Cabin* were headed for Liberia, the African nation established for formerly enslaved people. Colonization, he said to the "good lady," was no answer to ending slavery. "The truth is, dear madam," Douglass explained, "we are *here,* & here we are likely to remain."[4]

Yet they would be allies and occasional correspondents for many years to come. She tried to mend the rift between Douglass and William Lloyd Garrison, telling Garrison that "[Douglass] holds no opinion which he cannot defend . . . [and] his plans for the elevation of his own race, are manly, sensible, comprehensive."[5] In his speeches and his writings, Douglass often made reference to *Uncle Tom's Cabin* and its raw emotional truths, calling it "a work of marvelous depth and power. . . . No book on the subject of slavery had so generally and favorably touched the American heart."[6]

The success of her book dwarfed the sales of Douglass's *Narrative,* but he was more than happy that *Uncle Tom* made slavery a topic of dinner-table talk across the country. Mrs. Stowe's portrayal of slavery's cruelties outraged many in the South, but more importantly, it appealed to people of conscience of the North, whether they were farmers in Maine, factory workers in eastern cities, or settlers making their way in the West. By making everyone look more closely at slavery and by demanding slaveowners look in the mirror, *Uncle Tom's Cabin* raised the country's emotional temperature a good deal closer to the national boiling point.

# LINCOLN RISING

After completing his term in Congress, Lincoln once again pushed politics to the back of his mind.[7] For the next five years, his personal life was eventful, with the death of his three-year-old son, Eddie, taken by tuberculosis, in February 1850, and the birth of William Wallace that December. He and Mary welcomed a last child, Thomas—nicknamed "Tad," short for "Tadpole," because of his very large head—in 1853, so Lincoln spent much of the first half of the 1850s helping to raise his three boys, including the eldest, Robert, who turned ten in 1853.

His Illinois law practice prospered, partly because of his reputation for diligence and truthfulness. The man now widely known in Illinois as "Honest Old Abe" summed up his legal philosophy in a single line. "[I]f in your own judgment, you can not be an honest lawyer," he wrote, "resolve to be honest without being a lawyer."[8]

Then, in 1854, Lincoln heard the call to public life once more.

Signed into law on May 30, 1854, the Kansas–Nebraska Act sent a tremor across the country. The argument over slavery had become a heated debate over which of the western territories could become slave states and which free states. Sponsored by Lincoln's old rival Stephen Douglas, the Kansas–Nebraska legislation attempted to break a legislative logjam, but it did so by repealing a three-decades-old agreement, spelled out in the Missouri Compromise, that established latitude 36°30' as the northern boundary for slavery in territories and new states. Douglas's legislation erased that hard line and replaced it with the principle of "popular sovereignty." That meant residents would vote on permitting or prohibiting slavery in the upper half of the Louisiana Purchase, now the Nebraska and Kansas territories.

By blowing up the central principle of the Missouri Compromise, the Kansas–Nebraska Act ended a fragile truce that had prevailed for years.

Southerners rejoiced because new slave states could be established where once they could not, potentially adding more congressional representation to what was called the "slave power." In the North, opponents of slavery feared the balance of power would now shift permanently into Southern hands.

For Lincoln, it was as if he had been awakened from a slumber by a bucket of water. When the act became law he was "thunderstruck and stunned," and he felt compelled by the sudden change in his country's ground rules to leap into the unfolding national controversy.[9] But before he did, Lincoln, as a man who always lived by the book, went to the library.

For Frederick Douglass, anti-slavery was a cause he carried like a cross every hour of his life. For Abraham Lincoln, a White man who lived in a free state, slavery wasn't an everyday matter. Instinctively he hated the idea of it. He thought slavery was morally wrong and, some said, he had quietly contributed money to help fugitives on the Underground Railroad.[10] As a young politician, he admitted, "the slavery question often bothered me," but as he readied to weigh into the debate in 1854, he felt the need to master its history, economics, and politics.[11] That summer he set about improving his education at the State Library in Springfield.

For weeks he pored over historical and legal texts, reading what the Founders said about slavery. He analyzed the census records and studied earlier congressional debates. Wanting to know everything about the history of slavery in the United States, he assembled a mass of facts and accumulated "scraps of arguments against slavery."[12] At summer's end he emerged with a sheaf of papers and, in late August, gave the first of a dozen speeches around Illinois, speaking and debating as the election of 1854 approached. In Peoria, on October 16, he presented his final argument, one buttressed by a deep and careful reading of the American past.

## LINCOLN'S REBUTTAL

Stephen Douglas had spoken earlier, and after a break for dinner, the crowd reassembled to listen to Lincoln in front of the tall facade of Peoria's stone and brick courthouse. At seven o'clock he appeared, one leg first, maneuvering his angular frame through a window to stand atop the roof over the entrance portico. Lincoln looked down at the crowd that filled the town square, their faces lit in the autumn dark by lanterns and by candles in the windows of nearby houses.

He told his listeners he had long believed, along with many of the Founders, that slavery would die a natural death. He pointed out that the Framers omitted all mention of "slave" and "slavery" in the Constitution. "[T]he thing is hid away, in the constitution, just as an afflicted man hides away a wen or a cancer, which he dares not cut out at once, lest he bleed to death." He pointed to subsequent limitations put on the slave trade and noted that the Northwest Ordinance of 1787 forbade slavery in Ohio, Indiana, Illinois, Michigan, and Wisconsin. Lastly, he pointed to the Missouri Compromise, which had been "canonized," he said, "as a sacred thing."

Only now Stephen Douglas's Kansas–Nebraska Act had gutted it, making the spread of slavery seem inevitable.

His speech lasted for three hours, but "perfect silence prevailed" as he laid out his argument.[13] He argued for the restoration of the 36°30' boundary, though he knew that was unlikely. Nor did he have another answer. "If all earthly power were given me, I should not know what to do [though] . . . my first impulse would be to free all the slaves, and send them to Liberia." Despite its appeal—and he would advocate for it in the years to come—colonization was not a practical solution. But neither could Lincoln imagine freeing all Blacks to "make them politically and socially our equals." He did not believe they were.

What he did do was lay down a hard line of his own: a stubborn opposition to the extension of "the monstrous injustice of slavery itself." He hated slavery because it made Americans hypocrites and diminished his country's influence as a representative to the world of republican values. He felt in his bones that the further spread of slavery must be prevented.

The speaker that cool autumn evening in Peoria wasn't Lincoln the amusing storyteller who won over juries and audiences by poking fun at himself and others. Instead he stood as a passionate man who had found a topic that tested his intellect as he spoke from the heart. "Mr. Lincoln's eloquence," one young Chicago journalist observed, "produced conviction in others because of the conviction of the speaker himself. His listeners felt that he believed every word he said."[14]

After delivering his speech, he handed the manuscript to the editors of the *Illinois State Journal.* Its great length, some seventeen thousand words, necessitated serial publication in the single-sheet paper, and in late October the full text appeared piece by piece in seven consecutive issues of the *Journal.* Lincoln was announcing himself to his nation, and for the next few years, his Peoria speech would be his most essential position paper as he found his place in the politics of his state and country. His opposition to slavery—most specifically, to preventing its extension—was a cause equal to his ambitions.

The immediate consequences of the Kansas–Nebraska Act were on his mind, too. As he asked the crowd at Peoria, "Bowie-knives and six-shooters are seen plainly enough [in the territories] but never a glimpse of the ballot-box. . . . Is it not probable that the contest will come to blows, and bloodshed?" Events would prove him prescient: So many violent clashes between slavery and anti-slavery men occurred in the territory in the coming months that *New-York Tribune* editor Horace Greeley nicknamed the place "Bleeding Kansas." But the violence and intimidation would not be limited to Kansas or Nebraska. One bloodletting would soon occur in Washington, D.C., within the hallowed halls of the United States Congress.

# A FIGHT ON THE FLOOR

The Senate chamber was unusually quiet. After an early adjournment, the hush of the room was broken only by the voices of a few stragglers talking quietly. For these about-to-be witnesses, May 22, 1856, would be anything but a typical day in the Capitol.

Senator Charles Sumner of Massachusetts sat alone. At work on the correspondence spread across his desk, he was unaware of the arrival of the other player in this two-man drama, Congressman Preston Brooks. Elected from an upland district in South Carolina, Brooks spent most of his time in the House of Representatives at the opposite end of the building, but on this particular Thursday he had a pressing matter to take up with the senior senator from the Bay State.

Earlier that week, Sumner had delivered a long speech. He was a lawyer and a scholar, and at a time when few in Congress would call themselves abolitionists, he was proud to claim that label. He had spent weeks drafting his speech, which he titled "The Crimes Against Kansas." On the floor of the Senate, he made a full-throated argument that Kansas was falling into "the hateful embrace of slavery."[15]

His fears were well-founded. Just as Lincoln and others predicted, Kansas had become a battleground. After passage of the Kansas–Nebraska Act, immigrants on both sides of the slavery argument flooded into the territory, looking to establish residence and gain the right to vote. Towns like Lawrence and Topeka became hotbeds of abolitionism, while Leavenworth and Atchison filled with so-called "border ruffians," mostly pro-slavery Missourians. Widespread voter fraud led to unrest, with Kansans struggling to decide whether their state would be

*Gifted orator, brilliant lawyer, linguist, and committed reformer, Senator Charles Sumner of Massachusetts. The photograph dates to the early 1850s.*

free or slave. "Beecher's bibles" arrived, too. To avoid capture by the enemy, Sharps rifles, renamed for the Brooklyn-based minister Henry Ward Beecher, had been packaged in crates labeled "Books" to arm abolitionist forces.

Sumner's oration had lasted for hours on each of two consecutive days. Speaking from his Senate desk, he criticized the pro-slavery administration of President Franklin Pierce. He condemned Senator Stephen Douglas, too, and in particular his doctrine of popular sovereignty, which Sumner renamed "Popular Slavery." In Sumner's hot words, popular sovereignty was an evil idea that had emerged from Douglas's mind just as sin had from Satan's. But he had reserved his sharpest barbs for Senator Andrew Butler.

Sumner compared Butler to Don Quixote. "The senator from South Carolina . . . believes himself a chivalrous knight," Sumner began. But rather than taking as his mistress an innocent farm girl, as the title character in Cervantes's novel had done, Butler chose a woman "ugly to others [and] polluted in the sight of the world." She was, said Sumner, "the harlot slavery." Even an indirect allusion to sexuality violated the Senate's rules of decorum, but Sumner blew through that prohibition—and his meaning was clear to every informed listener. He was referencing the widespread accusation that slaveholders were sexual predators who fathered children with the women they owned.

For Preston Brooks, a cousin of Butler, Sumner's words were too much to take. After reading the speech in the newspaper, he set out for the Capitol, walking stick in hand, to complete what he viewed as an errand of honor. Sumner's words had besmirched the honor not only of his cousin, who was absent that week from Washington, but of their state. According to the Southern code of chivalry, that demanded a response.

Arriving at the mostly empty Senate floor, Brooks walked down the aisle, limping noticeably, the result of a gunshot wound sustained in a duel years before. When Brooks reached Sumner's desk, he leaned in.

*Congressman Brooks's assault on Charles Sumner shocked the nation. When this illustration was published, the caption read,* THE SYMBOL OF THE NORTH IS THE PEN; THE SYMBOL OF THE SOUTH IS THE BLUDGEON.

"Mr. Sumner," he began, his tone calm. He told Sumner he had read his Kansas speech and that he took exception to his slander of "a relative of mine." Even before he finished speaking—as Brooks remembered, his closing words were, "I feel it to be my duty to punish you for it"—he struck Sumner with his walking stick.[16]

The gold head of the heavy cane crashed into the senator's head. Before Sumner could rise, Brooks swung the walking stick again. And again and yet again, delivering a rapid series of blows with such force that the stick cut clean to Sumner's skull, opening deep lacerations in the flesh. With blood pouring down his face, Sumner, a sturdy man of six-foot-four, struggled to stand, but his long legs caught beneath the desk. He teetered, but Brooks, taking Sumner by the lapel, steadied him as he continued to strike blow after blow with the stick clenched in his other hand.

Blinded by the blood running into his eyes, Sumner raised his arms to protect himself. The shaft of Brooks's cane snapped, but he continued to batter Sumner with the length that remained. No one interfered; the attack was sudden, and most senators had departed for a midday meal. After tearing the desk free of the bolts that fastened it to the floor, Sumner finally managed to get to his feet. But almost as soon as he stood, dazed and concussed, he sank to the floor in the main aisle. Only then did Brooks step back, having delivered, by his own count, thirty blows to Sumner's head and shoulders. "I desisted," he told a congressional investigation a few days later, "simply because I had punished him to my satisfaction." Sumner lay unconscious, his head still bleeding freely, his waistcoat, shirt, and coat covered with blood.

Brooks's premeditated attack was over in a minute or two, but its impact would be lasting. News of the assault traveled quickly, with telegraph lines carrying word far and wide. In the North, people were angry at the "act of an assassin."[17] In the South, people were proud, proclaiming Brooks a hero, with the *Richmond Enquirer* announcing that "the press of the South applaud the conduct of Mr. Brooks, without condition or limitation."[18] In Kansas, however, a man named John Brown got a different message. He heard a call for retribution.

A passionate abolitionist caught up in the fight for Kansas's soul, Brown had been outraged to learn that, on May 21, 1856, pro-slavery forces from Missouri had ransacked Lawrence, Kansas, a town founded by Massachusetts abolitionists. He reached his flashpoint when, a few hours later, he got wind of the attack on Sumner in the Capitol. Brown reacted: As men on both sides had done, Brown had created an informal militia company under his leadership, its ranks including four sons and a son-in-law. Brown and his men then took what he called "radical retaliatory measures."[19] Marching into the Kansas night, they kidnapped five men associated with local pro-slavery violence and slashed them to death with broadswords.

Such carnage was exactly what Lincoln had feared—and predicted. News of what was called the Pottawatomie Massacre, named for a nearby creek, flashed across the country, a terrible counterblow to the beating Sumner had taken. Brown and company were the slaveholders' worst

*John Brown, pictured here in the 1850s, fathered twenty children, failed as a businessman, but committed himself absolutely to the cause of abolition.*

nightmare come to life. Abolitionism, previously a peaceable movement for change, had experienced a real-life transformation like Robert Louis Stevenson's Dr. Jekyll; this wing of the abolitionist movement was as savage and vengeful as the murderous Mr. Hyde of Stevenson's novel.

Overnight John Brown became the intimidating face of abolitionism and a man the entire South could hate. Even to Northerners, Brown seemed a dangerous man and a lawbreaker. A few years later, he would ignite an even larger firestorm.

# SIX

# A SUBTERRANEAN PASSWAY

[John Brown] is of the stuff of which martyrs are made.

—SAMUEL GRIDLEY HOWE, FEBRUARY 5, 1859

T he neighbors knew the tall, angular man in the storm-beaten hat as Isaac Smith. A dense beard worthy of an Old Testament prophet hid the sharp planes of his face, and the fishing rod he carried suggested he was about to try to hook his dinner in a nearby stream. But the disguise didn't fool Frederick Douglass, who recognized Captain John Brown in an instant. He was unmistakable, Douglass later recalled, "lean, strong, and sinewy, of the best New England mould, built for times of trouble, fitted to grapple with life's flintiest hardships."[1]

At Brown's request, the two were about to have a clandestine meeting in an abandoned quarry near Chambersburg, Pennsylvania. The month was August 1859, but their friendship went back a dozen years. They met when Douglass, traveling the lecture circuit to promote his just-launched newspaper, stopped in Springfield, Massachusetts. The orator had been welcomed by Brown's large family—Brown would father twenty children—and partook of a simple meal of beef soup, cabbage, and potatoes.

That evening years earlier Brown had confided his master plan for emancipation. Showing Douglass a map of the United States, Brown drew his finger along the Allegheny Mountains, the rugged ridge that extended from Pennsylvania through Virginia and into Kentucky. He would start small with just twenty-five handpicked men, Brown explained. From hiding places high in the Alleghenies, his volunteers would infiltrate nearby Virginia farms and find bondsmen eager to run away. Some fugitives would be sent north on the Underground Railroad, but the strongest and bravest would join Brown's little army in the mountains, expanding the effort to emancipate as many of the enslaved as possible.[2] And it would give Blacks a larger role in shaping their destiny, as they became soldiers fighting for their own freedom.

The two men had debated the bold plan for a "Subterranean Pass-Way" until three in the morning, their faces lit by candlelight. Brown impressed Douglass, who wrote in *The North Star* that his host was "deeply interested in our cause, as though his own soul had been pierced with the iron of slavery."[3] Brown had hated slavery since the age twelve, when, having himself been treated with kindness and consideration by a slaveholder his father knew, he was horrified at the man's mistreatment of a "*negro* boy . . . who was fully if not more than [my] equal." The enslaved child was badly clothed and fed. After watching the man beat the other boy mercilessly, Brown swore an "*eternal war*" on slavery.[4]

In the years since their first meeting, Brown and his family had devoted themselves to abolitionism. As homesteaders in Gerrit Smith's Adirondack experiment, Timbuctoo, Brown welcomed Black settlers to dine at his table. He spoke to them using their surnames—as in *Mr. Jefferson* and *Mrs. Wait*—which was an unheard-of politeness from a White man. One Black neighbor child remembered Brown would "walk up to our house . . . and come in and play with us children and talk to father. Many's the time I've sat on John Brown's knee."[5] In a way that few Whites of the time did, Brown treated the Black man as his equal.

Douglass and Brown were friends, meeting over the years in Rochester and at abolitionist meetings. They found different approaches, Douglass with his lectures, Brown with action in Kansas. Douglass looked to work inside the law, looking to rewrite it; Brown followed a path that sometimes veered outside of it. But both had been stunned, in 1857, when the United States Supreme Court handed down the Dred Scott decision. It made clear that the whole simmering stew of American politics was about to bubble over.

The ruling in *Dred Scott v. John F. A. Sandford* found that the plaintiff, Dred Scott, a man born into slavery, remained the legal property of John Sandford, despite having spent years living in free states. The broad strokes of Chief Justice Roger Taney's opinion further angered

*Dred Scott in an image published several decades after his death. Scott was the subject of what has been called the Supreme Court's worst-ever decision.*

*By the late 1850s, John Brown was notorious; he grew a beard as a disguise. In this lithograph published after his capture at Harper's Ferry, the imprisoned Brown holds a copy of the* New-York Tribune. *The newspaper's editor, Horace Greeley, observed, "[Brown] seems to have infected the citizens of Virginia with a delusion as great as his own . . . that a grand army of abolitionists were about to invade them from the North."*

abolitionists because it asserted that the "negro African race" was "of an inferior and subordinate class." Blacks, wrote Taney, "had no rights which the white man was bound to respect."[6]

In the eyes of the most powerful judge in the land, people of African descent *were not* and *could not* be citizens.

ON AUGUST 20, 1859, Douglass entered the abandoned stone quarry with caution; he knew that Brown, a wanted man, would be well armed. But Brown greeted him with his usual intense gaze, his blue-gray eyes "full of light and fire."

He explained why he had summoned Douglass. The ever-larger stakes, Brown believed, required bigger action. They had talked often over the years about fomenting a slave uprising in Virginia, but the plan now consisted of much more than the creation of a subterranean passway.

Brown aimed at a new and specific target, the federal arsenal at Harper's Ferry, Virginia.*

They sat amid the rocky debris. On hearing the new scheme, Douglass immediately opposed it. His thinking had shifted from the pacifism of his early Garrison days—violence at places like Pendleton, Indiana, ended that—but for many hours that day and the next Brown and Douglass again debated the cases for and against. The entire nation would see taking the arsenal as an attack on the government, Douglass said. The country needed to be shocked, countered Brown. The assault would make the original goal of opening a conduit for runaways to the North nearly impossible, Douglass argued. He also warned the older man that he would be "going into a perfect steel-trap, and that once in he would never get out alive."[7] In short, attacking Harper's Ferry was a suicide mission. Brown remained adamant.

At last, as Douglass prepared to depart, having refused to join Brown's troops, the White man embraced his Black friend and made one last argument. "Come with me, Douglass," Brown said urgently, "I want you for a special purpose. When I strike the bees will begin to swarm, and I shall want you to help hive them."[8] He understood that Douglass could rally the Black man like no one else.

Whether out of discretion or cowardice—he could never say—Douglass refused to participate. Had he agreed to go, his life would have been very much shorter.

---

* Douglass, *Life and Times* (1881), p. 279. West Virginia did not become a separate state until 1863; in time, the name of the town would lose its possessive, and is now officially known as Harpers Ferry.

# *INSURRECTION!*

On a moonless night eight Sundays later, John Brown held the reins of a four-horse team that pulled a wagon loaded with tools and weapons. Eighteen soldiers of his "provisional army" followed, thirteen of them White men, five Black; three others remained behind at a log school-house with more supplies and ammunition. Shouldering their rifles, the raiding party marched toward Harper's Ferry, the industrial town located at the confluence of the Potomac and Shenandoah Rivers in western Virginia.

At first, Brown's plan went like clockwork. Two of his men slipped into the woods and cut the east-bound telegraph lines. The little company then crossed the Potomac on a long, covered bridge, capturing the unsuspecting watchman, whose primary worry was locomotive sparks that might set the wooden structure afire. On entering the sleeping town—it was after ten o'clock on the Sabbath—Brown headed directly for the U.S. Armory, an expanse of buildings that contained the rifle works and an arsenal.

An elderly night watchman refused them entry, but one of Brown's men pried open the padlocked gate with a crowbar, and the guard, armed with only a sword, was taken prisoner. By midnight, the invading party secured a second bridge, this one stretching across the Shenandoah River. Without firing a shot, Brown was in possession of a hundred thousand guns.

Brown was poised to embark on the fulfillment of his life's mission. "I want to free all the Negroes in this state," he told his prisoners in the armory, ". . . and if the citizens interfere with me, I must only burn the town and have blood."

After midnight the tide shifted. The first blood flowed when a

Baltimore & Ohio express train chugged into town. A Black baggage-master was shot and mortally wounded. Brown permitted the train to proceed, but its departure meant that, at 7:05 A.M., a telegram sent by its conductor arrived at the B&O main offices in Baltimore. "[Train] stopped this morning at Harper's Ferry by armed abolitionists," the train conductor reported. "They say they have come to free the slaves and intend to do it at all hazards."[9]

Brown's identity remained a secret, since the telegram referred to him only as "the Captain." But the occupation of the U.S. Armory by this dangerous man would soon become national news. "SERVILE INSURRECTION," read the front-page headline on the next day's *New-York Times*. "The Federal Arsenal at Harper's Ferry in Possession of Insurgents. GENERAL STAMPEDE OF SLAVES."[10]

The shocking reports of the uprising and of Whites and Blacks in league with one another echoed near and far. But contrary to Brown's hopes, local enslaved persons did not fly to his aid. Instead, farmers and militiamen began to arrive to fight him, alerted by two riders who, Paul Revere–like, galloped into nearby towns hollering *Insurrection! Insurrection!* As tolling church bells alerted people to an emergency, rumors circulated. Some claimed the occupying force consisted of 150 men, others that the raiding party included hundreds of Blacks and a total force of more 750 men.

By late Monday morning, the town rallied in defense, and Brown's force at the U.S. Armory faced almost constant gunfire. Just before noon a contingent of militiamen from nearby Charles Town charged across the Potomac Bridge. All but one of Brown's sentinels fled to safety, but a freedman named Dangerfield Newby became the first of Brown's men to die. After a bullet tore through his neck, Newby's lifeless body was subjected to indignities by the infuriated townspeople. They sliced off his genitals, took the ears for souvenirs, and left his bloody corpse in a gutter for roaming hogs.[11]

By then Brown held a number of hostages, including a local slave-holder named Lewis Washington, a great-grandnephew of General Washington. Brown had plotted Colonel Washington's kidnapping, believing that an association with the name Washington—in the North and South alike, the first president was revered almost as a god—would send a message about the righteousness of his cause. But now Brown had to use his hostages to negotiate a ceasefire, and he sent out a team to talk. The white flag of truce they carried would mean nothing that day, and despite the rules of war, his representative was taken prisoner.

In a defensive move, Brown consolidated his remaining men and hostages in the armory's engine house, a solid, compact building in which fire engines were stored. Here he could make his stand, but "John Brown's Fort," though made of brick, would be a fulfillment of Frederick Douglass's "perfect steel-trap" prophecy.

Brown tried to parley again, but this time the white flag met with a spray of bullets. Brown's eldest son, Watson, shot in the gut, barely managed to crawl back to the engine house. Already several men down, Brown's little army lost another fighter when Oliver, the youngest Brown son, was shot as he sighted his rifle through a crack in the double door of the engine house. He fell motionless to the floor, dead within minutes.

# ENDGAME

At eleven o'clock that night, October 17, 1859, the U.S. military arrived. When word of Brown's raid had reached Washington, there had been a scramble to find a nearby fighting force. Ninety marines stationed at the Washington Navy Yard had been chosen; to command them, the secretary of war summoned Colonel Robert E. Lee, a veteran of the Mexican War and former superintendent of West Point. Lee and his troops marched in a light rain from the train station into Harper's Ferry, arriving before midnight. After reconnoitering the situation, Lee concluded that Brown and his men were not the large fighting force that had been reported, and out of concern for the safety of the hostages, he chose to take no action until morning.[12]

At 7:00 A.M., the company of marines, armed with bayonets and sledgehammers, stood just out of sight of the insurgents. Lieutenant James Ewell Brown ("Jeb") Stuart, Lee's second in command, approached the engine house under a flag of truce.

Inside, John Brown waited with what was left of his "provisional army," now down to four uninjured fighters. Despite the odds, Brown was calm. As hostage Lewis Washington later remembered, "With one son dead by his side, and another shot through, he felt the pulse of his dying son with one hand and held his rifle with the other, and commanded his men with the utmost composure, encouraging them to sell their lives as dearly as they could."[13]

An audience of some two thousand townspeople watched. Lee was in their midst, dressed in civilian garb, as Brown cracked open one of the heavy oak doors. Through the narrow gap Stuart recognized the bearded face of a man he had met once before, in Kansas, while serving in the U.S. Cavalry.

"You are Ossawattomie Brown, of Kansas?" he asked.

"Well," Brown replied, confirming the rumor that had begun to circulate in the town, "they do call me that sometimes."

Stuart delivered his message: Brown and men must surrender unconditionally.

Brown refused, asking instead for safe passage to Maryland in return for the release of the hostages. To that Stuart could not agree.

Brown remained resolute. After further back-and-forth, he said, "You have the numbers on me, but we soldiers are not afraid of death. I would as leave die by a bullet as on the gallows."

"Is that your final answer, Captain?" asked Stuart.

"Yes," replied Brown.[14]

The lieutenant bowed respectfully, but as he stepped away from the engine house, he doffed his cap, waving it high in the air. His gesture—the agreed-upon signal—meant a dozen marines leapt into action. Carrying sledgehammers, they sprinted to the building and began thumping the doors. Another team of marines ran at the building wielding a heavy ladder as a battering ram. Gunfire and smoke filled the air by the time ladder's third blow opened a ragged hole.

The first man who charged through recognized Lewis Washington, who pointed at Brown, crouching and reloading his rifle by the door. "Quicker than thought," as the marine remembered later, "I brought my saber down with all my strength upon his head."[15] Gripping the sword with two hands, he opened wounds on Brown's head and neck before delivering a thrust to the chest. Brown slumped to the ground, not dead but severely injured.

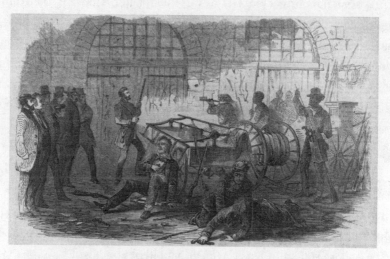

*A frozen moment, just before the Harper's Ferry engine house was stormed by federal troops. Colonel Lewis Washington and the other hostages stand at left, while one of John Brown's sons bleeds to death in the foreground, in a woodcut published shortly after Brown's raid.*

THE PRESIDENT AND THE FREEDOM FIGHTER

In a matter of a few minutes, the thirty-two-hour siege at Harper's Ferry was over. Ten of Brown's men were dead, five unaccounted for, and Brown and six others in custody. Despite the fact that Brown's army was decimated and defeated, that very afternoon the man himself rose again to do battle, this time in a war of words.

# "THE END OF THAT IS NOT YET"

Brown lay on the floor, covered by a grimy quilt, his head resting on a carpetbag. His face was gaunt, his beard and hair tangled and matted with blood. He looked up defiantly at a squad of interrogators, including Virginia governor Henry Wise, Robert E. Lee, Jeb Stuart, and several congressmen. They wanted answers—and Captain Brown was more than happy to talk.

As several reporters looked on, Virginia senator James Mason led the questioning. He tried first to get Brown to identify his coconspirators, but Brown told them the plan was his idea. He brushed away questions about who had helped him. "I will answer freely and faithfully about what concerns myself . . . but not about others."

When Mason asked the purpose of the raid, Brown gave him a simple and pointed reply. "We came to free the slaves, and only that."

"How do you justify your acts?" asked Mason.

This time Brown had an even sharper reply for Senator Mason, who had drafted the hated Fugitive Slave Act. "I think, my friend," said Brown, "you are guilty of a great wrong against God and humanity . . . and it would be perfectly right for any one to interfere with you so far as to free those you wilfully and wickedly hold in bondage."[16]

Later, as the interrogation came to an end, one of the reporters asked Brown if he had anything further he wished to say. He replied with a warning to the people of the South. "Prepare yourselves for a settlement of this [slavery] question, that must come up for settlement sooner than you are prepared for it. . . . You may dispose of me easily,—I am nearly disposed of now; but . . . this negro question I mean; the end of that is not yet."

A word-for-word transcript appeared later that week in the pages of the *New York Herald.* Readers found Brown was not only unrepentant, but full of accusations. There was clarity to his thinking, too, which made it difficult for the open-minded to dismiss him as a madman. His actions at Harper's Ferry might be wrong, but he was driven by a moral and religious rectitude. Yes, he had committed a violent act, but then the men who imprisoned him were slaveholders, men who owned other men.

## FREDERICK DOUGLASS, FUGITIVE

News of the Harper's Ferry raid reached Frederick Douglass in Philadelphia. It hit him "with the startling effect of an earthquake[,] . . . something to make the boldest hold his breath." But he went about his business, delivering his speech as scheduled.[17]

A few hours later, however, Douglass learned he had become the most wanted man in America.

Jeb Stuart's men had found John Brown's papers, which included maps of the Alleghenies, letters in code, and correspondence that suggested a much larger conspiracy. Tucked into the stack was a letter from Douglass to John Brown. In the estimation of Virginia governor Wise, eager to take action and quell the panic in his state over the insurrection, the letter provided sufficient evidence to charge Douglass with multiple crimes, although it made no mention of Harper's Ferry.

Despite the news, that day would be a lucky one for Douglass. A Philadelphia telegraph operator sympathetic to the abolitionist cause pocketed a wire from Washington ordering Douglass's arrest and sent word to the abolitionist of the imminent danger. By the time the telegram was delivered several hours later and the Philadelphia sheriff came knocking, Douglass was gone. Again a fugitive, he had hopped the first train to New York, where friends smuggled him onto another train for Rochester. He was on the run once more, heading for Canada, but stopping at home before he made for the border.

Douglass sent a telegram of his own, ordering one of his sons to clear out his desk, just in case the authorities arrived before he did. Though he reached his adopted hometown without incident, he soon learned that New York's lieutenant governor would honor a Virginia arrest warrant. With the authorities in hot pursuit, Douglass stepped aboard a ferry hours later, crossing Lake Ontario to Canada, like so many fugitives on the Underground Railroad before him. Six hours later, federal marshals knocked on his door in Rochester.

John Brown almost got him killed—as a Black man linked to Brown's conspiracy, Douglass believed, he would have been sentenced to death by a Virginia court. Even so, writing from Canada, Douglass defended his friend. In an essay for his paper, he called him a "glorious martyr of liberty" and compared Brown to the "heroes of Lexington, Concord, and Bunker Hill."[18] Unsure of his safety even in Canada, Douglass made his way to Quebec and sailed for England, though his thoughts remained with Brown. "John Brown has not failed," he wrote. "He has dropped an *idea*, equal to a thousand bombshells."[19]

Brown's crimes at Harper's Ferry would not go unpunished. Convicted of treason, murder, and inciting a slave insurrection, he received a death sentence. On December 2, 1859, thousands of soldiers and citizens gathered in a field outside Charles Town. In a strange glimpse of moments to come, the crowd included Professor Thomas J. Jackson of the Virginia Military Institute, soon to be a Confederate general honored with the nickname "Stonewall"; Edmund Ruffin, who would fire one of the first shots at Fort Sumter sixteen months later; and the actor John Wilkes Booth, costumed in a militia uniform. As his sentence was carried out, John Brown displayed the same extraordinary dignity he had during his interrogation and, later, at his trial, where he impressed even Governor Wise. With head hooded, arms and ankles tied, John Brown was hung by the neck until dead.

Douglass arrived in Liverpool after John Brown had met his fate on the gallows, but even across the sea Douglass recognized that John Brown had become a symbol of the national divide. Brown accomplished his goal of striking terror into the hearts of pro-slavery people, giving him the status of the devil incarnate in the South, where his actions boosted secession sentiments. In the North, the reaction was more complicated. People could see Brown as both a criminal and a holy warrior; in many towns, church bells tolled in his honor on the day he died. Henry David Thoreau equated him to Jesus Christ, calling them "two ends of a chain." The philosopher Ralph Waldo Emerson called him a saint.[20]

Almost single-handedly he pushed the national slavery debate from an angry conversation into the realm of violent combat. His actions at Harper's Ferry made people of conscience ask themselves how to carry the fight against the evil of slavery. Was such violence justified? Whether one condemned or admired John Brown, he was, in Herman Melville's words, "the meteor of war," a man who set the stakes for the immensely greater violence to follow in the new decade.[21]

# SEVEN

# THE DIVIDED HOUSE

We cannot be free men if this is, by our national choice, to be a land of slavery. Those who deny freedom to others, deserve it not for themselves; and, under the rule of a just God, cannot long retain it.

—ABRAHAM LINCOLN, MAY 19, 1856

The day before John Brown attacked Harper's Ferry, Abraham Lincoln found a telegram waiting for him on his desk in Springfield. Wired from New York, it was an invitation to speak in Brooklyn on "any subject you please." The compensation would be generous, a lecture fee of two hundred dollars.[1]

For lawyer Lincoln, fresh from traveling the circuit, the invite meant much more than money. He had speechified far and wide in the West, but never before in New York. Thus, the piece of paper he held in his hand represented a priceless political opportunity, one that dared him to think he really could find a place on the national scene.

Lincoln-the-politician was well known and well liked in Illinois, but outside his home state, his reputation had risen more slowly. At least one newspaper in the East, when deigning to mention him at all, spelled his name *Abrahm* Lincoln. His single term in Congress was a decade in the past, though stump speeches on behalf of other politicians and his occasional public pronouncements had gained him enough respect that, to his complete surprise, his name had been entered in nomination for vice president at the 1856 Republican Party convention. But that had come to nothing since he lost on the second ballot, and the ticket went nowhere when a pro-slavery Democrat, Pennsylvanian James Buchanan, became the nation's fifteenth president that autumn.

More recently, in 1858, Lincoln had run for the U.S. Senate. After winning the Republican Party nomination that June, he had delivered a speech that got people talking. Attempting to reframe the slavery debate, he had borrowed Jesus's words to proclaim that "a house divided cannot stand."* "I believe this government cannot endure," he had told his audience, "permanently half *slave* and half *free*."[2]

These were strong words, and they reverberated beyond the Illinois border. Although Lincoln softened them with a disclaimer—"I do not expect the Union to be *dissolved*—I do not expect the house to *fall*"—he also made a prediction, "I *do* expect it will cease to be divided. It will become *all* one thing or *all* the other." In his view, slavery was very much more than a regional disagreement; it posed a challenge to the country's very survival.

The "House Divided" speech, as it came to be known, had also set the stage for a series of debates with Stephen Douglas, the Democratic incumbent. Though the senator was a well-established national politician, thanks in part to his controversial promotion of popular sovereignty, Douglas understood that this time his old rival Lincoln could

---

* "And Jesus knew their thoughts, and said unto them, 'Every kingdom divided against itself is brought to desolation; and *every city or house divided against itself shall not stand.*'" Matthew, 12:25. Italics added.

*Lincoln, at the podium, with Douglas, at left, on the dais, in an early twentieth-century re-creation of one of their 1858 debates.*

be a real threat to both his reelection to the Senate and to Douglas's hope of running for president in 1860. "I shall have my hands full," he told one reporter, ". . . and if I beat [Lincoln], my victory will be hardly won."[3]

## IT BEGINS

When Lincoln and Douglas faced off in Ottawa, Illinois, Lincoln was on a mission to change the national argument about slavery. As a sitting senator, Stephen Douglas wanted to crush his opponent, get back to Washington, and run for president two years later. Their debate that day was the first of what would be an epic series of seven across the state.

Taking the stage in Ottawa on August 21, 1858, the two could hardly have looked more different. The gangly Lincoln was a foot taller than Douglas, who was a portly bulldog of a man. Douglas was a natty dresser, while Lincoln's ill-fitting suits tended to look as if he had slept

*Senator Stephen Douglas of Illinois in a campaign photograph taken when he was the Democratic nominee for president in 1860.*

in them. Douglas was a polished debater with a booming voice, while Lincoln's listeners complained his near-falsetto sounded shrill.

Douglas began on the attack. He accused Lincoln of trying to create "an Abolition party, under the name and disguise of the Republican party."

Flustered at Douglas's description, Lincoln struggled to respond. He hurried through his speech, reading a large chunk of his 1854 Peoria speech. Afterward, worried at his performance, he called a meeting of his advisers to discuss strategy.

Douglas seemed to have the upper hand, but word of the contest spread. People flocked to the second debate to see and hear the verbal fireworks as "the Little Giant," as Douglas was known, tried to fight off upstart "Honest Abe." This time, at Freeport, Illinois, Lincoln went on offense. But he sounded lawyerly, his arguments overly technical. A better showing, but he still wasn't able to dominate Douglas.

The attention of the state was now on the candidates, and crowds of twelve, fifteen, and even eighteen thousand attended as the debates became even more heated. Douglas had damned Lincoln as a "black Republican," claiming that Lincoln was allied with "fred douglass, the negro," a man who, unlike Lincoln, was already an established national figure, and insisted that "Lincoln [was] the champion of the black man." In a bold-faced lie, Stephen Douglas put it out that Frederick Douglass was campaigning for Lincoln in Illinois and had been seen "reclin[ing] in a carriage next to the white driver's wife."

Lincoln responded that he did not believe in full racial equality. "I agree with Judge Douglas that [the negro] is not my equal in many respects—certainly not in color, perhaps not in moral or intellectual endowment." The furthest he could go speaking in the Black man's favor was his bread-for-work argument:

> In the right to put into his mouth the bread that his own hands
> have earned, he is the equal of every other man, white or black.
> In pointing out that more has been given you, you cannot be
> justified in taking away the little which has been given him. All
> I ask for the negro is, that if you do not like him, let him alone.
> If God gave him but little, that little let him enjoy.[4]

In Lincoln's mind, in the late 1850s, equality ended there. Though ahead of his time—it was his conviction that slavery must be dealt with as a moral wrong—he was still a man of his time.

In the course of the debates, Lincoln gained confidence. His energy and persuasiveness rose in the final three meetings, and he outperformed the incumbent; Douglass seemed tired and, in the last debate, hoarse. By then word of the spirited debates had spread well beyond Illinois. With big city and national papers reporting on the debates, some reprinting word for word what the candidates said, more and more people across the country began to recognize Lincoln's name.

Despite his good efforts, however, Lincoln's campaign fell short. Senate seats were still decided by state legislatures in 1858 (that wouldn't change for another half century, with the ratification of the Seventeenth Amendment), and since the Democrats managed to retain control of the Illinois house that November, Douglas was chosen by a 54–26 vote once again to represent the state in the U.S. Senate.

Yet Lincoln was far from vanquished. Illinois had been the perfect place for the larger national discussion to play out as the two brilliant orators wrestled over slavery. With his name now on many people's lips, Lincoln had become a politician many thought belonged in the discussion beside Stephen Douglas when the conversation turned to the next presidential race. Americans were beginning to recognize Lincoln's voice just might be the clearest in the Republican Party—and that he might very possibly be the party's future.

# BECOMING A NATIONAL CHARACTER

The invitation a year later to speak in Brooklyn was a recognition of Lincoln's new role in national politics. The tens of thousands of people had attended the debates and the many more who had read the published transcripts, not only in Illinois but elsewhere, now had a sense of what the man stood for. In the final debate, in Alton, Illinois, he had been clear. "The real issue of this controversy," he insisted, was between "one class that looks upon the institution of a slavery *as a wrong*, and of another class that *does not* look upon it as wrong."[5]

His words appealed particularly to Republicans in the East, and they wanted to hear from the man himself; as for Lincoln, he saw that a lecture in New York was a door opened where there hadn't been one. He would get a chance to rub shoulders with men like Reverend Henry Ward Beecher, the internationally famous social reformer, whose sister was Mrs. Stowe, author of *Uncle Tom's Cabin*. Lincoln could meet mighty newspapermen like William Cullen Bryant, editor of the *Evening Post*, which had published full reports of his debates with Stephen Douglas, and attract the attention of Horace Greeley of the *New-York Tribune*, the country's only truly national newspaper. The audience would be full of other New Yorkers who ran the nation's most important city.

Lincoln could only say yes, and a date was agreed upon for him to lecture at the end of February 1860. That gave him time to prepare his speech and to organize a side trip to visit his eldest son, Robert, preparing for college at Phillips Academy in Exeter, New Hampshire. Lincoln even ordered a suit tailored for the occasion—the cost amounted to half his speaker's fee—and by the time he boarded a train headed east, the carpetbag he carried contained a thick stack of blue foolscap paper. It was his handwritten speech, one he had labored over for weeks.

In the months after Lincoln received the New York invitation, John Brown had changed everything. His actions resulted in a sudden shift in electoral politics, one that gave Lincoln another lift. Before the Harper's Ferry story broke, the odds-on favorite for the Republican nomination had been Senator William H. Seward, a patrician former New York governor and sitting senator. But as the nation recoiled from the bloodbath at the engine house, Seward's well-known slavery views—he had memorably asserted in his first speech on the Senate floor that "there is a higher law than the constitution"—seemed suddenly dangerous.[6] Adding fuel to the fire, the papers also reported that Seward once contributed twenty-five dollars to John Brown's efforts in Kansas. Now, after John Brown had taken the law into his own hands—and paid for it with his life—Lincoln's moderate perspective on slavery seemed less risky than Seward's.

Lincoln hoped his speech would be the means by which he could complete his transformation, making a formerly obscure western man a genuine contender for the Republican presidential nomination in 1860.

# "THE PRINCE OF PHOTOGRAPHERS"[7]

On Monday, February 27, 1860, the day of his New York appearance, Lincoln walked north on Broadway from his hotel, together with four members of the Young Men's Central Republican Union, the sponsor of the evening's lecture. He might be from the provinces, but Lincoln understood that to promote himself he needed a suitable photograph—Mary disliked the ones he had—and he was worldly enough to know that Mathew Brady, the foremost American photographer of the day, was the man for the job.

When Lincoln entered the grand reception room at Brady's gallery on the corner of Broadway and Bleecker Street, he took in the elegant carpets, chandeliers, and gilt walls. There was an array of Brady's images on display, including one of Stephen Douglas.

Lincoln was soon introduced to George Bancroft, another man who had come to get his picture taken. Bancroft was a diplomat, two-time cabinet secretary, and the distinguished author of a book Lincoln admired, the multivolume *History of the United States of America*.

The contrast between Brady's two customers struck one of Lincoln's companions. "One [was] courtly and precise in every word and gesture," the young New Yorker observed, "with the air of a trans-Atlantic statesman; the other bluff and awkward."[8] Even before meeting the genteel Bancroft, however, Lincoln grasped that he faced a large challenge in the hours that followed. He needed to win over an elite audience full of sophisticated men like Bancroft.

On arriving two days earlier, Lincoln had checked into the busy

Astor House, one of the premier hotels in the city. The watershed in his party's politics had meant his room immediately became a reception area for visitors, some of whom he knew, though many others came to meet and to pay their respects to the stranger emerging as a plausible candidate for the Republican nomination for president. A few party people had endorsed Lincoln, and the *Chicago Press and Tribune* had announced its support back in January. While Seward remained the favorite, the dark horse from Illinois was gaining unexpected momentum.

When his turn came to go before Brady's camera, Lincoln climbed the stairs to the "operating room" to meet the man who would take his picture.[9] Brady, his face half-hidden by a flowing mustache and spade-like goatee, had spent the preceding two decades taking pictures of anybody who was anybody, making trademark images of aging historic figures like Andrew Jackson, Henry Clay, and Dolley Madison, as well as current headline-makers such as Chief Justice Roger B. Taney and President Buchanan.

Brady studied his subject, who that morning looked notably "haggard and careworn."[10] Even Lincoln's friends agreed he was an odd-looking man, his ears, Adam's apple, and blunt nose too big, his chin too sharp, with a mole that marred his right cheek.[11] Brady had his work cut out for him.

The photographer's usual preference was to make bust images, portraits that that framed the head and shoulders. But looking at Lincoln, Brady decided to make a standing portrait to call attention to his subject's imposing stature rather than to his craggy face. A table was positioned so Lincoln could rest his left hand on a small stack of books, suggesting erudition. An assistant straightened Lincoln's ribbon tie, but Brady, standing by his immense box camera and examining his subject, still wasn't satisfied. The problem, he decided, was Lincoln's collar. He asked him to pull it up a little.

*The Mathew Brady likeness shot on the same day as Lincoln's Cooper Union speech. "Honest Abe" himself would later observe that the picture, which introduced him to countless Americans, put him in the White House.*

"Ah," said Lincoln, a man always quick to make a joke at his own expense, "I see you want to shorten my neck."

"That's just it!" crowed Brady. The two men, one short, one tall, laughed as one.[12]

## THE COOPER UNION

Just after 8:00 P.M. that evening, William Cullen Bryant introduced "an eminent citizen of the West, hitherto known to you only by reputation, . . . Abraham Lincoln of Illinois."[13] To prolonged applause, the evening's main speaker stood and made his way the podium. People were struck by his great height, rumpled black suit, and unruly black hair as he waited for the room to quiet.

When he began to speak, Lincoln looked out upon a blur of faces.

Audience members had paid twenty-five cents for admission to the Cooper Union for the Advancement of Science and Art in Manhattan, and despite snow falling and slushy streets, the great hall was nearly full. "His manner was to a New York audience a very strange one," thought one observer. But Lincoln set about presenting his methodically constructed constitutional argument.[14]

His debates with Douglas a year and a half earlier had been superb practice, the dialectic of their back-and-forth sharpening his thinking. But in the four months since receiving the invitation to speak here in New York, Lincoln had spent uncounted hours in the Illinois State Library where, guided by his training as a lawyer, he drafted what was in effect a legal brief. This evening he would reargue the Dred Scott case and refute Chief Justice Taney's insistence that the Framers of the Constitution approved of slavery in the territories.

Lincoln went back in time to count heads. As he told the roughly 1,500 people in the room, he found that "a clear majority" of the signers, twenty-one of thirty-nine, had opposed the extension of slavery into the territories.[15] Thus, said Lincoln, *Dred Scott v. Sandford* had been wrongly decided.

His argument was detailed, but he won the rapt attention of his audience. Moving from the subject of Dred Scott, he took issue with the Southerners who tried to demonize him and his party. He defended the Republicans from the accusation that they were "revolutionary." Not so, he argued. "You charge that we stir up insurrections among your slaves. We deny it; and what is your proof? Harper's Ferry!" Lincoln insisted that "John Brown was no Republican; and you have failed to implicate a single Republican in his Harper's Ferry enterprise." In fact, Lincoln said, "John Brown's effort was peculiar. It was not a slave insurrection. It was an attempt by white men to get up a revolt among slaves, in which the slaves refused to participate. In fact, it was so absurd that the slaves, with all their ignorance, saw plainly enough it could not succeed."[16] Although Lincoln held a quiet admiration for the man, he carefully distanced himself from John Brown.

The long speech required an hour and a half to deliver, with frequent interruptions for cheers and loud applause from his listeners. But his central argument was clear: Slavery could not, must not, be extended to the territories. It wasn't a matter of abolishing slavery; in fact, the Fugitive Slave Act, hateful though it might be, was the law of the land and, Lincoln said, had to be enforced. "Wrong as we think slavery is," he said in conclusion, "we can yet afford it to leave it alone where it is." But in his final words, he sent a clarion call to all good men. "Let us have faith that right makes might, and in that faith, let us, to the end, dare do our duty as we understand it."

Lincoln had chosen not to deliver a stump speech. Instead, he offered an argument, a statement of principles, a defense, and a call to arms. He held his audience spellbound as he persuaded them of his positions. He won their admiration for him as a man and—all importantly—as a candidate. As one partisan reported, "the house broke out in wild and prolonged enthusiasm. I think I never saw an audience more carried away by an orator."[17] People tossed handkerchiefs in the air and gave the speaker an ovation that lasted ten minutes.

The evening was a triumph. Lincoln himself was surprised at the wave of congratulations and hearty handshakes that came his way. After the full text of his speech appeared, as previously arranged, in five New York newspapers the following day, he received multiple invitations inviting him to speak. His trip to visit his son in southern New Hampshire rapidly became a campaign tour, with nine addresses in Connecticut, Rhode Island, and New Hampshire. He would turn down invitations from Philadelphia and other eastern cities in order to return to Illinois, but the Cooper Union speech elevated him. If Senator Seward remained the front-runner, he now had a worthy challenger in the contest for the Republican nomination for president, which would be decided in Chicago, in the month of May, at the party convention.

Whatever private doubts Lincoln had about running were banished, too. When Illinois senator Lyman Trumbull inquired about the coming fight for office, Lincoln wrote back, with wry understatement, "I will be entirely frank. The taste *is* in my mouth a little."[18]

# DEATH OF A DAUGHTER

In exile on the other side of the Atlantic, Frederick Douglass sheltered with friends in Yorkshire, England. In the early months of 1860, he used their home in the mill town of Halifax as a base from which he traveled to speaking engagements in England and Scotland, making stops in Newcastle, Edinburgh, and other large cities. His expanding gifts as a writer were on full display in the lectures he gave. One in particular he would deliver dozens of times over a period of years; he called it "The Trials and Triumphs of Self-Made Men." He espoused a theory: Success, he believed, was to be credited to the individual, "ascribed to brave, honest, earnest, ceaseless heart and soul industry. By this simple means—open and free to all men—whatever may be said of chances, circumstances, and natural endowments—the simple man may become wise, the wise man wiser."[19]

The separation was difficult for Douglass's wife and children back in Rochester, but ten-year-old Annie took it the hardest. The baby of the family, she was born in 1849 after her father's return from his long first exile to the British Isles. Knowing only the stability of their Rochester lives, she was a lively and happy child, much cherished by her family. But the departure of her father weighed on her.

The trial and execution of John Brown was an added burden for the young girl. In early 1858, Annie had become a nearly constant companion of Brown when the old man spent several weeks as a boarder in the Douglass household, insisting upon paying his host three dollars a week. Quietly planning his passway escape plan, he employed Annie's older brother Lewis to courier his letters to and from the post office. Like a man playing with toy soldiers, he engaged the Douglass children with model fortifications he made of boards and showed them drawings of his mountain installations. The young Douglasses found it all more intriguing than their father did, and to Annie their eccentric boarder became "dear old John Brown, upon whose knee she . . . often sat."[20]

Early in 1860, Douglass received a letter from Annie. "I am proceeding in my grammar very well for my teacher says so," she wrote to her distant father. Well aware of his passions, she transcribed a poem she had memorized for school: "He is not the man for me / Who buys or sells a slave / Not he who will not set him free / But send him to his grave." More ominously, the innocent, ordinarily cheerful girl acknowledged her sense of loss. "Poor Mr. Brown is dead," she told her father. "[T]hey took him in an open field and . . . hung him."[21]

*Frederick Douglass and his high-spirited youngest child, Annie, when she was about five years old. Her unexpected death at age eleven brought her father back from his exile in England in early 1860.*

On March 13, 1860, Frederick Douglass was rocked by the news that his beloved daughter, "the light and life of my house," was dead.[22] He was shocked and surprised; it was worst possible piece of news he could have received and the most unexpected. The circumstances were inexplicable; after having written to him, in December, she had become withdrawn and lost the ability to speak and to hear. No doctor could explain why, beyond guesswork about a possible fever of the brain. Douglass himself would attribute her retreat from life to "over-anxiety for the safety of her father and deep sorrow for the death of dear old John Brown."[23]

Brokenhearted at the loss, Douglass's fear for his own safety seemed suddenly unimportant. The report of her death reached him in Glasgow and, after collecting his things in Halifax, he hurried to Liverpool and found passage on the first available ship. He made landfall in Portland, Maine, then traveled across Canada to Rochester, taking care not to call attention to himself. A funeral cortege of thirty-five carriages had long since delivered Annie's remains to her grave, but Douglass did his best to console his family. Friends would report that the father would mourn the loss of his little daughter for years to come.[24]

During the spring of 1860, Douglass lay low, wary that he might still be a wanted man. But the feverish pursuit of Brown's alleged co-conspirators was rapidly cooling. A congressional committee formed to investigate had found no evidence of a larger conspiracy involving Douglass or anyone else beyond Brown and his provisional army.* Even before the June publication of the Senate Select Committee report,

---

* "There is no evidence that any other citizens than those there with Brown were accessory to this outbreak." "Select Committee Report on the Invasion and Seizure of the Armory and Arsenal at Harper's Ferry, June 15, 1860." Senator Mason, the man who had interrogated the bloody Brown hours after his capture, chaired the committee. Senator Jefferson Davis, who would soon resign from the U.S. Senate and become president of the Confederate States of America, was also a member.

Douglass resumed his public life, traveling and speaking without fear of arrest. The nation's central focus had become the future. Electoral politics—in particular, the race for the presidency—filled the air.

# THE RAIL SPLITTER

In the month of May, Lincoln made his first and last major appearance of the 1860 presidential campaign.

His nomination was far from a certainty even in Illinois, but when he arrived in Decatur, the site of the state's Republican convention, he did have a national strategy in mind. If he could win the unanimous support of the Illinois delegation, together with a few delegates from other states, he might prevent Seward from winning a majority on the first ballot. That would give his supporters a chance to harvest delegates previously committed to others for subsequent tallies. Going in, however, everyone in Lincoln's camp agreed: He needed a boost to win big among his in-state neighbors and to enhance his appeal beyond his region.

Richard Oglesby, Lincoln's Illinois campaign manager and, later, a governor of Illinois, cogitated on how to generate enthusiasm for his rawboned candidate. He wondered whether they might devise a down-to-earth nickname, something like Andrew Jackson's "Old Hickory." Or a catchy slogan, such as "Tippecanoe and Tyler, Too," the memorable phrase that had helped power William Henry Harrison, victor at the Battle of Tippecanoe, along with his running mate, John Tyler, to victory in the election of 1840. Oglesby wanted to capitalize on Lincoln's folksy and likable manner, maybe with a moniker that conveyed not that he was a fine lawyer but that he was a down-to-earth westerner who could spin a yarn and speak for the common man.

A conversation with Lincoln's cousin John Hanks provided the answer.

A dozen miles down the road from Decatur lay the fields that Lincoln helped clear as a last act of family duty before leaving his father's homestead. Lincoln and Hanks had enclosed the acres with split-rail fences.

"John," Oglesby asked Hanks, "did you split rails down there with old Abe?"

"Yes, every day," was the reply.

"Do you suppose you could find any of them now?"

Hanks thought he could.

"Then," said Oglesby, "come around and get in my buggy, and we will drive down there."[25] A plan was taking shape in Oglesby's mind.

With no building large enough to house the convention, the citizens of Decatur constructed an oversized tent of canvas and lumber, which they called a wigwam, complete with stands for the delegates, a platform, and a podium. When the convention opened, on May 9, the wigwam was packed with an overflow crowd estimated at more than four thousand. But the undoubted high point of the two-day meeting came when Oglesby announced from the dais that John Hanks "desired to make a contribution to the Convention." Right on cue, Hanks and an assistant marched down the center aisle carrying two well-worn fence rails of split walnut. They were decorated with flags, streamers, and a banner that read, "Abraham Lincoln, The Rail Candidate for President in 1860."

According to one newspaper account, "the effect was electrical." The spontaneous applause was deafening, and Lincoln, seated in the tent, rose to speak. He hadn't split a rail in years, but with his long lean frame and weathered features, he looked like a man who had. He told the crowd he could not be certain that these ones in particular were his handiwork, but that, yes, certainly he "had mauled many and many better ones" as he had "grown to manhood."[26] After he finished speaking, he was met with another long ovation. When he left Decatur the following day, he did so with the unanimous support of the Illinois delegation.

For purposes of the campaign, he became "the Rail Splitter." A week later, the national Republican convention convened in a Chicago auditorium, its entrance framed with a pair of fence rails. Observing tradition, Lincoln himself did not attend, but waited in Springfield. A local newspaperman found Lincoln in his law office with encouraging news: On the first ballot, Seward outpolled him only 173½ to 102, with the other 40 percent of the votes almost evenly divided among three other candidates.

Lincoln made his way to the telegraph office, where he learned the second ballot was closer, the count Seward 185½, Lincoln 181. Lincoln, as one congressman put it, became "the second choice of everybody" because people thought he might be more electable than Seward, despite his relative lack of experience.[27] At the candidate's next stop, the offices of the *Illinois State Journal*, Lincoln opened a telegram addressed to him: The nomination was his. He shook hands all around before heading for home to Mary and his boys. "Well, Gentlemen," he said in parting, "there is a little woman at our house who is probably more interested in this dispatch than I am."[28]

EIGHT

# THE ELECTION OF 1860

*I want every man to have the chance—and I believe a black
man is entitled to it—in which he can better his condition.*

—ABRAHAM LINCOLN, SPEECH IN NEW HAVEN,
CONNECTICUT, MARCH 6, 1860

D uring the summer and fall, Lincoln did no campaigning. At
the insistence of his advisers, the Republican nominee remained in Springfield, since whistle-stop tours and other
city-to-city campaigning would not become a standard part of American
presidential politics for another two decades. But Lincoln found other
ways to keep himself in the conversation.

For one, he had compiled transcripts of his debates with Stephen Douglas, pasting them in a scrapbook. He arranged with an Ohio publisher to
set them into type and publish them as a book, thinking they might be
useful as a campaign document. He was right: Just as his ideas had reso-
nated with the large crowds from the debate stage in 1858, the published
debates fueled curiosity about the rising political star in 1860. The book
became an unexpected bestseller, selling more than thirty thousand copies and finding its way into parlors and taverns across the North.

Then there was the picture. Immediately after the convention, Mathew Brady released his photograph of Lincoln, as recorded on the day of the Cooper Union speech, and within a week, the covers of two major national publications, *Harper's Weekly* and *Frank Leslie's Illustrated Newspaper*, featured woodcuts based on the picture.* Brady had touched up the image in the darkroom, softening the lines and shadows on Lincoln's face. To those inclined to think so, the man looked positively presidential—somber and serious, tall and confident, unafraid

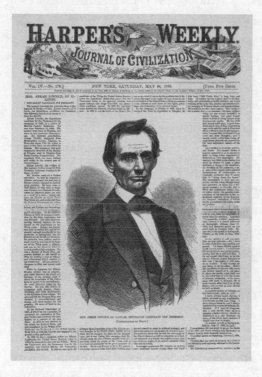

*Brady's first photograph of Lincoln, cropped to his head and upper torso and reworked as a woodcut for newspaper publication.*

---

* *Harper's Weekly*, May 26, 1860, which rendered the candidate's name *Abram*; and *Frank Leslie's Illustrated Newspaper*, May 20, 1860. Twenty and thirty years, respectively, would elapse before the technology permitted photographs to appear in newspapers and magazines.

to engage the viewer's eye. Lincoln's Cooper Union speech, already widely reprinted in newspapers, appeared in numerous new editions.

Lincoln set up shop in the Illinois State House in offices lent to him by the governor, but on issues of policy, he made a point of keeping his thoughts to himself. At the Republican national convention he had put out the word he would make no deals—"I authorize no bargain and will be bound by none"—and he steadfastly refused to associate himself with the liberal, anti-slavery wing of the party. He wanted to appeal to easterners and westerners, to radicals and conservatives, to former Whigs and wavering Democrats. The strategy seemed to work, as the common ground he shared with most Republicans helped consolidate the party behind him.

He hired a new secretary, a bright young journalist name John Nicolay. A reporter from the *Chicago Press and Tribune* arrived, and with Lincoln's cooperation, John Locke Scripps published a thirty-two-page biography. A nation hungry to learn more about Illinois's little-known man bought more than a million copies of the brief life. Hundreds, perhaps even thousands, of biographies and profiles appeared in print, and lithographers Currier & Ives soon found a market for frameable prints. Painters and sculptors arrived to take Lincoln's likeness. Countless images of Lincoln-as-rail-splitter proliferated.[1] The symbolism reverberated just as Oglesby hoped. As one letter to the editor of the *Illinois State Journal* put it, "[Lincoln's] rails, like his political record, are straight, sound and out of good timber."[2]

In June his candidacy got a large boost when the opposition Democrats split. His old nemesis Douglas won the support of the Northern wing of the party with his promise of popular sovereignty. The South chose a Kentuckian named John C. Breckenridge who favored imposing a strict slave code on the territories. A fourth major candidate, Tennessean John Bell, would also be on the ballot, running under the banner of the anti-secessionist Constitutional Union Party, further dividing the

*The political mythology of rail-splitter Lincoln has produced countless artistic renditions of Lincoln in his homesteading days.*

electorate. But a dark cloud had rolled in, shading all the candidates and parties, Lincoln especially.

The threat of disunion hung over the election. Lincoln's outspoken opposition to the spread of slavery—and the growing chance that he might actually win—meant that leaders in some Southern states had begun to threaten they would withdraw from the Union if he did. That would be a calamity, everyone agreed, but as the preelection months slowly passed, Lincoln continued to insist the slave states would never carry out such a threat.

## ELECTION DAY 1860

In Springfield, Lincoln, though growing cautiously optimistic at his chances, was "bored—*bored badly*."[3] Since he wasn't campaigning, he had little to do but wait and read news reports—until 2:00 A.M. on

Wednesday, November 7, when a telegram arrived carrying the news that New York's voters had put him over the top. "I then felt as I never had before," Lincoln remembered, "the responsibility was upon me."[4]

He won only 40 percent of the popular vote, but his 180 Electoral College votes, out of 303, were more than enough for a solid victory. Breckenridge led the rest of the field with 72. Douglas finished last with a mere 12 electoral votes.

After decades in which slaveholders—the "slave power," the "slavocracy"—controlled national politics, a president who wanted to steer his country away from slavery won the White House. However, because of his anti-slavery stance, Lincoln collected zero votes—literally none—in most of the South. In the nine states south of Virginia his name did not even appear on the ballot.

## THE TREMONT TEMPLE RIOT

Three days after the presidential election of 1860, South Carolina began the process of secession. The move to disunion was driven by the prospect that Lincoln would interfere with slavery, which was the very foundation of Southern culture and prosperity. There was much anger in other Southern states, too, but Lincoln still insisted he wasn't particularly worried, assuring a Kentucky friend in a confidential letter that "the good people of the South [will] . . . find no cause to complain of me."[5] As president-elect, he waited quietly in Springfield for his March 4 inauguration day; until then he could do little but instruct his supporters to "Stand firm."[6]

In contrast, Frederick Douglass boarded a train in Rochester, his destination Boston. As engaged in the battle for freedom as ever, he was booked to deliver a lecture in honor of John Brown, who had been executed exactly one year earlier. To Douglass's surprise, he found that the anger evident in the South had infected even staid old Boston.

For most of 1860, Douglass observed the election from a distance. After the Republican convention, he told subscribers of *Douglass' Monthly* that "Mr. Lincoln is a man of unblemished private character . . . one of the most frank, honest men in political life."[7] But for Douglass, that was not enough. Lincoln neither favored giving the vote to Black citizens nor thought them the White man's equal. He wasn't promising abolition in slave states, since his anti-slavery policy ended with the territories, where he swore to prevent slavery's spread. That left Douglass with no choice. "I cannot support Lincoln," he had told Gerrit Smith in July.[8]

Despite being disgruntled that Lincoln didn't take a radical abolitionist position, Douglass recognized what a Lincoln win could mean to his cause. It would be a victory for "anti-slavery sentiment," he wrote in the September issue of his newspaper. It would be a major blow to the slavocracy if the "government [was] divorced from the active support" of slavery.[9] After decades of controlling Washington politics, "The slaveholders know that the day of their power is over when a Republican President is Elected."[10] Now, with Lincoln set to take up residence on Pennsylvania Avenue, the slave states began their exodus.

To Douglass, it smacked of revolutionary change. He did not want war, but he wasn't afraid of that; he worried about compromises that might be made to avoid it. There was talk in Washington and many Northern states of walking back protections for the Black man in order to placate angry Southerners. Douglass felt certain that concessions granted to the South could only undermine his quest for freedom.

The site of the John Brown commemoration was the Baptist Tremont Temple, a converted theater a block from Boston Common. At first, the arriving crowd consisted of mostly Black faces, since the church was racially integrated, as were the local schools (Boston had been the first city in the United States to integrate its classrooms five years before). But as the hall filled, the audience grew more varied. From wealthy Beacon Hill came well-dressed gentlemen, many of whom were merchants and millowners dependent upon cotton from the plantation South. Dockworkers who unloaded cotton bales in the port of Boston founds seats. So did laborers from the city's rough-and-tumble North End, men who competed for jobs with free Blacks. The balance of the crowd had shifted from African Americans and abolitionists to a "mob of gentlemen," some of whom were simply ruffians, hired by the merchants, to cause trouble.[11] They came to condemn—not to celebrate—"John Brown and his aiders and abettors."[12]

The unruly crowd greeted the call to order with loud hissing and catcalls. When they refused to quiet, the moderator stepped from the stage, walked down the aisle, and took a man who had been heckling him by the collar. Before he could drag him to the door, the man's companions separated the two men.

A Black minister called for order, but the crowd shouted him down. Abolitionists responded by offering three cheers for their featured speaker, Frederick Douglass, who was seated on the stage. The disrupters shouted, "Put him out." With the room filling with shouting, mad laughter, and scuffles, the police arrived to quell the growing chaos.

Douglass rose to his feet, asking to be heard. The chair refused to recognize him, and this time it was the abolitionists who screamed. When Douglass tried to yell over the din, someone in the audience screamed, "Throttle him!" In Boston, the nation's intellectual center, a genteel place and a longtime stronghold of abolitionism, the scene was set for a riot.

A resolution was offered condemning Brown and the "fanatics of the Northern States" who had supported him and "even now [are] attempting to subvert the Constitution and the Union."[13] Douglass demanded to be heard, and the police struggled to keep order, breaking up fights in

*The normally peaceful Tremont Temple in Boston was the scene of a
violent riot when Douglass was invited to speak on December 3, 1860,
the one-year anniversary of John Brown's execution.*

the crowd. This time the chair permitted Douglass to speak, but warned
him to be brief.

He bellowed over the jeers and shouts, quoting the Bible. "The freedom of all mankind was written on the law by the finger of God!" He
condemned the proceedings, yelling, "You are serving the slaveholders!"

"Put a rope around his neck," someone yelled back.

When a large man in the front threw fresh insults at him, Douglass
fired back. "If I was a slave driver, and had hold of that man for five
minutes, I would let more daylight through his skin than ever got there
before." When the outraged crowd began throwing chairs at the stage,
the police, who stood between Douglass and the angry crowd, tried to
seize him; when he slipped from their grasp his supporters cheered.
"We will not yield our place on the platform! No, by God," he swore,

still fighting off policemen intent upon subduing him. One grabbed him by the hair; several dragged him to the edge of the stage and threw him down the stairs. He jumped to his feet and ran, pursued by some of the rabble.

Douglass was finally gone. But before a vote could be taken on any resolutions, he was back. His hair disheveled and clothes torn, he walked with dignity down the aisle. This time no one put a hand on him. He mounted the stage, with every eye fixed on him. The incandescently angry man resumed his seat without saying a word. On orders from the police, the chairman declared the meeting over.[14]

With passions running high from Boston to Baton Rouge, Mr. Lincoln's war was about to begin. It would be a war that jeopardized the basic beliefs of the nation as stated in the Constitution, and the president would be at the center of the conflict, always seeking strategies to bind the nation together. As an outsider, as an agent for change, Frederick Douglass would play a very different—and yet essential—part in determining the outcome.

NINE

## MR. LINCOLN'S WAR

I have no purpose, directly or indirectly, to interfere with
the institution of slavery in the States where it exists.

—ABRAHAM LINCOLN, FIRST INAUGURAL ADDRESS,
MARCH 4, 1861

Chilled by the cold drizzle, the crowd of more than a thousand admirers waited at Springfield's Great Western Railroad depot. Just before 8:00 A.M. on the morning of February 11, 1861, the throng of friends and neighbors got what they were waiting for: an opportunity to bid Illinois's favorite son farewell before he traveled east to be sworn in as president of the United States.

When President-Elect Abraham Lincoln emerged from the station, the crowd parted as he walked toward the train. He shook many hands and offered greetings to familiar faces. He climbed aboard the last car and, standing on its rear platform, turned to face his well-wishers, solemnly removing his tall beaver hat. At first, he said nothing, honoring the silence. His bodyguard, the six-foot-four, barrel-chested Ward Hill

Lamon, remembered that the seconds that ticked by "were as full of melancholy eloquence as any words he could have uttered."[1]

Lincoln had prepared no words for this moment, but memory and emotion provided them.

My Friends,

No one not in my situation can appreciate my feeling of sadness at this parting. To this place, and the kindness of these people, I owe everything. Here I have lived a quarter of a century, and have passed from a young to an old man. Here my children have been born, and one is buried. I now leave, not knowing when or whether ever I may return, with a task before me greater than that which rested upon Washington. Without the assistance of that Divine Being who ever attended him I cannot succeed. With that assistance I cannot fail. Trusting in Him, who can go with me and remain with you, and be everywhere for good, let us confidently hope that all will yet be well. To His care commending you, as I hope in your prayers you will commend me, I bid you an affectionate farewell.[2]

As scheduled, at eight o'clock sharp, the train departed for his journey to Washington, D.C.

In the preceding weeks, Lincoln had endured what some called the "secession winter." As South Carolina's convention debated whether to secede, he considered how he could respond if states actually left the Union. He read a book about the 1832 nullification crisis, during which President Jackson angrily warned South Carolina he could at any time order an army into the Palmetto State to enforce the federal law the state threatened to defy. Finding no easy answer in Jackson's threats, the new president also focused on his cabinet appointments. As a relatively inexperienced politician, he chose to nominate previous political rivals for their experience. He made a key choice in December, selecting William Seward to become his secretary of state. However, by the time the New Yorker accepted Lincoln's offer shortly after Christmas, South Carolina had withdrawn from the Union. There was no denying that the nation was coming apart.

Yet, until his inauguration, scheduled for March 4, 1861, Lincoln lacked legal standing to act. He could and did attempt to exercise a quiet persuasion, writing to Alexander H. Stephens, an influential voice in the South and a friend from his time in Congress. Stephens went on the record after Lincoln's election as opposing secession, and the president wrote to ask the diminutive Georgian to pass the word that he had no plans to interfere with the internal workings of the Southern states. In a letter he marked as "for your eye only," Lincoln wrote, "Do the people of the South really entertain fears that a Republican administration would, *directly*, or *indirectly*, interfere with their slaves?" Not so, he promised Stephens. "I wish to assure you, as once a friend, and still, I hope not an enemy, that there is no cause for such fears."[3] Unfortunately for Lincoln, his assurances had little or no impact, and in the new year six states—Mississippi, Florida, Alabama, Louisiana, Texas, and Georgia—followed South Carolina's lead, seceding in a period of four weeks. Adding insult to injury, on the very day Lincoln departed Springfield, his erstwhile friend Stephens took the oath of office as provisional vice president of the newly established Confederate States of America.

Above all else, Lincoln wished to preserve the Union. Many years before, as a self-tutored youth looking for an anchor in his life, he embraced the law and in particular the principles laid out in the Constitution. More recently, in the wake of the wrongheaded interpretation offered by Roger Taney and others, Lincoln retrenched, placing his faith in the simpler fabric of the Declaration of Independence with its promise of liberty for all. That premise—*liberty for all*—became his benchmark, his ultimate point of reference in the months and years to come.

# GLIMPSES OF LINCOLN

Frederick Douglass and Abraham Lincoln had yet to meet. Nor would they come face-to-face on February 18, 1861, although Douglass did lay distant eyes on Lincoln early that Monday morning, when the Presidential Special hissed to a halt in Rochester, New York.

The train ran late so Lincoln's planned speech from the balcony of the Waverly Hotel had to be scrapped. Instead, he again stood on the rear platform at the end of the four-car train. His family rode in a saloon car, which was accompanied by a passenger car for dignitaries and the press, and one for baggage.

"The train only stopped a few minutes," Douglass reported in the next issue of *Douglass' Monthly*, "but Mr. Lincoln had to make a speech to the assembled thousands who had come to greet him." Douglass found what Lincoln said disappointing. "His short speech here," he told his readers, "did not touch on the great question of the day."[4]

For the most part, Lincoln's frequent addresses on the twelve-day trip east would not focus on policy; it was planned to be a getting-to-know-you tour. He would glad-hand political supporters at important stops while, in lesser towns, he showed himself briefly to give the curious the opportunity, as he put it in typically self-deprecating terms, "of observing my very interesting countenance." One youthful Ohio politician who came for a look, future president Rutherford B. Hayes, thought that Lincoln's bow to his public was oddly mechanical. "His chin rises," Hayes wrote to a friend, "his body breaks in two at the hips—there is a bend of the knees at a queer angle."[5]

Lincoln revealed little about his plan for a rapidly dividing nation. He told a Cincinnati audience that "I deem it my duty . . . [to] wait until the last moment, for a development of the present national difficulties, before I express myself decidedly what course I shall pursue."[6] He reassured the citizens of Cleveland that "the crisis, as it is called, is altogether an artificial crisis."[7] But his calm words were contradicted by actions elsewhere when the Confederate States of America declared its existence in its new capital of Montgomery, Alabama. In the eyes of Southerners, one nation officially became two with the inauguration of Jefferson Davis on February 18. Even if the CSA had yet to gain formal recognition as anything more than an illegal rebel conclave, the dilemma Lincoln faced grew by the day.

A light note was struck at what became the best-remembered stop on the trip. In the weeks before the election, Lincoln had received a letter from a girl named Grace Bedell. "If you let your whiskers grow," the eleven-year-old advised, ". . . you would look a great deal better for your face is so thin. All the ladies like whiskers and they would tease their husbands to vote for you and then you would be president." Lincoln wrote back, offering no promises but musing that people might think a beard "a silly affectation."[8] Yet by the time his train paused four months later in Westfield, New York, Miss Bedell's hometown, a Quaker's beard lined Lincoln's chin. To the delight of onlookers, he invited young Miss Bedell to join him on the platform. He planted an appreciative kiss on the young girl's head, and many of the newspapermen accompanying him had a field day. "WHISKERS WIN WINSOME MISS" read one headline; another, "OLD ABE KISSES PRETTY GIRL."[9]

# PINKERTON'S PLOT

A few days later, a man named Allan Pinkerton brought much darker news. Lincoln had been getting hate mail for months and, more recently, there had been nonstop rumors that he was in physical danger. He refused to take any of them seriously, but this new warning came from a well-regarded Chicago detective agency that specialized in railroad security. At a meeting behind closed doors in his Philadelphia hotel, said Lincoln, "Pinkerton informed me, that a plan had been laid for my assassination."[10]

Pinkerton explained that in Baltimore, a pro-South city in a slave state, secessionist sentiments were at a boil. The presidential entourage was supposed to arrive in the Maryland city, change trains, and then proceed to Washington. With Lincoln's travel schedule public knowledge, a group of conspirators, according to Pinkerton, intended "to create a mob of the most excitable elements of society" at Baltimore's Camden Street Station. In the confusion, hired assassins would "rush forward, shoot or stab the President elect" and then "fly back to the shelter of the rioters."

Pinkerton urged Lincoln to proceed immediately—and secretly—to Washington. Still unwilling to believe the murder plot was real, Lincoln refused Pinkerton's plea to cancel the rest of his appearances. But the warning shook him, and his speech on Washington's birthday, at the very place where the Declaration of Independence had been signed, was almost a confession.

"I have never had a feeling politically that did not spring from the sentiments embodied in the Declaration," Lincoln said, and the crowd at Independence Hall erupted in cheers. He promised to try to save the country to protect liberty, the principle he honored above all others. Then, perhaps for the first time, he admitted to a shadow of doubt. "But, if this country cannot be saved without giving up that principle— I was about to say I would rather be assassinated on this spot than to surrender it." His strong words met with applause, though few knew what was really on Lincoln's mind.[11]

A second warning of the danger to Lincoln arrived when Frederick Seward, son of the soon-to-be secretary of state, delivered a report of the plot to kill the president; it came from Winfield Scott, the commanding general of the U.S. Army. This time, Lincoln agreed to cut short his tour, and Pinkerton quickly put in place a scheme for Lincoln's safe passage.

After delivering a speech that evening in Harrisburg, Lincoln ate a quick supper. Leaving all but the burly Lamon behind, the guest of honor then slipped out, exiting through the side door of his hotel, an overcoat draped over his shoulders to disguise his narrow physique. In place of his widely recognized stovepipe hat, Lincoln drew a soft woolen hat over his head. He and Lamon then stepped into a waiting carriage, which carried them to a special Pennsylvania Railroad train.

The party became three with the addition of Allan Pinkerton. By midnight the train for Baltimore—this time with Lincoln hidden behind the curtains of a sleeping berth that one of Pinkerton's agents had reserved purportedly for an invalid—was racing southward. At 3:30 A.M. it arrived in slumbering Baltimore, where the sleeper car was pulled by a team of horses to Camden Street Station, from which southbound trains departed. By sunrise, the unfinished U.S. Capitol, its dome half-obscured by scaffolding and cranes, came into view.

Lincoln arrived in Washington sleepless, but safe, in time for breakfast at the Willard Hotel. He was joined in the afternoon by Mary and their

*This photograph of the unfinished Capitol—Lincoln made the completion of the dome an objective during his first term—was taken the day of the sixteenth president's inauguration.*

(3.) THE SPECIAL TRAIN.

"He wore a Scotch plaid Cap and a very long Military Cloak, so that he was entirely unrecognizable."

*Opposition Democratic newspapers satirized Lincoln's furtive trip to Washington after he was warned of a possible assassination plot. In this cartoon he is portrayed running fearfully for his life.*

sons, who, still aboard the Presidential Special, had passed through Baltimore without incident.

When word got out, Lincoln's enemies were quick to mock his midnight escape. A prominent national magazine ran a scathing political cartoon, lampooning him as a coward, running for his life, with the heading "The Flight of Abraham."[12] But Frederick Douglass understood why Lincoln acted as he had. As he saw it, Lincoln had run a dangerous gauntlet, very much like "the poor, hunted fugitive slave [who] reaches the North, in disguise, . . . crawling and dodging under the sable wing of night.[13] Douglass could not help but look back to 1838 when, as Fred Bailey, his younger self made his own dangerous escape.

## INAUGURAL BLUES

A week later, soldiers were everywhere. On inauguration day, March 4, 1861, sharpshooters scanned the crowd from the rooftops. Infantrymen patrolled Pennsylvania Avenue. Companies of cavalry blocked the side streets, and there was even a battery of howitzers on a nearby hill, just in case. The air was alive with fears not only for Lincoln's safety but of impending war.

An open carriage and military escort arrived at noon to ferry Lincoln from his hotel to the Capitol. Once there he made his way to a large platform constructed on the east portico. He removed his new silk hat, preparing to address the crowd, but after a moment of confusion—*where would he put it?*—Stephen Douglas, one of the several hundred dignitaries arrayed behind him, stepped forward. "Permit me, sir," he said, taking the hat. Lincoln put on his steel-rimmed spectacles and began to read. Twenty-five thousand listeners were spread before him on the Capitol grounds.

His address attempted to heal the nation's wounds, but it fell largely on deaf ears. In faraway Rochester, New York, Frederick Douglass in particular saw Lincoln's words as nothing short of an abject betrayal. He had wanted from Lincoln an explicit damnation of slavery, but when Douglass read the speech, the new president's promises fell far short of that.

Instead of denouncing secessionists, Lincoln was cool and reasonable. "I have no purpose," he explained, "directly or indirectly, to interfere with the institution of slavery in the States where it exists." He appealed to Unionists in the South, promising to uphold existing laws, including the Fugitive Slave Act. He did take a hard line regarding secession, calling it unlawful, but added, "there needs to be no bloodshed or violence; and there shall be none, unless it be forced upon the national authority." Above all, he saw defending and maintaining the Union as his duty, but he would not order the first gun fired. He wanted "harmony," not "anarchy."

The tightly crafted ending to his speech was a poetic plea:

> We must not be enemies. Though passion may have strained, it
> must not break our bonds of affection. The mystic chords of

memory, stretching from every battle-field, and patriot grave, to every living heart and hearthstone, all over this broad land, will yet swell the chorus of the Union, when again touched, as surely they will be, by the better angels of our nature.[14]

With the speech at an end, Chief Justice Roger Taney, withered, bent, and nearly as tall as Lincoln, administered the oath of office to the sixteenth president. Afterward the crowd cheered and cannons were fired in tribute. But in the days to come, none of the seven states that seceded accepted Lincoln's olive branch. John Bell, one of Lincoln's opponents in the election, thought Lincoln's speech amounted to a declaration of war. President Buchanan was uncertain what to think. "I cannot understand the secret meaning of the document," he told one reporter. Some observers suspected they knew why Buchanan seemed confused; he appeared to them to have fallen asleep.

## FREDERICK'S FRUSTRATION

After Frederick Douglass read the published version of Lincoln's address, he penned a screed that was one and a half times its length. The speech was pure hypocrisy, he concluded, a "double-tongued document." The angry and disappointed Douglass condemned Lincoln: His willingness to enforce the Fugitive Slave Act made him nothing less than "an excellent slave hound," said Douglass, adding in disgust that Lincoln thought "the poor bondman should [be] returned to the hell of slavery."[15] Douglass was furious that Lincoln had said he would sign a proposed amendment to the Constitution, then under consideration in Congress, which would guarantee slavery in the Southern states *forever.* In Douglass's eyes, Lincoln's "better angels," so oblivious to the freedom of the Black man, were poor angels indeed. Lincoln's words shattered Douglass's hopes that this man would end slavery.

Douglass's disappointment was so great he considered leaving his country. No fan of colonization, he was on record as strongly opposed to sending his people back to Africa. But abolitionist friends had begun advocating for African American emigration to the Republic of Haiti, the largely Black island nation that had gained independence from France. In the next issue of his newspaper, he reported having booked tickets to travel there, departing New Haven, together with his eldest child, daughter Rosetta. The Haitian consulate invited him, and he told his readers that, as a journalist, he wanted to "do justice to Haiti, to paint her as she is."[16]

The first guns of war, fired on April 12, would change his—and Mr. Lincoln's—plans.

## THE FALL OF FORT SUMTER

In his first hours as president, Abraham Lincoln found a ticking time bomb on his desk. It took the form of a dispatch from the commander of Fort Sumter. U.S. Army major Robert Anderson reported that food and other supplies were running low. Unless provisions arrived soon, his small garrison would have no choice but to surrender to Confederate forces. In the time it took Lincoln to read Anderson's words, the immense national challenge of the seceding South shrank to the fate of a tiny, two-acre island in Charleston Harbor.

Lincoln asked the advice of the men he'd selected for his cabinet. At first, most of them, including Seward, saw no alternative to withdrawal from the fort. The head military man, General Winfield Scott, concurred. But Lincoln refused to give up Fort Sumter so easily, and he dispatched his friend Ward Lamon to Charleston to talk with South Carolina governor Francis Pickens and Major Anderson. As days became weeks, the president heard voices pro and con from Congress—*You must do something!* said some, while others warned, *Anything you do could start war!*—but he ordered preliminary preparations be made to ship supplies to Anderson. Finally, on April 4, he issued the order that humanitarian aid of food and medicine be sent to Fort Sumter. It was to be done "peaceably," Lincoln ordered, if at all possible.

A lifelong insomniac, Lincoln stayed awake nights worrying about much more than Sumter. Holding the fort was a point of principle, since he had sworn in his inaugural speech to "hold, occupy, and possess" federal property, but he devoted a great deal of thought to the much larger canvas of slave country. His hope had been that Unionists in the South would persuade hotheaded "fire-eaters," the angry men who wanted war, to rethink secession and voluntarily rejoin the Union. That now seemed laughably unlikely—and giving up Sumter would amount to both capitulation and recognition of the Confederacy.

Some newspapers began to question the new president's leadership: "HAVE WE A GOVERNMENT?" screamed one headline.[17] But Lincoln knew one thing for certain: He wanted to avoid firing the first shot. He did not want to be the aggressor, which might provoke more states to leave the Union. In particular, he worried about Virginia, just across the Potomac, where the state's politicians waited and watched.

On Friday morning, April 12, 1861, Confederate president Jefferson Davis brought the stalemate to a crashing conclusion. On Davis's order, Confederate cannons boomed in Charleston at 4:30 A.M., firing the first of some four thousand shots and shells from what seemed like all directions. With first light, Fort Sumter's artillerists began to return fire, but Major Anderson ordered his gunners to fire sparingly to conserve limited supplies of powder and cartridges.

Confederate cannonballs preheated in a furnace ignited fires in

*Before becoming president of the Confederate States of America, Jefferson Davis served honorably as a soldier, secretary of war, and, at the time this picture was taken just before the Civil War, U.S. senator from Mississippi.*

Fort Sumter's wooden barracks. The projectiles traced soaring arcs in the sky, remaining in the air for thirty seconds and more as spotters shouted warnings of incoming shot, shells, or mortars.[18] Remarkably, no one was killed during the artillery exchange, but fighters on both sides knew what the result of the assault would be.

The Union men managed to hold on until the next day, when Anderson negotiated terms. His men marched out of the fort with heads high and saluted the Stars and Stripes as the flag was lowered. They would not be prisoners of war, instead boarding a civilian ship bound for New York. But Fort Sumter was lost, surrendered to an enemy in the first battle of what could now only be called civil war.

In Washington, Lincoln was far from shocked; in a way, he had engineered this fight. The surprise was that the nation immediately rose from the sleepy limbo in which it had been suspended for months. When Lincoln acted quickly to issue a proclamation, calling upon the remaining

Union states to muster seventy-five thousand militiamen to put down what he called the "insurrection," men raced to volunteer. The Northern states unified in a way that had seemed impossible days before. Stephen Douglas, addressing a huge rally in Chicago, defined the new stakes. "There are only two sides to the question. Every man must be for the United States or against it. There can be no neutrals in this, *only patriots— or traitors.*"[19] No one in the North seemed to disagree.

The South reacted differently: They believed Union troops were being assembled to suppress their rebellion. The response of North Carolina's chief executive was typical. "I can be no party to this wicked violation of the laws of the country," said Governor John Ellis, "and to this war upon the liberties of free people."[20] In a matter of weeks, his state, along with Virginia, Tennessee, and Arkansas, joined the Confederacy. Mr. Lincoln's play for peace had failed spectacularly. He truly had a war on his hands.

# REACTION IN ROCHESTER

"God be Praised!" wrote Frederick Douglass in response to the news. "As a friend of freedom, . . . we have no tears to shed, no lamentations to make over the fall of Fort Sumter." His worry that Lincoln would compromise on slavery to keep the peace went up in the billowing gun smoke over Charleston. "The slaveholders themselves," Douglass continued, "have saved our cause from ruin!"[21]

He canceled his trip to Haiti. "The last ten days have made a tremendous revolution in all things pertaining to the possible future of colored people in the United States," he told readers of *Douglass' Monthly.* "This is not the time to leave the country."[22]

Douglass saw with his own eyes his countrymen rising to defend the Union. On May 3, eight companies of militia volunteers boarded trains in Rochester. "[Their] departure was a thrilling spectacle," he noted in his paper, yet also a sad one. He saw the tears of wives wishing their husbands farewell and heard the "mournful sobs of mothers, as they part from their sons."[23] The safe return of their men was far from certain.

As one of the twenty thousand who crowded State Street to cheer the departing soldiers-to-be, Douglass was seized by another powerful emotion. No person of color—not a single one—departed Rochester that day to fight for liberty and for the freedom of his people in particular. This was not out of fear or a reluctance to join the ranks; dark-skinned men, even in the North, were simply not welcome to go to war shoulder to shoulder with Whites.

Douglass never doubted he and his brethren could fight. He claimed that "One black regiment alone would be . . . the full equal of two white ones." When asked what his people were prepared to do "in the present solemn crisis," Douglass could only express his frustration. "Would to God you would let us do something!"[24]

Douglass himself would do everything in his power to persuade the government to let freedmen and fugitives fight to liberate their brothers, an unwinnable fight in the spring of 1861. Though he failed initially, his words would prove prophetic. "If this conflict shall expand to the grand dimensions which events seem to indicate, the iron arm of the black man may be called into service."[25]

# CONTRABANDS OF WAR

A month after the fall of Fort Sumter, three men in a boat approached another Union fort. They were fugitive bondsmen seeking sanctuary, and after rowing across Norfolk harbor on the night of May 23, 1861, the unarmed Black men presented themselves to the sentries at the five-sided federal stronghold called Fortress Monroe.

CONTRABAND OF WAR.

VOLUNTEER SAPPERS AND MINERS, from the F. F. V's.

Massa Butler, we's jest seceded from Harper's Ferry, where we larnd de trade of making Trenches and Fortifcations. we's de niggers to call upon in dese ar line. We borrowed des yer tools at de Ferry, and of des isent *Contraban*, we's gwine to carry em back at the close of horsetilities.

*A crude rendering on a Civil War–era envelope that pictured General Benjamin Butler, on horseback, meeting up with Black sappers and miners volunteering to work for the Union.*

They were taken to the fort's commanding officer, Major General Benjamin Butler, a large and pugnacious man with a walrus mustache. He had only just arrived to take charge of the strategically placed citadel, which overlooked the channel linking the James River and the Chesapeake Bay, but General Butler already knew he needed all the help he could get to improve the dilapidated installation.

While the Confederacy had bondsmen to dig ditches, build fortifications, and perform a hundred other support duties, the Union did not. So when Frank Baker, Shepard Mallory, and James Townsend explained they had been working on enemy artillery earthworks but escaped across Confederate lines out of fear of being shipped south— which, to them, might mean permanent separation from their families— Butler put them to work right then and right there. Unexpectedly, his snap decision also put him in the middle of a new and heated debate about enslaved people.

Before the day was out, a messenger arrived under a flag of truce. Acting as agent for the local Confederate commander, the officer claimed that Butler, given his "constitutional obligations," was compelled to return Baker, Mallory, and Townsend as human property under the terms of the Fugitive Slave Act. Having been a lawyer in Boston before Lincoln commissioned him a general, Butler considered the facts of the case. Even in the absence of a clear precedent, Butler saw his duty. He was quick to reject the man's demands.

"Virginia passed an ordinance of secession and claims to be a foreign country," he reminded his visitor. Thus, the Union general explained, "I am under no constitutional obligations to a foreign country, which Virginia now claims to be."

Butler's argument went further. The two sides were, after all, at war, and the men were "being used against the government by its foes." To return them to their owner would aid and abet the enemy. The three runaways were, under the terms of international law as Butler saw it, military goods and could be lawfully seized by a combatant in wartime.

"I shall hold them," he said firmly, "as *contraband of war*."[26]

That ended the two men's conversation—but opened a much broader one. The term "contraband of war" came immediately into general use after other enslaved persons heard about the "freedom fort" and presented themselves at the gate of Fortress Monroe. Within two months, the contraband count of men, women, and children neared nine hundred at Fortress Monroe alone; eventually there were many thousands at other Union outposts. Contraband camps and contraband schools were created after Congress memorialized the legality of Butler's position with the Confiscation Act, which stated that a slaveholder forfeited his bondsmen if he permitted them to be used in service to the Confederacy.

But the new law had another immediate and important effect, too. It made the old Fugitive Slave Act unenforceable.

Lincoln signed the Confiscation Act into law, though not without misgivings. He found himself making a hard choice. He recognized he must do everything he could to appease the border states of Kentucky, Missouri, Maryland, and Delaware, since he could not afford to lose any more states to the Confederacy. None of the four in question had seceded yet, but each of the states did permit slavery. That meant Lincoln, like a tightrope walker, had to find just the right balance in his slavery policy. He could tip only so far in either direction as he tried to satisfy the free states' anti-slavery demands and to appease the slaveholders in the border states to keep them in the fold. If he had to choose between freeing enslaved people and saving the country, he felt he had no choice but to choose unity.

The strategy was a delicate one, only made more so by the contraband controversy, since the Confiscation Act represented a new stage in putting the powers of the Constitution to use regarding what was clearly the war's central issue. As Frederick Douglass saw it, the whole conversation was just "another compromise, [with] the old virus left to heal over."[27] He was interested less in a cautious balance than in radical change.

The president had other problems to confront, the biggest one the reality of a war about to unfold. In military terms, the bombardment in Charleston Harbor had been a small matter and a total mismatch. The outcome was never really in doubt, with forty-three Confederate artillery pieces firing upon just eighty-seven ill-fed Union soldiers. Now, however, both sides were raising large new armies to confront each other.

The North had certain large advantages. Its population numbered more than twenty million, compared to nine million in the South, where more than a third were enslaved people. The Union's industrial capacity was vastly greater, too, with roughly 90 percent of the nation's factories and double the railroad lines. As a result of this calculus, many a Union man thought the war would be short, perhaps a simple matter of capturing the new Confederate capital at Richmond, Virginia, a hundred miles into Confederate territory. Lincoln's first request for seventy-five thousand volunteers reflected this expectation, with a term of enlistment of just ninety days.

On the other side, Southerners, who believed they were fighting to preserve their honor and their way of life, chose not to see the war in stark David-and-Goliath terms. They had the distinct advantage of fighting a defensive war, and they would be fighting it with some of the best military minds that West Point had produced. Many in the South looked forward to the first land battle of war, confident they would prevail, while many Northerners told one another their army would easily overpower the undermanned South. July 21, 1861, would be the first test.

## THE BATTLE BY BULL RUN

On that Sunday, three months after Sumter's fall, on July 21, 1861, the armies faced off in Manassas, Virginia. Goaded by such newspaper headlines as the *Tribune*'s "FORWARD TO RICHMOND! FORWARD TO RICHMOND!," an impatient Lincoln had ordered General Irvin McDowell's army to move south. Although headed for the capital of the Confederacy, the Army of the Potomac would first have to deal with the enemy's line of defense at Manassas Junction. Just twenty-five miles from Washington, it was a railroad hub alongside a tributary to the Occoquan River called Bull Run.

Slowed by a shortage of horses and mules, McDowell's army of thirty thousand men marched into nearby Centreville on July 18. His opponent, General Pierre Gustave Toutant-Beauregard, the man who had been in charge at Fort Sumter, camped nearby with some twenty thousand soldiers. McDowell chose not attack immediately, and Confederate president Jefferson Davis took advantage of the pause, ordering rein-forcements. General Joe Johnston's army of ten thousand men, then in the Shenandoah Mountains, clambered into train cars for the long ride to Manassas.

By the time McDowell took the offensive three days later, every-one knew a battle was about to unfold. Half a dozen senators and their wives, newspaper correspondents, and other spectators rode out from Washington in their carriages, arriving with picnic baskets and opera glasses, anticipating a day's entertainment as the Union army won a great victory. Lincoln chose to remain in Washington, attending church that Sunday morning, but on his return to the President's House, he got his first reports of the battle.

Under a clear blue sky, a large Union force moved on the left flank of the Confederate line. As one Virginia soldier reported, "The enemy were thick in the field, and the long lines of blue could not be counted."[28] The spectators cheered the puffs of artillery smoke. The woods lining Bull Run rang with gunfire and the shouts of combatants. Early on, the Rebels were forced to retreat, and Lincoln was informed late in the af-ternoon that the battle looked like a clear Union victory. A *New York Herald* reporter telegraphed his editor, "I am en route to Washington with details of a great battle. We have carried the day."[29]

Such optimistic reports could not have been more wrong, as Lincoln learned when a despondent Secretary of State Seward arrived at 6:00 P.M. The same man who had repeatedly predicted the war would end in thirty days brought devastating news: McDowell's army was in full re-treat. The momentum of the battle had shifted when a Confederate gen-eral, rallying his men in the face of Union attack, gestured with his sword at a nearby hilltop. He called to his troops, "Look, men, there is Jackson standing like a stone wall! Let us determine to die here, and we will conquer! Follow me!" The man on the hill—who at that moment gained the nickname "Stonewall"—was Thomas J. Jackson. He and his

*Lincoln's Republican rival for the presidency and later his secretary of state, William Henry Seward. As one contemporary said of him, he "had a head like a wise macaw."*

men bought the Rebels time, holding their position until late afternoon. By then the trains carrying Joe Johnston's fresh troops arrived, and their fierce counterattack shifted the momentum of battle.

Lincoln lay awake all night at the White House, prone on a couch in the Cabinet Room, listening to a series of firsthand accounts of the battle. The Union army had cut and run, he was told. The scene had been utter chaos as soldiers and civilians retreated in disorder and humiliation to Washington, terrified the enemy might be in hot pursuit.

The follow-up attack never came, but at dawn Lincoln looked down on Pennsylvania Avenue. From his window he saw stragglers stumbling back from the battle in a driving rain, some of them collapsing and being tended to by medical staff. The Union had lost its first big battle, and Lincoln suspected perhaps for the first time that he faced a long, hard-fought war.

# TEN

# WAR IN THE WEST

Fire must be met with water, darkness with light, and war for the destruction of liberty must be met with war for the destruction of slavery.

—FREDERICK DOUGLASS, *Douglass' Monthly*, MAY 1861

E ight hundred miles west, the Civil War was playing out in miniature. More than half of Missouri's White citizens were pro-Union but, as a slave state settled by Southerners, it was also home to powerful and militant secessionists. Its pro-slavery governor confronted a legislature dominated by Unionists. Bloody guerrilla fighting broke out across the state, and a worried President Lincoln dispatched Major General John C. Frémont to keep the peace. He wanted the famous and charismatic general to keep Missouri in the Union—but he underestimated the size of Frémont's ego.

Frémont was famous, known as "the Pathfinder" after his heroic expeditions with the United States Topographical Corps. People admired him as if, in making his maps, he had lassoed the great beauty of the boundless Far West. He had been acting governor and one of California's first senators before becoming the Republican nominee in the three-man 1856 presidential election. Having resumed his army service after Fort Sumter, he was rich, well connected, and a man John Hay, one of Lincoln's secretaries, extolled as "upright, brave, generous, enterprising, learned and eminently practical."[1] He also held strong anti-slavery convictions.

On the very day of the Manassas debacle, Frémont boarded a train headed for St. Louis to take charge of the war's western theater. There, far from Washington, his job would be to create an army out of almost nothing, with little help from the distant federal government, and to figure out how to keep the Mississippi River open to trade. Lincoln personally told Frémont he had "carte blanche," trusting him to "use your own judgement."[2] The general soon made one visionary call when he put a former army captain of dubious reputation in charge of Missouri's Southeastern District, and Ulysses S. Grant thus began his rapid rise. But another Frémont decision seriously undermined Lincoln's border-state strategy.

In St. Louis, a town with strong Southern sympathies, Frémont was widely despised as a Yankee whose troops more or less occupied their city. It didn't help that his wife, Jessie Benton Frémont, daughter of Missouri's late senator Thomas Hart Benton, chafed at the social limitations imposed on women; "she had a man's power, a man's education, and she did a man's work in the world," remarked one friend.[3]

As instructed, Frémont attempted to consolidate Union control in Missouri. He took over railroads, converted ferry boats to gun boats, and trained recruits. But Confederates had swept into southern Missouri. Insurgents from Arkansas and Tennessee stole horses, burned bridges, cut telegraph lines, and attacked Unionist settlements. They recruited some forty thousand Missourians, too, some of whom, after taking part in guerrilla activities, would quietly return to their farms. Missouri appeared to be on the verge of falling into Confederate hands.

*General John C. Frémont—famous as the "The Pathfinder" for
his mapping expeditions in California and the West—and
his formidable wife, Jessie Benton Frémont, daughter
of Senator Thomas Hart Benton.*

On August 30, 1861, Frémont declared martial law across the state.
Set into type, his proclamation was nailed to posts and trees. Its harsh
terms ordered that guerrilla fighters arrested behind Union lines be
tried by court-martial; if found guilty, they would be executed. But
Frémont didn't stop there. The property of Confederate sympathizers
would "be confiscated," stated the order, "and their slaves, if any they
have, are hereby declared free men."[4]

In addressing slavery, an institution he despised, Frémont went a
long step further than General Benjamin Butler. In an unprecedented
move, one he made without consulting Lincoln, the Pathfinder had issued an emancipation proclamation.

WAR IN THE WEST

# A NOBLE DEED

Many Republicans back east enthusiastically embraced Frémont's decree. Gerrit Smith called it "a noble deed of a noble man." There were torchlight parades in Northern cities in celebration. Newspapers endorsed the proclamation, among them the *New York Evening Post*, which told its readers, "Mr. Frémont has done what the Government ought to have done from the beginning."[5]

To Harriet Beecher Stowe, Frémont's gesture had the aura of revelation: "The hour has come," she wrote, "and [so has] the man."[6] As far as she was concerned, the hero Frémont had earned another star to pin on his chest.

Frederick Douglass was more practical. He wanted to believe Frémont's order was "the hinge, the pivot upon which the war was to turn." But having been disappointed before, he also understood that the news from St. Louis might be too good to be true. He admitted to readers of his newspaper that he experienced "the deepest anxiety" as he waited and wondered "whether that remarkable and startling document was the utterance of the Major-General, or that of the Cabinet at Washington [and] whether . . . the President would approve it or condemn it."[7]

He did not have to wait long.

# TIMING IS EVERYTHING

Like so many others, Lincoln learned of Frémont's martial law declaration from a newspaper. He could hardly believe his eyes: His carefully calibrated border-state strategy, based on the promise not to interfere with slavery where it legally existed, was suddenly worth less than the paper he held in his hand. Sent west to put out a fire, Frémont had fueled it.

Lincoln rarely revealed his emotions in public and, though deeply angry, he kept his temper. Writing confidentially in what he called "a spirit of caution and not of censure," he told Frémont that the promise to liberate the enslaved would "alarm our southern Union friends"— and *that* he did not wish to do. Frémont's policy, Lincoln pointed out, could lead not only to Missouri's secession but might also "ruin our rather fair prospect" for keeping Kentucky in the Union. The president asked Frémont—but did not order him—to amend his proclamation to align with the terms of the recently passed Confiscation Act. In short, Lincoln wanted Frémont's promise of emancipation to go away.[8]

Despite the reasonable tone of Lincoln's letter, Frémont took offense. As a man steeped in the ways of the military, he read it as a reprimand. He sat down and wrote a firm response, in which the self-satisfied general assured his commander in chief that he remained quite certain of his own judgment. His proclamation, he assured Lincoln, was "right and neces-sary." He had decided to buck the chain of command. He wasn't going to admit he was wrong. Nor would he comply with Lincoln's soft order to amend the proclamation. Unless the president publicly directed him to modify his proclamation, Frémont would make no "correction."[9]

This second surprise from Frémont's pen came to Lincoln's attention on September 10, 1861, when Jessie Benton Frémont arrived at the White House. At 10:00 P.M., after spending more than fifty hours on a train from St. Louis, Mrs. Frémont waited for Lincoln in the Red Parlor. Her dress was smudged with coal soot, but, tired as she was, she felt at home, having known nine previous occupants of the White House, extending back to Andrew Jackson. Decades before, Old Hickory had played with her hair as he talked politics with her father, Senator Thomas Hart Benton, for decades one of the most powerful politicians in Wash-ington.

To Mrs. Frémont, the wait seemed like forever. Then, when Lincoln finally did appear, he took the sealed letter but did not meet her eye.

This was not the welcome Mrs. Frémont expected. Nor did Lincoln offer her a seat as he stood beneath the chandelier reading her husband's pointed rejection of his thinking. He folded and pocketed the letter before he spoke.

"I have written to the General and he knows what I want done," he said coldly.

His unhappiness with the situation was painfully obvious. Not only had Frémont refused to do as he was told, he had sent his wife to deliver the message. This meeting was virtually unprecedented: Women in mid-nineteenth-century America played no direct role in government, and they certainly didn't seek meetings with presidents. But Jessie Frémont was not a conventional woman. She was her father's daughter, confident and almost fearless, and, like her husband, she possessed a cocky certainty that he was right.

Despite Lincoln's obvious displeasure, she launched into a detailed justification of her husband's action, explaining to the president the workings of international politics. The nation needed England, France, and Spain, she argued, and in order to win their support, emancipation was necessary. Her foreign policy knowledge was considerable, her presentation clear and impassioned.

But Lincoln wasn't going to be lectured to. "I had to exercise all the awkward tact I have to avoid quarrelling with her," he told John Hay. Before she could complete her case, the frowning Lincoln, his patience at an end, interrupted.[10]

"You are quite a female politician," he said dismissively.

Although his words signaled their conversation was at an end, Lincoln did offer Jessie Frémont a few parting words. Her husband should have sought consultation before issuing his edict, he scolded. Furthermore, he said, "The General should never have dragged the Negro into the war. It is a war for a great national object and the Negro has nothing to do with it." For once, Lincoln put the matter in bold terms: Whatever his heart told him about the evils of slavery, his brain, ever pragmatic, put saving the country first.

The next day a letter bearing Lincoln's signature went west, ordering General Frémont to rescind the emancipation provision in his proclamation. As Frémont demanded, Lincoln took responsibility, releasing a copy of his letter to the newspapers. The notion of an emancipation proclamation was off the table, but the subject was far from closed.

## DISCOURAGED, NOT DEFEATED

For Frederick Douglass and his allies, the joy they shared at Frémont's declaration soured after Lincoln made public his order gutting the proclamation. Douglass saw the retraction as the work of a "crafty lawyer." He wrote that he still wanted to believe that Lincoln's reputation for being "honest and humane" was deserved, but what he actually saw was a willingness to pacify slaveholders. He did not for a moment accept the border-state argument. Missouri, Kentucky, Delaware, and Maryland were the "mill-stone about the neck of the government," he wrote, "and their so-called loyalty has been the very best shield to the treason of the cotton States."[11] Lincoln's rejection of Frémont's policy was appeasement, plain and simple.

Although Douglass wanted to appeal to the president directly, he had no channel to the White House; his best option was his *Douglass' Monthly*. In an essay he titled "Fighting Rebels with Only One Hand," he asked, "Why does the Government reject the Negro? Is he not a man? Can he not wield a sword, fire a gun, march and countermarch, and obey orders like any other?" Douglass was convinced that not only could a Black man fight as well as a White one, but, as he wrote that September, "in a war such as this, [one Black regiment] . . . would be worth to the government more than two of any other." The refusal to arm Blacks was foolish. "Men in earnest don't fight with one hand, when they might fight with two, and a man drowning would not refuse to be saved even by a colored hand."[12]

Douglass's words may have reached Lincoln, but his harsh criticisms of Lincoln's border-state policy certainly angered a great many people. When he arrived that November to lecture in Syracuse, New York, he saw advertisements promoting his speeches—but side by side were handbills that called him "Thief!," "Rescal," "Traitor!!!"—and worse. It invited all comers to "give him a warm reception at this time for his insolence, as he deserves."[13]

Yet his appearance on Thursday evening, November 14, would not be a repeat of the Tremont Temple riot the previous year. As Douglass told the story, "even the rattlesnake sounds an alarm . . . and in this instance the Mayor of the city, the police authorities and citizens took the alarm and provided amply for the attack."

The owner of the theater rejected calls from his neighbors to the close the doors to his hall. When he was reminded that "Frederick Douglass was a Negro," he replied that his "principles of freedom applied to humanity not to color." The mayor reached into the city coffers and came up with three hundred dollars to pay for regular police and a special fifty-man security force.

Additional recruits were summoned. They marched into Syracuse, where they guarded the theater entrance, bayonets fixed on their rifles. When Douglass arrived, the mayor locked arms with Douglass, endangering his own safety to shield his guest from mob violence.

Once at the podium, Douglass looked out over a packed house, and spoke freely of Lincoln, Frémont, the war, and emancipation. His reward was a standing ovation and a sense on leaving Syracuse that he was far from alone. As the tumultuous year 1861 came to an end, Douglass could only hope that his voice would carry to faraway Washington.

ELEVEN

# TO PROCLAIM OR NOT TO PROCLAIM

*I may walk slowly but I don't walk backward.*

—ABRAHAM LINCOLN

In the early months of 1862, reports of real military progress reached Washington. Ulysses S. Grant captured Forts Henry and Donelson in Tennessee. Newspapers dubbed him "Unconditional Surrender Grant," playfully adapting the hero's initials, and President Lincoln promoted him to major general. Unfortunately, while Grant demonstrated he was a man willing to fight, George B. McClellan, the commanding general of the entire army, seemed to lack that desire. To his frustration, the president saw much planning and preparation but little action in the eastern theater. Adding to his burden was a family tragedy.

On February 20, 1862, eleven-year-old Willie, the son said to be most like his father, lost a battle with typhoid. "My boy is gone—he is actually gone," Lincoln told one of his young secretaries before burying his face in his hands. "He was too good for this earth. God has called him home."[1]

The grieving president then nursed and consoled his youngest boy, Tad, age eight, still ill with the disease, and coped with his wife's devastating grief. Mary took to her bed, unable even to attend her son's funeral, which left Washington tongues wagging about her mental stability. Dressed in widow's weeds, she consulted with spiritualists in hopes of communing with Willie.

Despite the other pressures, Lincoln remained attentive to the ebb and flow of public opinion regarding slavery. He had long foreseen an eventual end to enslavement, but he sensed growing pressure in the country to do something sooner rather than later. An organization called the Emancipation League had been formed the previous November by Boston abolitionists. And in late February, at New York's Cooper Union, Frederick Douglass called for the destruction of the slave system. His well-publicized and persuasive address to the league met with "most hearty and enthusiastic applause."[2]

*Mary Lincoln during her husband's first term, all dressed up as if for a ball.*

Hoping to make at least a little progress, Lincoln looked for a legal framework. He understood that most slaveholders had more invested in their bondsmen than they did in their land. That meant, he reasoned, they needed to be compensated if they were to give up their bondsmen willingly. In a close rereading of the Constitution, he focused on the founding document's promise of "just compensation" for private property appropriated by the federal government.

Thinking the principle might apply to slavery, he chose Delaware as a test case. It was a slave state but one where less than 1 percent of Whites were slaveholders. When he proposed to several influential Delaware men that the federal government might pay four hundred dollars per person in return for emancipation, they expressed a willingness to move the idea forward. Lincoln drafted sample legislation for their consideration, but when once the discussion became public, vocal opposition immediately arose. The biggest objection was that emancipation could lead to equality—and few Whites, north or south, were ready to acknowledge racial equality in 1862. The bill was never formally introduced.

Lincoln also began talking, once again, about colonization. He mentioned it in his annual message, the precursor of today's State of the Union address, urging Congress to appropriate funds for establishing contraband colonies. He called for recognition of Haiti and Liberia, possible destinations for American freedmen. But these ideas, too, met with more opposition than enthusiasm, since even his own Republican Party remained deeply divided on almost every matter concerning the Black man.

On the other hand, the radical wing of the party wasn't about to let the matter drop. When pressed in one meeting, Lincoln shifted the conversation as he often did by telling a story. He told his guests that he first heard the yarn as a boy.

One spring, a group of Methodist preachers made their way across

Illinois. Two of the parsons discussed how, with its waters running high, they could get across a fast-moving river some distance ahead. The two talked and talked, and the more they talked, the more heated their words became. When their argument turned into a quarrel, a third member of their company stepped in.

"Brethren," said the older man, "this here talk ain't no use. I never cross a river until I come to it."[3]

Lincoln the raconteur left his visitors laughing, releasing the tension. Yet the moment also cleverly conveyed to them his attitude toward emancipation: *Not yet, gentlemen. That decision lies in our future.*

## SLAVERY IN THE CAPITAL

From a distance, Frederick Douglass observed the president. Some of what he saw, he liked; just as often, Lincoln's words and actions made him angry. But in April 1862, Lincoln gave him reason to rejoice.

Early in the month, Grant and his forces in the west prevailed at the bloody two-day Battle of Shiloh, fought on April 6–7. The cost was staggering, with the combined Union and Confederate casualties numbering 23,746, losses greater than those in all previous American wars combined. In the east, the Union continued to pin its hopes on General McClellan's army, which, after months of delays, again had the Confederate capital of Richmond in its sights. But the outcome of McClellan's so-called Peninsula Campaign could not be known for some time, since his strategy involved moving the Army of the Potomac by ship to a Virginia peninsula between the James and York Rivers and then marching fifty miles to the Confederate capital. Lincoln had no choice but to be patient.

In Washington, however, the issue of slavery emerged as a matter of intense local interest. A dozen years earlier, during Lincoln's one term as congressman, his bill to end the slave trade in the District of Columbia went nowhere. Now, as president, he watched as new legislation to end slavery altogether in the nation's capital worked its way through the legislative process. Introduced in January, the two-pronged bill called for the immediate emancipation of the enslaved in Washington and three hundred dollars in compensation to owners for each man freed.

One of its most outspoken supporters was Charles Sumner. After his brutal beating at the hands of Preston Brooks in 1856, the Massachusetts senator had not returned to the Senate for three years. His flesh wounds repaired quickly enough, but, concussed and traumatized, Sumner consulted a series of more than a dozen doctors, even going to Europe to seek care. During his long absence from Washington, his chair remained vacant, a perpetual reminder of the violence perpetrated on his person by South Carolina congressman Brooks. When he had finally returned to the Capitol, he demonstrated that his hatred of slavery and his contempt for slaveholders remained unshaken. In June 1860, he proclaimed in a major speech to the Senate that "barbarous in origin; barbarous in law; . . . barbarous in spirit; barbarous wherever it shows itself, Slavery must breed Barbarians."[4] Sumner was a man the slavocracy loved to hate. He reciprocated the feeling with a hard passion, which he displayed on March 30, 1862, when he took to the floor of Congress to speak in favor of ending slavery in Washington.

"It is the first instalment of the great debt," he told his fellow senators, "which we all owe to an enslaved race, and will be recognized as one of the victories of humanity." There was an ongoing argument about whether people raised in bondage and deprived of education could live and thrive independently; the dispute continued, too, on where they should go. Yet the Senate approved the measure within a week of Sumner's impassioned pitch, and eight days later the House passed the measure. On April 16, 1862, Lincoln signed into law the District of Columbia Compensated Emancipation Act.

Never before in the nation's history had a federal statute given freedom to the enslaved, and Frederick Douglass felt a joy he had not since the war began. He wrote directly to Sumner. "I trust I am not dreaming but the events taking place seem like a dream."[5] On Douglass's good days, he imagined Lincoln might do more to right racial injustice. In light of this new law, Douglass felt a cautious optimism. "A blind man can see where the president's heart is," he told an audience in Rochester. "He is tall and strong but he is not done growing, he grows as the nation grows."[6]

# THE GO-BETWEEN

Mary Todd grew up with enslaved servants in her household, people she remembered lovingly. Influenced as a girl by family friend Henry Clay and, later, by her husband, Mrs. Lincoln believed that compensated emancipation was the best route to ending slavery. But after the arrival of Charles Sumner in the Lincolns' lives, in early 1861, Mary's thinking shifted. As she herself admitted, she became an "ardent abolitionist."*

Sumner had hoped the national attitude toward emancipation would shift with Lincoln's election, and when the president-elect first reached Washington, in February 1861, Sumner had gone to visit the stranger who would lead the country. The senator left their meeting at Willard's Hotel with mixed feelings. He thought the man lacked dignity and social poise: Lincoln, on noting they were roughly the same height, suggested in his lighthearted way that they "measure backs" by standing back-to-back to determine who was taller. The solemn Sumner refused, observing that this was "the time for uniting our fronts against

---

* "Mr. Sumner says he wishes my husband was as ardent an abolitionist as I am." Randall, *Mary Lincoln* (1953), p. 355.

the enemy and not our backs." To his credit, however, Sumner also recognized "flashes of thought and bursts of illuminating expression" in
Lincoln's conversation.[7] As for the savvy Lincoln, he saw clearly what
sort of man Sumner was. "I have never had much to do with bishops
where I live," he told a journalist, "but, do you know, Sumner is my idea
of a bishop."[8]

Yet the humorless and pompous Sumner had gained easy access to
the White House after Mary took a liking to him; she and the senator
began to have "delightful conversations & often later in the evening."[9]
She thought the aging and cultured bachelor was good company, and he
devotedly came to their open evenings at the White House. He went
with the Lincolns to the theater and escorted Mary to the opera when
Mr. Lincoln was too busy. Mary and Sumner corresponded, too, cover-
ing topics from poetry to politics, from military news to "the great cause
of abolition."[10]

In part through Sumner's influence, Mary became a convert to the
cause. And Sumner emerged as the man in the middle, a link between
the worlds of Frederick Douglass—a Sumner confidant—and Mr. and
Mrs. Lincoln.

# JULY FOURTH

On Independence Day 1862, Charles Sumner visited the White House.
His mission was to persuade Lincoln to make emancipation his cause, too.

This was a regular topic for the two men. On the very day that the
fighting began at Fort Sumter sixteen months before, the senator tried
to convince the president that emancipation would not only be right but
legal. As Sumner recalled that April 1861 conversation, "I . . . told . . .
him that under the war power the right had come to him to emancipate
the slaves."[11] Lincoln had listened respectfully, then ignored the advice,

since it flew in the face of his larger promises to the country and his border-state strategy.

Despite mixed feelings about the bossy Bostonian, Lincoln had learned to work with Sumner. As chairman of the Senate Committee on Foreign Relations, Sumner was an ally as the president navigated the unfamiliar waters of international affairs, and his counsel proved particularly valuable when Lincoln and Secretary of State Seward did not see eye to eye. Mary described evenings when Sumner visited Pennsylvania Avenue, and he and "my darling husband would laugh together, like *two* school boys."[12]

On July 4, 1862, Seward arrived dressed to the nines, wearing a maroon vest and lavender trousers. Lincoln's attitude toward ending slavery continued to evolve; after much brooding, he now agreed in private that slavery must forcefully be abolished.[13] He said as much the previous December to Sumner, observing that "the only difference between you and me on this subject of emancipation is a month or six weeks in time."[14] Slavery must not be a permanent institution, Lincoln now believed, although he continued to resist a broad emancipation order, calling it a "thunderbolt" that he would use only as a last resort. But Sumner was insistent: *This is the time, Mr. President, to unleash that thunderbolt.*

The timing was significant. For more than a decade, abolitionists had held July Fourth celebrations. Their festivals were patriotic, and often included a reading of the Declaration of Independence. But the commemoration by Black and White abolitionists had also been critiques of the oppression and cruelty of slavery.

In 1852, Frederick Douglass had given an in-your-face speech at an Independence Day celebration, asking his audience of mostly White abolitionists, "What to the American slave, is your Fourth of July?"[15] He answered his own pregnant question: "To him, your celebration is a sham; your boasted liberty, an unholy license; your national greatness, swelling vanity; your sounds of rejoicing are empty and heartless."

Two years later at another July Fourth celebration, this one in Massachusetts, William Lloyd Garrison went further, burning a copy of the U.S. Constitution, along with the Fugitive Slave Act, warning that "the only remedy" to slavery was a dissolution of the union."[16]

When he had walked back Frémont's declaration the previous fall, Lincoln did so in part because he believed Frémont's decree illegal. According to Lincoln's interpretation, seizing property under the guise of military necessity was legitimate only "as long as the necessity lasts." To take an enemy's "property, real and personal" forever, he confided in a friend, was *purely political, and not within the range of military* law." It wasn't the proper province of a general, he felt, and as president he could not permit Frémont to make political decisions.[17]

But in July 1862, when Sumner renewed his argument, he argued that, as the nation's chief executive, Lincoln *could* legally issue an emancipation proclamation. And on this day of all days, Sumner told Lincoln, an emancipation decree would be a "reconsecration" of independence and freedom.

Lincoln listened, but still he could not agree. In his homespun way he said no, telling Sumner that across-the-board emancipation would be "too big a lick."

Even in the face of a counterargument—namely, that "big licks" were exactly what the present situation called for—Lincoln stayed firm, and Sumner departed unsatisfied. Never one to give up the high ground, however, he was undeterred and returned two hours later. This time he told Lincoln, "You need more men, not only at the North, but at the South, in the rear of the Rebels: *you need the slaves.*"[18] This was a different argument: *Arm the freedmen. They can help you win the war.*

On this day, this argument also failed to persuade, and Senator Sumner left the White House twice disappointed at the president's refusal to act.

# THE PROPOSAL

Less than three weeks later, on July 22, 1862, Lincoln called a cabinet meeting to order. Everyone in the room knew the war effort was going badly. With McClellan in retreat from Richmond, the Peninsula Campaign was a failure. Lincoln saw few good military options, and as he later told the story, he believed "that we had about played our last card, and must change our tactics or lose the game."[19]

With these dark thoughts in mind, he had set to work on an executive order to alter the nation's war strategy. With the draft before him, he told his advisers that he'd summoned them "[not] to ask their advice

PUNCH, OR THE LONDON CHARIVARI.—October 18, 1862.

ABE LINCOLN'S LAST CARD; OR, ROUGE-ET-NOIR.

*In this political cartoon, English artist John Tenniel portrayed a desperate but wily Lincoln. The caption reads "Lincoln's last card," a metaphor for the Emancipation Proclamation, and an accompanying poem reads, in part, "From the Slaves of Southern rebels / Thus I strike the chain."*

but to lay the subject matter of a proclamation before them." After they heard him out, he wanted their "suggestions" as to how to proceed.

Then he read aloud the Preliminary Emancipation Proclamation. It contained the extraordinary promise that that, as of January 1, 1863, "all persons held as slaves" within the rebellious states "henceforth shall be free." The proclamation would not declare all the enslaved free, since it specifically excluded those in the border states that remained in the Union.

The response to Lincoln's recitation was a mix of doubts, hopes, and surprise. The secretary of the treasury worried that financial instability could result. The postmaster general expressed concern its release might seriously reduce the Republican Party's prospects in the November elections. The attorney general thought Lincoln should publish the proclamation, but Secretary of State Seward offered the shrewdest advice.

"Mr. President, I approve of the proclamation, but I question the expediency of its issue at this juncture." With the recent military setbacks in mind, he proposed a delay. "I suggest, sir, that you postpone its issue until you can give it to the country supported by military success." Seward worried it would be seen as "the last measure of an exhausted government, a cry for help . . . on the retreat."

Lincoln saw the wisdom of the secretary of state's suggestion. As he later remembered, "I put the draft of the proclamation aside, . . . waiting for a victory." The war would go relentlessly on, and the document that could—and would—change American history remained a closely held secret as Lincoln waited for the tide to turn in the Union's favor.

## PROPOSAL NOT ACCEPTED

Though Frederick Douglass knew nothing about Lincoln's July 22 meeting, he had plenty to say about a small, invitation-only gathering at the

White House on August 14, 1862. Of the five Black guests, none was a well-known abolitionist or a man of national stature; four had been enslaved and not all could read and write. Even so, the meeting was unprecedented. No president had ever summoned a "Deputation of Negroes," as Lincoln called it, to talk about a matter of national interest.

Though he did not utter the word, *emancipation* was the great weight that burdened Lincoln's thoughts. If he were to free the enslaved, would his war strategy collapse like a house of cards? He understood that, as one senator told his brethren in the Capitol, "There is a very great aversion . . . [to] having free negroes come among us."[20] Northern citizens who feared that freedmen would take their jobs and marry their daughters might reject such a change. Could emancipation lead to another secession? The departure of even one border state might just tip the balance in favor of the Confederacy.

After he shook hands with his Black guests, Lincoln began to talk about the relocation of people of African descent to other countries. This wasn't going to be an exchange of ideas about colonization—"I do not propose to discuss this," he told his guests—but he wished to present a plan. And he wanted their cooperation.

As he rarely did, Lincoln talked at and down to his guests. "You and we are different races. . . . Whether it is right or wrong I need not discuss, but this physical difference is a great disadvantage to us both, as I think your race suffer very greatly, many of them by living among us, while ours suffers from your presence. In a word, we suffer on each side. If this is admitted, it affords a reason why we should be separated. . . .

"The institution of Slavery," he continued, has "evil effects on the white race. See our present condition—the country engaged in war!— our white men cutting one another's throats. . . . But for your race among us there would not be war."

Lincoln offered a proposal. He wanted a vanguard of African American volunteers, prominent men and their families, to pack up and leave.

He hoped their departure would launch an exodus. "I want you to let me know whether this can be done." It would be, he concluded, "for the good of mankind."

His words were met by a stunned silence.

As the men rose to leave, one of them, a minister, promised to "hold a consultation and in a short time give an answer" to Lincoln's proposal.

"Take your full time," Lincoln replied, "no hurry at all."[21]

The audience ended, but a reporter from the *New-York Tribune* in attendance produced a full transcript of the meeting, and as Lincoln had hoped, many newspapers published in full what he had said. His words were a message intended to mollify a very much larger audience of White men.

When Frederick Douglass read Lincoln's verbatim words, he was enraged. He fired back angrily in *Douglass' Monthly*, ripping into the fallacy of Lincoln's arguments. Lincoln was wrong to suggest that both the war and slavery could be blamed on the enslaved. To Douglass, that notion was laughable, and he turned Lincoln's fondness for the folksy back at him. "No, Mr. President," Douglass wrote sarcastically, "it is not the innocent horse that makes the horse thief, not the traveler's purse that makes the highway robber, it is not the presence of the negro that causes this foul and unnatural war, but [the fault] of those who wish to possess horses, money and negroes by means of theft, robbery, and rebellion." No, Douglass insisted, blame for the Civil War does not belong to the Black man.

In his bitter response, Douglass also called Lincoln "a genuine representative of American prejudice." The president appeared "silly and ridiculous," said Douglass, and the facts affirmed it. For anyone who could do basic arithmetic, the idea of colonization was preposterous: In 1860, there had been more than four million enslaved persons and another half million free Blacks. That made the president's request for volunteers—he asked his five visitors to find him "twenty-five able-bodied men, with a mixture of women and children"—ridiculous in the extreme. Sending millions of Douglass's brothers and sisters abroad or to Africa? That wasn't remotely feasible.

To Douglass, the meeting demonstrated Lincoln's "hypocrisy." After the joy at the emancipation in the capital, Douglass's estimation of Lincoln crashed to a new low. He feared above all that this supposedly antislavery president had just demonstrated "his pride of race and blood [and] his contempt for negroes."[22]

When a member of Lincoln's cabinet, Postmaster General Montgomery Blair, reached out to try to enlist Douglass's help in the colonization scheme, Douglass responded as he no doubt would have if he had been in the room when Lincoln delivered his colonization lecture. "We have readily adapted ourselves to your civilization," Douglass wrote to Blair. "We are American by birth and education, and have a preference for American institutions. . . . [W]hy, oh why! may not men of different races inhabit in peace and happiness this vast and wealthy country?" Having rejected colonization, Douglass offered a better idea. "Instead of sending any of the loyal people out of the country, it seems to me that at this time our great nation should hail with joy every loyal man, who has an arm and a heart to fight as a kinsman and clansman, to be marshalled to the defence and protection of a common country."[23] It was an argument he had made before and would again: *Let us Black men be soldiers!*

The voice from Rochester was far from the only one to mock Lincoln's proposal. The idea of exporting Blacks was rejected outright by many, and signatures were collected for a petition that advocated the deportation not of formerly enslaved people but of slaveholders.

IN AUGUST, LINCOLN made a camouflaged pronouncement in his quiet campaign. Horace Greeley, the widely admired editor of the *New-York*

*Tribune,* provided an opening to Lincoln that he used to prepare the public for the emancipation document locked in his desk drawer.

In the August 20, 1862, issue of his paper, Greeley's editorial addressed President Lincoln directly. Titled "The Prayer for Twenty Millions," the editor's passionate plea called for emancipation; Greeley argued that eradicating slavery was necessary for the Union to prevail. Two days later, Lincoln responded by taking sides—all of them— without settling upon one.

"My paramount object in this struggle," Lincoln wrote, "*is* to save the Union, and is *not* either to save or to destroy slavery. If I could save the Union without freeing *any* slave I would do it, and if I could save it by freeing *all* the slaves I would do it; and if I could save it by freeing some and leaving others alone I would also do that."[24]

Lincoln's political dance was delicate: He offered assurance to nervous Northerners that he did not wish to turn this war into a crusade for abolition. At the same time, he alerted anti-slavery advocates that abolition also featured in his thinking. Although Douglass was pleased to see Lincoln's restatement that it was his "personal wish that men everywhere could be free," he also wrote to his friend Gerrit Smith, "I think the nation was never more completely in the hands of the slave power."[25]

Lincoln continued to bide his time as the debate whirled around him. He still needed the U.S. Army to deliver a victory before he could make his move.

## THE BATTLE OF ANTIETAM

August brought little good news. As the month ended, Lincoln absorbed the shock of a second military defeat at Bull Run, a failure that meant Confederate troops now camped within easy striking distance of Union territory.

Emboldened by his smashing win, Confederate general Robert E. Lee took the offensive, marching his fifty-five thousand men into Maryland. This played into Lincoln's fears, because the citizens of Maryland, a border and slaveholding state, could still switch sides. A Southern victory on Northern soil might also sway foreign opinion, winning the CSA valuable recognition in Europe. Lincoln could envision a chilling scenario in which Lee was about to set the stage to win the war.

The situation was shocking enough that Lincoln, though not a deeply religious man, "made a solemn vow before God." The loss of son Willie may have disposed him to see worldly matters in a more spiritual light, but whatever the cause, Lincoln resolved that if his army managed to drive Lee back across the Potomac, "I would send the Proclamation after him."[26] Freeing the enslaved became a matter of waiting for divine intervention.

When it came to earthly practicalities, Lincoln put his faith in General McClellan one last time, and on September 15, he got good news. Waiting in the telegraph office near the White House, Lincoln was among the first to hear that the Army of the Potomac had driven back the Rebels at the Battle of South Mountain, Maryland. He wired McClellan back, "God bless you, and all with you. Destroy the rebel army, if possible. A. Lincoln."[27]

George McClellan possessed a talent for painstaking preparation but no genius for strategy. By the time McClellan was satisfied his troops were ready to reengage with the enemy, Lee's army had advanced another ten miles and settled into a defensive position on a low ridge near Antietam Creek, in Sharpsburg, Maryland. On the other side of the stream, McClellan's eighty-thousand-man Army of the Potomac was ready on September 17, 1861.

The fight began with an early-morning engagement in a cornfield near a plain but picturesque whitewashed church. For hours, combatants on the ground fought hand to hand with bayonets and rifle butts, while cannoneers on both sides turned the formerly peaceful farmland

*Photographer Alexander Gardner's image of the aftermath at the Battle of
Antietam. When this image of the Dunker Church and other detailed images
of the battlefield were put on display in Mathew Brady's New York gallery,
the* New-York Times *said of the pictures that they "[brought] home
to us the terrible reality and earnestness of War."*

into "artillery hell." The thirty-acre stand of tall, browning stalks changed
hands more than a dozen times in the chaotic combat.

By late morning, the fighting shifted south to a sunken road, which
would be remembered as Bloody Lane. The carnage would leave some
five thousand men in both blue and gray uniforms lying in a river of
blood. By midafternoon the center of action moved again, this time to
the vicinity of a stone bridge. Strategic blunders by Union general Am-
brose Burnside—his army was stymied by a bottleneck of his own making as it attempted to cross "Burnside's Bridge"—gave the outnumbered
Confederates precious time, and reinforcements arrived to join the fight.

Lincoln scrutinized the battle reports as they arrived in Washington, but neither side seemed on its way to a resounding victory; still, if only because of its sheer numbers, the Union army did manage to hold the upper hand when the day ended. On Thursday both sides remained in place, stacking their dead and treating the wounded—and the casualty numbers were appalling. More than ten thousand men fell on each side, making that smoke-filled Wednesday the bloodiest day not only of the war but in all of American history, before and since. At last, on Friday, reports arrived that Lee and his army had begun to retreat.

Lincoln retired for the weekend to his cottage at the Soldiers' Home, a sprawling national cemetery on a hilltop four miles from the White House. There, on Saturday, he finally learned that Lee had gone back across the Potomac to Virginia soil. Antietam was the success that Seward prescribed, even if the battle was, in strictly military terms, little better than a draw. The next day when the president returned to Pennsylvania Avenue, honoring his holy promise, he locked himself in his office to work on his executive order.

Before he issued the Emancipation Proclamation on Monday, September 22, 1862, he remarked to a friend, "It is my last card, and I will play it and may win the trick."[28]

## "THIS RIGHTEOUS DECREE"

Four hundred miles separate the White House from Rochester, New York, but after Frederick Douglass read the newspaper on Tuesday, September 23, 1862, the distance seemed much shorter. "We shout for joy that we live to record this righteous decree," he wrote on behalf of himself, his readership, and the four million in bondage.[29] He believed—he hoped—deliverance was at hand.

*Forever free* were the magic words. As of January 1, 1863, Lincoln promised, "all persons held as slaves"—albeit those in the designated states and territories—"shall be then, thenceforward, and forever free." And the promise was delivered with an iron fist: Lincoln commanded that the U.S. Army and Navy were to perform "no act or acts" that would interfere with freedmen exercising "their actual freedom." Had Douglass drafted it, the language might have been different; Lincoln had written it not in the manner of an abolitionist tract, making no mention of the Almighty or even righteousness. Despite the lawyer talk, which put the order in military terms as a necessity of war, Douglass understood the Emancipation Proclamation could be "the turning-point in the conflict between freedom and slavery."[30]

Lincoln did not free all the enslaved: As in the preliminary draft, the proclamation excluded those in the border states and in the occupied areas of Virginia, Louisiana, and Tennessee. In practice, it would have little impact in Confederate territory, over which the United States no longer had jurisdiction, but it did enunciate a new policy. It shifted the relationship of the government to slavery. In boldface, it meant Lincoln had extended the idea of liberty to the Black man.

Yet in autumn 1862, elated as he was, Douglass worried whether or not Lincoln would make the preliminary permanent. He wanted to believe that Lincoln would issue the proclamation in one hundred days, as promised, making it a legal instrument with the force of law, but until he did, it was merely a contingency. Douglass could only wait and hope that nothing transpired to dampen Lincoln's enthusiasm.

In November, such concerns did arise after Lincoln's party suffered serious setbacks in the midterm elections, even in his home state of Illinois. Some voter frustration could no doubt be blamed on war weariness, but no one doubted that emancipation had cost the party, too.

A concerned Harriet Beecher Stowe traveled to the White House for tea on December 2, hoping to get confirmation. When she entered the room, the long tall Lincoln rose from a seat before the fire to greet the famous author. He took Mrs. Stowe's tiny hand in his—the small-boned woman weighed less than a hundred pounds—and offered a welcoming witticism. "So this is the little lady who made this big war," he said to the author of *Uncle Tom's Cabin*. Warm as their meeting was, Lincoln did not confide his intentions, though their mutual friend Charles Sumner soon wrote to Stowe that "the Presdt. has repeatedly assured me of his purpose to stand by his proclamation."[31]

On January 1, 1863, the president and first lady took their place in the Blue Room at the White House at 11:00 A.M. for the traditional New Year's Day presidential reception. They greeted hundreds of diplomats, military officers, members of Congress, judges, and other worthies. They shook the hands of a great mass of average people, too, who had waited in line to wish the president well. When the doors finally closed in the early afternoon, Lincoln retired upstairs to his office.

In the preceding weeks and days, he had repeatedly reworked and revised the proclamation. He amended some wording and added a solemn closing line that made reference to the law, military necessity, the principle of justice, and even the Lord. "Upon this act," he wrote, "sincerely believed to be an act of justice, warranted by the Constitution, upon military necessity, I invoke the considerate judgement of mankind, and the gracious favor of Almighty God."

With a freshly inked copy of the final version before him, he raised his wooden pen, dipped its steel nib into the inkwell, and moved to affix his signature. But his large hand trembled badly as "a superstitious feeling came over me." When he recalled he had just spent three hours having his hand pumped by hundreds of people, the sensation passed quickly. "I never in my life felt more certain that I was doing right than I do in signing this paper," he said to Secretary of State Seward as he slowly, carefully, signed his full name.

With that he looked up, smiled, and said quietly, "That will do."[32] Lincoln had traveled many miles to reach this juncture, but his thinking about the Black man was still evolving.

*Francis Carpenter's 1864 painting,* The First Reading of the Emancipation Proclamation before the Cabinet, *which memorialized the first hearing of Lincoln's landmark decree two years earlier. Edwin M. Stanton, secretary of war, is at left, and Secretary of State Seward sits across the table from Lincoln.*

THE PRELIMINARY EMANCIPATION PROCLAMATION announced the previous September had been a promise; the document itself stated that Lincoln's presidential order would not take legal effect until he issued the final version, on January 1, 1863. That moment was awaited with great anticipation, not least in Boston.

In the Massachusetts capital, Henry Wadsworth Longfellow, the nation's most famous poet, organized a jubilee concert, held on New Year's Day, at the Music Hall, an event much ballyhooed in the papers. The White audience came to listen to Ralph Waldo Emerson, Beethoven's Fifth Symphony, and the cheers that greeted Mrs. Stowe, who took a bow from the balcony rail with tears in her eyes. Less than two blocks away, a largely Black audience of some three thousand people attended a day-long vigil at the Tremont Temple, as ministers delivered prayers and abolitionists spoke. With expectation in the air, everyone—whether of African or European ancestry—waited for the final word from Washington.

There was still no news when Frederick Douglass stepped to the Tremont Temple podium that evening; the absence of news was worrisome, and he sensed "a visible shadow . . . falling on the expecting throng." But the good news did arrive when a messenger burst into the hall, shouting, "It is coming! It is on the wires!" The audience leapt to its feet. People uttered prayers, clapped, unleashed shouts of joy, and tossed their hats in the air. Lincoln had honored his word.

Front and center, Douglass broke into song, his deep baritone leading the ecstatic crowd in singing "Blow Ye the Trumpet, Blow," a favorite of his friend John Brown. *"The year of jubilee is come,"* they sang. *"The year of jubilee is come! / Return, ye ransomed sinners, home."* The songs and celebrations, the embraces and tears, lasted well into the night.

Before dawn, however, Douglass exited, leaving the warmth of the hall for the cold January night. Snowflakes gently fell as he made his way to the train station. He would remember this night as the happiest of his life. Yet the war wasn't over; the Confederacy hadn't been vanquished. Joyful as the moment was, Douglass knew his work was not yet complete.[33]

# TWELVE

# TURNING POINT AT GETTYSBURG

We are not to be saved by the captain, at this time, but by
the crew. We are not to be saved by Abraham Lincoln, but
by that power behind the throne.

—FREDERICK DOUGLASS, "OUR WORK IS
NOT DONE," DECEMBER 1863

F rederick Douglass answered a knock at his door. On February 23, 1863, he greeted a small man with a great bushy beard
that reached his chest and clothes that might have belonged to a bigger brother. Recognizable behind the whiskers were the
familiar features of Douglass's old abolitionist comrade George Luther
Stearns.

Stearns had accumulated a large fortune as an industrialist and mer-
chant, but, like Gerrit Smith and Charles Sumner, he adopted anti-
slavery as the great public passion in his life. His estate outside Boston
had been an important station on the Underground Railroad, and

Stearns helped underwrite John Brown's little army at Harper's Ferry several years before.

He and Douglass exchanged greetings before Stearns, a shy man who spoke with a pronounced stutter, explained he was freshly off the train from Boston. His trip was prompted partly by the Emancipation Proclamation, since Lincoln had added to its final version a new section concerning Black enlistments. It stated that Blacks "will be received into the armed service of the United States to garrison forts, positions, stations, and other places, and to man vessels of all sorts."[1] The Black man could now go officially to the front lines to fight for his freedom.

Stearns needed Douglass's help in implementation. The governor of Massachusetts had obtained President Lincoln's permission to organize a Black regiment, but since the Bay State had fewer than two thousand Black male inhabitants of military age, the Massachusetts Fifty-Fourth Regiment would have to reach beyond the commonwealth's borders to recruit soldiers. Who better than Frederick Douglass to help create what Stearns called "a true John Brown corps"?[2]

Emancipation thus represented a transformation, and not only for Black Americans. With Lincoln's shift in policy, the U.S. Army could now fairly be called an army of liberation. The stubborn refusal of the Rebels to listen meant Lincoln had been forced to abandon his hopes for reconciliation. That also meant Douglass and Lincoln now shared the same objective: Nothing, absolutely nothing else, was more important to either man than winning this war. Lincoln's presidency and the survival of the Union depended upon defeating the Rebels—but so did emancipation. Both men understood the proclamation was a war measure: If the South won independence, emancipation in the region would almost certainly be proclaimed at an end, disappearing into thin air. Only victory—and a constitutional amendment—could assure permanent freedom for Black Americans.

The idea of arming Black men was obviously not new. Almost two

*Massachusetts abolitionist George Luther Stearns. Commissioned a major by Secretary of War Stanton, he recruited some 13,000 Black troops to fight for the Union.*

years before, just after Fort Sumter fell, Douglass himself wrote an essay titled "How to End the War" for his newspaper. Typeset in all caps, he pleaded, "LET THE SLAVES AND FREE COLORED PEOPLE BE CALLED INTO SER-VICE, AND FORMED INTO A LIBERATING ARMY."[3] He made the case again after the first disaster at Bull Run. But his, Sumner's, and other men's calls to arms had met with stony resistance.

Many in the upper ranks of the military doubted the bravery and intelligence of African Americans and worried that White soldiers would refuse to serve with them. Early in the war Lincoln had feared that putting formerly enslaved men in uniform would undo his administration's argument that this was a war about Union rather than abolition. If he enlisted Blacks, he told Sumner in mid-1862, "Half the army would lay down their arms and three other States would join the rebellion."[4]

During that year, however, cracks appeared in the no-Black-soldiers policy when several generals quietly raised Black units. The Kansas

Colored Volunteers came into being. The War Department authorized recruitment of up to five thousand former bondsmen in South Carolina, although the secretary of war also warned that his order "must never see daylight, because it is so much in advance of public opinion."[5] Attitudes had been slowly shifting. Speaking of his role in the First Regiment Louisiana Native Guards, also known as the Corps d'Afrique, one officer saw both sides of the argument. "I felt a little repugnance at having anything to do with negroes, but having got fairly over that, am in the work. They are just as good tools to crush rebellion with as any that can be got."[6]

In the weeks before Stearns knocked at the door, Douglass had given a series of speeches. He brought new fervor to audiences from Massachusetts to Michigan. At each engagement, his three-hour lecture was interrupted by applause and cheers, and sometimes his words provoked laughter, too. But never was he more serious than when he spoke of an army of Black soldiers.

"I want to assure you," he told audiences in Philadelphia, Chicago, and New York's Cooper Union, "that the colored man only waits for honorable admission into the service of the country."[7]

Stearns's invitation to join the effort delighted Douglass, who leapt at the chance to find men for the Massachusetts Fifty-Fourth. Within days, he published a broadside titled "Men of Color, to Arms!" He urged other Black men to prove themselves, to disprove the doubters. "This is our golden opportunity. Let us accept it, and forever wipe out the dark reproaches unsparingly hurled against us by our enemies. Let us win for ourselves the gratitude of our country."[8]

The Emancipation Proclamation also produced a valuable shift in attitudes abroad. Great Britain, France, and other European countries previously wavered on whether to recognize the Confederate States of America as a new nation. But Lincoln's proclamation cleared the air. As one American ambassador put it, "Everyone can understand the significance of a war where emancipation is written on one banner and slavery on the other."⁹ One Londoner who grasped the larger significance was Karl Marx, the German scholar who watched events in America carefully from his seat in the reading room at the British Museum. To Marx, the Emancipation Proclamation was "the most important document of American history since the founding of the Union."¹⁰

Opening the door to Black enlistment was also crucial to the Union's military fortunes, and as reports drifted in about the effectiveness of the units, Lincoln overcame his earlier doubts as he saw a double opportunity: He needed more men, since recruitment was down, but now he also embraced a psychological advantage. When he wrote to Tennessee governor Andrew Johnson to try to persuade him to form a Black fighting force, he made the case. "The bare sight of fifty thousand armed, and drilled black soldiers upon the banks of the Mississippi, would end the rebellion at once."¹¹ Frederick Douglass couldn't have agreed more. Yet these troops faced a double danger. As if marching into battle weren't enough, men of color faced the added risk of mistreatment in the event they were captured. Jefferson Davis and his generals made clear the rules of war regarding the humane treatment of prisoners of war did not extend to the Union's new recruits.

By the time George Stearns departed, just hours after he arrived, the Douglass family had made a deeply personal contribution to the new "sable arm" of the military. Among the first volunteers recruited for the Massachusetts Fifty-Fourth were Frederick Douglass's sons Charles and Lewis. In a matter of weeks, Frederick Douglass himself would travel to Boston, where, on May 28, 1863, the ladies of Boston society waved their handkerchiefs in farewell as Black soldiers marched up Beacon Street before entering Boston Common. A crowd of more than a thousand people cheered the regiment as it drilled. From there the troops marched on to Battery Wharf, where they were serenaded by throngs of well-wishers singing "John Brown's Body."

At the docks, Frederick Douglass went aboard the steamer *De Molay*

*The eldest of Frederick Douglass's three sons, Lewis Henry Douglass joined the Massachusetts 54th in 1863, fought at Fort Wagner, and gained the rank of sergeant major. Prior to one battle, he wrote home to his future wife, "Should I fall in the next fight killed or wounded I hope to fall with my face to the foe. If I survive I shall write you a long letter."*

to wish the soldiers well. Among them were Sergeant Major Lewis Douglass and another hundred men that the elder Douglass had personally recruited. The Fifty-Fourth was a cross section of African American society, with freemen and former bondsmen from twenty-four states, including five that had seceded. They were off to war, bound for South Carolina.

## "WHAT WILL THE COUNTRY SAY!"

The Civil War ground cruelly on. Despite new commanders—at last, Lincoln gave in to his frustrations and replaced George McClellan—no one seemed able to best General "Bobby" Lee. At Fredericksburg, Virginia, in December, Lee's forces had routed the Army of the Potomac, which sustained nearly three times the casualties of Lee's troops. As Lincoln watched thousands of wounded and defeated men arrive in Washington, he lamented, "If there is a worse place than hell, I am in it."[12]

With the arrival of spring, he tried to take an optimistic view. After four days spent reviewing the army in northern Virginia, he thought his generals might be in a position to engineer a major victory. On May 6, 1863, at the White House, he awaited word of just such a hoped-for triumph at Chancellorsville, a crossroads town some sixty miles south of the capital. "I expect the best, but I am prepared for the worst," Lincoln admitted to a reporter from the *Chicago Tribune*.[13]

Two friends who arrived that afternoon waited in an anteroom for the president. At three o'clock he appeared, but both Noah Brooks, a California journalist, and Dr. Anson Henry, whom Lincoln knew from his days as a young lawyer in Springfield, Illinois, were shocked at his appearance. As ashen as the gray wallpaper, he held out a telegram.

"Read it. News from the army." His voice trembled with emotion.

*In a celebratory image painted more than three decades after the war, General Robert E. Lee is being cheered by his troops after the resounding victory at Chancellorsville, Virginia.*

The report from the front was bad—worse than bad. Union commander "Fighting Joe" Hooker had been manhandled by Lee, his army forced to retreat back across the Rappahannock River. The battle at Chancellorsville was over, a catastrophic loss for the Union.

Brooks kept his composure. Dr. Henry's eyes filled with tears; he was so swamped with emotion he could not speak.

Lincoln paced, his hands clasped behind his back. Brooks thought he never looked "so broken, so dispirited, and so ghostlike." Finally, the president broke the silence.

"My God! my God! What will the country say! What will the country say!"[14]

Before the question could be answered, a carriage pulled up below and Lincoln hurried out of the room, headed for the army encampment to meet with his defeated generals. Trying to absorb another battle lost, despite the fact that the Union fielded a much larger force, Lincoln was asking himself, *What does this mean?* He was afraid the answer was, *The Union could lose this war.*

## THE INVASION OF PENNSYLVANIA

A few scraps of better news arrived. On May 27, official reports lauded the bravery of two African American regiments that marched repeatedly into deadly Confederate fire at Port Hudson, Louisiana. The performance of the Black troops defied widely held racist views. "It is no longer possible," acknowledged their commanding general, "to doubt the bravery and steadiness of the colored race."[15] At a base near Vicksburg, Mississippi, on June 7, Black troops fought off a Confederate bayonet charge, leading a War Department official to observe that "the bravery of the blacks in the battle of Milliken's Bend completely revolutionized the sentiment of the army with regard to the employment of negro troops."[16] The racist prejudice against Black soldiers showed signs of fading into history.

Closer to the capital, however, the news remained bad. On the heels of his big win at Chancellorsville, Robert E. Lee persuaded Confederate president Jefferson Davis to take the fight to Northern soil. By mid-June, reports reached Lincoln of the Army of Northern Virginia crossing the Potomac into Union territory, and by June 27, the invaders marched over the Mason-Dixon Line into Pennsylvania. Although Lee had lost his most trusted general, "Stonewall" Jackson, killed at Chancellorsville, his army was headed for Harrisburg, the state capital, and perhaps Baltimore, Philadelphia, or even Washington. No one could be sure.

Lincoln saw a larger danger. If Lee's campaign succeeded, he might cleave the country in two and thereby force peace talks. So far, Lincoln refused to speak the name of the Confederate States of America; there was no such country in his mind, just an illegal brotherhood of traitors with no legal standing. However, if he were forced to accept a negotiated end to the war, the CSA might become a separate nation, permanently dividing the Union and ending the war on slavery.

Nervous and agitated, Lincoln changed generals again, giving command in the east to Pennsylvanian George Meade. Meanwhile, the Confederates continued their campaign, taking the Pennsylvania cities of Carlisle and York. A major military confrontation became inevitable when Meade's army, strategically positioned to shield Washington, reached the Maryland–Pennsylvania line on June 30, and Lee concentrated his forces near a little college town named Gettysburg.

On July 1, a Confederate division seeking supplies in open farmland north of the town encountered two Union cavalry brigades. After skirmishing with the much larger enemy force, the Federals beat a hurried retreat through the streets of Gettysburg, halting just south of the village. By daybreak on day two of the Gettysburg fight, four Union corps arrived and established defensive positions on Cemetery and Culp's Hills.

The pastoral setting—a fertile valley surrounded by low ridges, with a mix of wooded hills and babbling brooks—became an immense campground for two armies, with some seventy thousand men in gray facing off against roughly one hundred thousand dressed in Union blue.

That day, the Rebels directed heavy assaults on a number of Union positions, including those remembered today as Little Round Top, the Devil's Den, and the Wheatfield. At three o'clock on the afternoon of July 2, Meade telegraphed the War Department. "If I find . . . the enemy is endeavoring to move to my rear and interpose between me and Washington, I shall fall back."[17]

The possibility of retreat was not at all what Lincoln wanted to hear, but, as if he didn't have enough to concern him, a messenger arrived with word that Mary Lincoln had been thrown from her carriage, striking her head violently on the road. He arranged for a nurse to care for her, but he parked himself at the telegraph office for hour after hour, monitoring the faraway battle, waiting for news. He simply could not draw his attention away from Gettysburg.

Day three at Gettysburg would be decisive. Lee directed his attack at the center of the Union line at Cemetery Ridge, delivering one of the largest artillery bombardments of the war to soften up Union resistance; then he ordered his infantry to attack. At 2:00 P.M. nine brigades, commanded by Major General George Pickett and two other officers, numbering more than twelve thousand men, began to march deliberately across open fields. As they covered the thousand-yard distance, shell and solid shot from Union artillery tore holes in the oncoming formation. Once the Rebels were within four hundred yards, the Federals' canister, rifle, and then musket fire proved equally murderous. In barely an hour, the assault was over. In one of the best-remembered and most analyzed military moments of all time, Pickett's charge had failed. A decimated Confederate force retreated, leaving dead and wounded strewn across the landscape. The battle over, Meade's army held the field, though the casualty total for the

*Some military historians believe that artist Peter Rothermel was trying to capture the carnage of Pickett's Charge in this 1872 image. Although the war's outcome remained uncertain in July 1863, the Battle of Gettysburg, in retrospect, was clearly a turning point.*

two armies exceeded fifty-one thousand dead, wounded, and missing. Gettysburg set a terrible new record for the deadliest battle of the war.

The next day, Lincoln went to visit General Daniel Sickles, a New Yorker who had been wounded at Gettysburg. Just back in Washington, his right leg amputated, he lay on a blood-stained stretcher in a house on F Street. When Lincoln arrived with son Tad, aged ten, at his side, he took a chair next to Sickles. The two men "discussed the great battle and its probable consequences." Lincoln wanted to know everything about the victory.

When Sickles completed his account of the battle, he asked, "Well, Mr. President, I beg pardon, but what did you think about Gettysburg?"

"I suppose some of us were a bit 'rattled,'" Lincoln admitted. "[But] we did right handsomely."[18] He kept his feelings, his worries, his hand-wringing to himself.

In the coming days, Lincoln faced good news and bad. Mary took a turn for the worse, her head wound infected, before recovering. Lee managed to slip back into Confederate territory—Lincoln was deeply frustrated at the Confederates' escape—but, still, Lee's northern offensive was at an end. Then news from the west arrived. After weeks of resisting a Union siege, Confederate forces at Vicksburg, Mississippi, had surrendered to Ulysses S. Grant on July 4. Vicksburg's strategic location meant the Union gained control of the Mississippi, the key supply line to the heart of the country.

Although the momentum of the war shifted, the Confederacy was far from defeated. The Union still needed more soldiers and, with the Mississippi now controlled by Union ships, Lincoln wanted to broaden his recruitment campaign among Blacks. "I believe it is a resource," he wrote to Grant, "which, if vigorously applied now, will soon close the contest."[19]

# FORT WAGNER

For Frederick Douglass, July was an unhappy month. His high spirits tumbled after a recruitment speech, delivered in Philadelphia on July 6, to some five thousand people. The applause was thunderous, but only a few volunteers stepped forward. Arguments that had worked for months—hundreds upon hundreds of men enlisted after hearing his pitch—rang hollow when everyone in the room knew about the recent slaughter in Gettysburg.

On his way home to Rochester, Douglass narrowly escaped the Draft Riots that rocked New York for three days and three nights. What began as a protest of recent draft laws degenerated into a race riot, with Whites lynching Black men on light poles, murdering Black women, and setting fire to their homes, businesses, and even the Colored Orphan Asylum;

"the cry of the crowd," Douglass wrote, was "beat, shoot, hang, stab, kill, burn and destroy the Negro."[20] Passing through the city, he escaped the mob's wrath only because the "high carnival of crime and reign of terror" was unfolding well uptown from the Chambers Street rail station where he changed trains.[21]

In Rochester, the news got suddenly personal with reports of the Fifty-Fourth's assault on Fort Wagner. The Massachusetts regiment exhibited great bravery in attacking the fortification at the mouth of Charleston Harbor, on July 16, but enemy artillery took a terrible toll on Sergeant Major Lewis Douglass and his men. Their commanding officer, a young White Bostonian named Robert Gould Shaw, was killed. Half of his six hundred men became casualties, including Lewis, and many of the officers. "Men fell all around me," the wounded Lewis

*In this 1890 lithograph, the commander of the Massachusetts 54th, Colonel Robert Gould Shaw, brandishes his sword over his head as the soldiers in his regiment engage in hand-to-hand combat with the enemy. Shaw was killed at the Battle of Fort Wagner, along with 272 of his men.*

Douglass wrote home. "A shell would explode and clear a space of twenty feet, our men would close up again. . . . How I got out of that fight alive I cannot tell."[22]

His father, though relieved his son survived, was deeply upset about bureaucratic issues. For one, White soldiers were paid thirteen dollars a month, while the new Black soldiers, 80 percent of whom had been in bondage, received the wages of laborers, seven dollars a month plus a clothing allowance. Even worse, Douglass felt a new sense of betrayal at the government's failure to stand up for the soldiers he recruited. According to reports from the front, many captured Black troops were executed by their Confederate captors, and others returned to slavery and forced labor.

Douglass stewed for a few days before writing to George Stearns, who had been commissioned a major in the army to aid in his recruitment efforts. He directed his anger at the president's inaction: "No word comes from Mr. Lincoln or from the War Department, sternly assuring the Rebel Chief that inquisitions shall yet be made . . . when a black man is slain by a rebel in cold blood . . . or caught and sold into slavery."[23] Douglass had decided he was finished with recruiting "until the President shall give the same protection [to Black] . . . as to white soldiers."

Major Stearns, who could ill afford to lose his best recruiter, wrote back promptly. He suggested Douglass take the matter into his own hands and pay "a flying visit to Washington."[24] Douglass took Stearns's urging seriously, and in a matter of days he departed on the two-day rail journey to the nation's capital.

At last, the time had come for the president and the freedom fighter to meet.

# THIRTEEN

# A BLACK VISITOR TO THE WHITE HOUSE

You say you will not fight to free negroes. Some of them seem willing to fight for you.

—ABRAHAM LINCOLN TO JAMES CONKLING, AUGUST 26, 1863

M any years earlier, another kind of railroad—the Underground Railroad, that mix of the real and the metaphorical—carried a runaway named Fred Bailey to freedom. By August 1863, things had changed. A free man for many years, the former fugitive bore the surname Douglass. A world-famous writer and lecturer, he rode in a first-class sleeper, befitting his elevated station, on the Baltimore & Ohio Railroad. But for the first time in twenty-five years, he was again in slaveholder territory, with slavery still legal in border state Maryland.

At his destination, the most important residence in the land, the White House, the weary traveler hoped to meet with the president of the United States.

When Frederick Douglass emerged from the rail station in Washington, his body humming from two long days of continuous rail travel, he stood just a few blocks from the Capitol with its still unfinished dome. Even on a Sunday night, the city around him was a teeming military depot, its streets alive with the rumbling of army wagons and the clatter of galloping cavalry. Markets, saloons, and slaughterhouses lined Pennsylvania Avenue. Almost two dozen mansions, schools, churches, and hotels converted to makeshift hospitals were crowded with wounded. Peddlers occupied street corners, and many a storefront offered the services of an undertaker. Crippled veterans maneuvered on crutches, some of them missing limbs. The smell of sewage, death, and garbage hung in the air.

In the fading evening light, Douglass could see he was far from the only visitor. Strangers looking to find loved ones wounded in the war flooded the city. Washington's new citizens also included many formerly enslaved people hoping to establish new lives as free men and women in a place where bondage was now forbidden.

The well-dressed Douglass stood out amid the hustle-bustle. Wherever he went people noticed this proud forty-four-year-old. The long black coat he habitually wore could not disguise his muscular build, and his large head of salt-and-pepper hair was combed back to frame his handsome face. "[His] appearance," as one friend observed, looked "stamped by past storms and struggles, [and] bespeaks great energy and will power . . . in the face of all odds."[1]

He would need that confidence the next day when he went about the business of persuading President Lincoln to come to the aid of the Black soldier.


ON AUGUST 10, 1863, Frederick Douglass took a place in line. The White House reception room was crowded with people waiting, since

President Lincoln made it a practice to meet with idea men, office seekers, the curious, and even foreign visitors who came to his door. Douglass handed his calling card to an assistant, and as "the only dark spot" among a roomful of White visitors, he readied himself to wait for hours or even days.[2] Rumor had it that some people waited a week.

The White House was his second stop that sultry Monday morning. The thermometer was well on its way to the hundred-degree mark when Douglass had arrived at the War Department, accompanied by Samuel Pomeroy, a Massachusetts-born reformer who went to the territories during the days of Bleeding Kansas. Now a senator from his adopted state, Pomeroy added authority to Douglass's mission, and the pair were ushered into the office of Secretary of War Edwin Stanton.

They were allotted a half hour. Stanton, famous for his brusque and impatient manner, listened intently as Douglass articulated his argument that all soldiers be paid the same. Stanton hedged—equal pay, he said, was a hard sell in the face of prejudice in the ranks—but he said he believed equal treatment could come in time.

*With his large scraggly beard and small wire-framed glasses, Ohioan Edwin Stanton became the secretary of war in 1862, the year this photo was taken. He was an able man doing a demanding job and uninterested in small talk. Douglass reported after their half-hour meeting that Stanton's "manner was cold and business like throughout but earnest."*

Much more surprising, the secretary countered with a proposition. *Would Douglass join recruiting efforts in the Mississippi Valley?* Now, barely an hour later, Douglass waited at the White House, his head spinning. Stanton had offered him the post of assistant adjutant. He had asked him how soon he could be ready; Douglass had told him two weeks. After meeting with the president, he would go home, where, Stanton promised, he would soon receive an official legal document making him an officer. Douglass felt deeply honored at being granted an officer's commission, perhaps the first ever to a Black man in the U.S. Army. Yet he could not help but worry about the great personal danger of working in the deep South. Many a Black man had been murdered or lynched for much less, and his fame would surely put a target on his back.

His thoughts were interrupted.

"Mr. Douglass?"

Barely two minutes had elapsed since he'd submitted his card, but one of the president's aides invited Douglass and Senator Pomeroy to follow him. As the trio shouldered their way through the throng, Douglass heard one voice complain, "Yes, dammit, I knew they would let the n—r through." He left the room to the crackle of bitter laughter.

Moments from meeting the president, Douglass did not know what to expect. For years, he had been writing and speaking publicly about Lincoln's politics and positions, and more often than not, his remarks were highly critical. His personal feelings about the man fluctuated between hopeful and impatient, exhilarated and angry. Lincoln wielded immense power and at last had done right with the Emancipation Proclamation, yet at other times he fell far short of Douglass's expectations. Just days before, the president rose in Douglass's estimation after he declared a one-for-one policy: For every Union soldier executed by the Rebels, a Rebel soldier would be put to death. Douglass was grateful, but he still held many reservations about Mr. Lincoln.

Douglass took in Lincoln's office, a moderate-sized room and a hub of activity. A desk with an overflowing pigeonhole organizer rested against one wall, a marble fireplace on another. A small mountain of documents obscured an oak table. There were two sofas, chairs arranged in no apparent pattern, and several young men, secretaries and clerks, came and went, their conversation a low buzz. Inevitably, Douglass's gaze fell upon the tall man sitting between two west-facing windows, surrounded by maps and books and stacks of paperwork. Lincoln's long legs stretched out in front of him.

The stresses of his job had robbed Lincoln of twenty pounds. The well-muscled torso of his younger years had narrowed, his face grown more angular. Even on first look, Douglass noticed the "long lines of care . . . deeply written on Mr. Lincoln's brow." But the president's expression opened and brightened with the announcement of his visitors.

Lincoln rose laboriously from the low chair. On reaching his full height, he extended his hand in cordial welcome. As they shook, Douglass again was struck by Lincoln's face. This time, as he wrote to Stearns the next day, "[I] saw at a glance the justice of the popular estimate of his qualities expressed in the prefix 'Honest' to the name of Abraham Lincoln. I have never seen a more transparent countenance."

Seizing the moment, Douglass launched into an explanation of his reason for calling. But Lincoln stopped him.

"Mr. Douglass," said the president kindly, "I know you; I have read about you, and Mr. Seward has told me about you. Sit down. I am glad to see you."

A candid conversation followed. Douglass thanked Lincoln for extending protections to Black soldiers, but added that, in his estimation, the president had been "somewhat slow" in doing so.

In great earnestness, Lincoln acknowledged that, yes, he had been accused—by others, as well as Douglass—of a reluctance to confront the problems of the Black man. As Stanton had done an hour before, he cited the need to overcome popular prejudices. The best means of meeting the objections to treating the races equally, Lincoln said, would be the performance of Black soldiers on the battlefield. As fighters and patriots, their "bravery and general good conduct," said Lincoln, would set the stage for him to protect the proclamation.

But Lincoln wasn't finished. He clearly took Douglass seriously, wanting his guest to understand his larger approach to such a matter. "I have been charged with being tardy," he acknowledged. "[B]ut, Mr. Douglass, I do not think that charge can be sustained." He was firm. "I think it can be shown that when I take a position, I think no man can say I retreat from it."

Douglass had underestimated Lincoln; as had so many others, he found himself captivated by the manner in which Lincoln listened patiently to his every word, then responded in measured and thoughtful ways; he spoke, Douglass thought, "with an earnestness and fluency of which I had not suspected him." Lincoln would ask for particulars; Douglass replied in detail. Their exchange was truly a conversation; they did not speak at cross-purposes as Lincoln looked to find common ground. If the justifications the president offered for actions or inaction did not always wholly satisfy Douglass—and they did not—the Black man nonetheless recognized he was in the presence of a "humane spirit."

As the meeting drew to a close and Douglass prepared to leave, he told Lincoln of Stanton's invitation to be a recruiter in Mississippi. He showed him the pass he was issued, which bore Stanton's name. Lincoln examined it then put his own pen to it.

"I concur," he wrote. "A. Lincoln. Aug. 10, 1863."

When Douglass departed, Lincoln was left with a sense that his guest deserved his reputation as a tough-minded, articulate, and passionate man who could hold his own in a discussion with any man. The Black man arrived as both adversary and ally; perhaps their exchange could tip the balance toward cooperation? With his parting words, Lincoln tried to leave that door open.

*Douglass in a photograph taken in January 1863 when he was in Michigan on a speaking tour.*

"Douglass," he said in farewell, "never come to Washington without calling upon me." In fact, they might have met again just a few days later, when Douglass was invited to tea, but had previously agreed to deliver a lecture that afternoon. The carriage Lincoln had dispatched to bring Douglass back for the afternoon returned without a passenger. Both men anticipated there would be other days and more conversations.

DOUGLASS'S MEETING WITH LINCOLN left him deeply impressed by "the gravity of his character," and for the first time, he felt that he could take Lincoln at his word. He wrote to Stearns saying he believed the president would "stand firm," that he felt confident "slavery would not survive the war." For Douglass, that was a very large leap of faith. He accepted both that Lincoln's thinking was evolving and that the pragmatic president might be right in thinking that if he moved too quickly with regard to the rights of African Americans, the move toward equality could blow up in their faces.

Douglass's trip to Washington was a watershed moment for him personally, too, with Stanton's offer of a job and a commission. The opportunity prompted him to change his life: He would immerse himself in the work of recruiting, reinventing the life he had lived for decades. He decided to complete one final issue of *Douglass' Monthly*, publishing it as a valedictory in which he bid goodbye to his devoted readers. He would move on from his publishing life to this new and important work.

The visit to the White House changed him in another way, too. "I tell you I felt big there," he told a Philadelphia audience a few months later. Lincoln received him, a man once enslaved, "precisely as one gentleman would be received by another." The president shook his hand, offered him a seat, listened to his concerns, and responded with directness and honesty. The reassurance stayed with him, and his respect for Lincoln grew. He believed that if the country survived, the name "Honest Abraham" would be written "side by side with that of Washington."

Although Lincoln left no record of their conversation—Douglass wrote several—their meeting sent a loud message to the country.* The president of the United States had opened the doors of his office—and opened his mind—to the most essential representative of a largely voiceless population of millions. The terms were set for an unprecedented partnership of two self-made men concerned most of all with what Lincoln would soon call "a new birth of freedom."

---

* John Hay, one of Lincoln's secretaries, noted in his diary on August 11 that "Fred Douglass in company with Sen. Pomeroy visited the president yesterday." Hay, *Inside Lincoln's White House* (1997), p. 309.

# A NEW CEMETERY IN GETTYSBURG

In the autumn, Abraham Lincoln received an invitation: *Would he deliver "a few appropriate remarks" at the dedication of a cemetery in Gettysburg?*[3] Although the busy president turned down most requests to speak, this one he accepted, agreeing to travel to Pennsylvania for the solemn event. The purpose of the war had shifted in his mind, and the time to say so publicly just might be November 19, 1863, in front of acres of mourners at a new rural cemetery.

After the July battle, teams of soldiers, Confederate prisoners, and civilians had raced to bury the eight thousand dead. With the stench of decaying flesh poisoning their nostrils, the gravediggers choked on smoke as nearby fires consumed immense pyres of dead horses and mules. Many graves were so shallow that the fresh soil could not disguise the human silhouettes beneath. The gravediggers scrawled the names of some Union soldiers on crude wooden markers, but the Confederate dead were buried anonymously in trenches.

Since the fallen were interred where they died, unquiet graves dotted Gettysburg's cornfields, orchards, gardens, and woodlands. But survivors of the dead soon began to arrive. They opened some of the fresh graves, looking for the remains of beloved husbands, fathers, and sons to take them home for burial; the strangers they uncovered were hastily reburied. According to one local civic leader, the result was that "in many instances arms and legs and sometimes heads protrude and my attention has been directed to several places where the hogs were actually rooting out the bodies and devouring them."[4] The whole town had become a graveyard, with fetid air and fouled streams, and the dead dishonored. Something had to be done.

An interstate commission was established to create a proper cemetery. Acreage was purchased. A landscape designer laid out the burial ground, arranging the graves not in rank and file but in curves that fit the contours of the site and gave the dead of no one state a higher status than another's. The federal government agreed to provide pine coffins, and over a period of weeks and months, the Union dead would be methodically exhumed, identified, and reinterred. No Rebel corpses would be welcome on this hallowed ground.

In preparing his remarks for Gettysburg, Lincoln could not follow his usual writing routine. With only two weeks' notice prior to the dedication of the new Soldiers' National Cemetery, he simply didn't have time for his usual extensive library research and writing. But the president already had a template in his head.

Back in July, just after the victories at Gettysburg and Vicksburg, he spoke to a small crowd outside the White House. The good war news put him in a philosophical mood, and after a band serenaded him, he gave a short speech. He mused aloud about the Declaration of Independence. How long ago was it, he asked his audience—perhaps "eighty odd years"?—since that memorable July Fourth? He cited the "self-evident truth" at the core of that founding document, namely, "that all men had been created equal." Rather than develop the thought, however, he stopped short and thanked the band for the music.

"Gentlemen, this is a glorious theme, and the occasion for a speech," he said, "but I am not prepared to make one worthy of the occasion." Now, a few months later, as he prepared to fulfill his duty in Pennsylvania, he decided to complete those thoughts.[5]

His would not be a long oration, he told his friend Noah Brooks, but "short, short, short."[6] That suited the organizers, who had invited Edward Everett, a former senator and secretary of state and a renowned orator, to give the main address. As his last-minute invitation indicated, Lincoln's inclusion was almost an afterthought.

When Lincoln began the six-hour trip to Gettysburg the day before the event, he carried a sheet of paper with a few lines jotted on it, amounting to perhaps half the speech. Working on a piece of cardboard during the train journey, he added to his text, then in his room that night and early the following morning, he worked on the draft. By the time he left his room to join Seward on a carriage tour of the battlefield, he carried a completed manuscript copied out in his steady, even handwriting, a few last edits squiggled between the lines.

With the dedication scheduled for two o'clock, every road into town was jammed with carriages, buggies, wagons, and carts filled with out-of-towners. Special excursion trains brought visitors, too, and Gettysburg's population of three thousand would be at least five or six times that with the visitors who made their way to the new cemetery's hilltop a half mile south of town. The fighting had taken place on every side, with Culp's Hill just northeast and Seminary Hill to the north and west. Well south lay Little Roundtop, Big Roundtop, and Devil's Den.

The speakers and other notables gathered on a platform lined with chairs. The program began with the invocation, a long and emotional prayer, followed by a hymn played by a band. Edward Everett came next. As Everett delivered a two-hour address, Lincoln listened intently, and Secretary of State Seward sat nearby with his arms folded, his hat drawn down over his eyes to shield them from the bright sun. When Everett finished, he bowed to the audience, and they responded with polite applause. A hymn followed.

Lincoln's turn came next. Rising from his chair, he stepped forward, carrying his address in his left hand. He adjusted his spectacles but delivered the speech from memory. He spoke slowly, clearly, so his tenor voice would carry his words to listeners at the greatest distance, to whom the speakers resembled doll-like figures on a toy wagon.

# 272 WORDS

In the brief speech destined to be remembered as the Gettysburg Address, Lincoln told no stories. In speaking to the thousands gathered to mourn the death of many good men on the field of battle, he offered no parables. But he did compress layers of meaning into just ten sentences.

Four score and seven years ago our fathers brought forth on this continent, a new nation, conceived in Liberty, and dedicated to the proposition that all men are created equal.

Now we are engaged in a great civil war, testing whether that nation, or any nation so conceived and so dedicated, can long endure. We are met on a great battle-field of that war. We have come to dedicate a portion of that field, as a final resting place for those who here gave their lives that that nation might live. It is altogether fitting and proper that we should do this.

But, in a larger sense, we can not dedicate—we can not consecrate—we can not hallow—this ground. The brave men, living and dead, who struggled here, have consecrated it, far above our poor power to add or detract. The world will little note, nor long remember what we say here, but it can never forget what they did here. It is for us the living, rather, to be dedicated here to the unfinished work which they who fought here have thus far so nobly advanced. It is rather for us to be here dedicated to the great task remaining before us—that from these honored dead we take increased devotion to that cause for which they gave the last full measure of devotion—that we here highly resolve that these dead shall not have died in vain—that this nation, under God, shall have a new birth of freedom—and that government of the people, by the people, for the people, shall not perish from the earth.[7]

As he had done in his off-the-cuff speech on July 7, Lincoln reminded his listeners of the founding proposition that "all men are created equal." This time he got the year exactly right—the Declaration of Independence, he noted, had been issued "four score and seven years ago"—but then went straight to the purpose of the day. They assembled to dedicate "a final resting place for those who here gave their lives."

Lincoln rooted his words in the earth ("this ground," he called it) and "the brave men" who fought upon it. But his message was not only a matter of mourning. His called to his listeners, to his countrymen, "for us the living," to dedicate themselves to "the unfinished work."

The last sentence of his artfully crafted speech laid out his challenge clearly.

Without saying so directly, the president acknowledged the passing not only of the Gettysburg dead but of the old republic, wounded and divided by war. In its place, he proclaimed a reborn nation, one in which freedom would be redefined, not solely as freedom from tyranny but by adopting the even higher standard of equality. Lincoln had already extended the pledge of freedom to the enslaved; here, in Gettysburg, Lincoln was asking his countrymen to join him in carrying out a transformation of the nation's society, extending freedom to all, Black and White.

The great underlying truth of Lincoln's 272 words was that the president no longer regarded the war as a battle to restore the Union to what it had been. His goal was to reconstitute the nation based upon human liberty, making explicit what was implied in the Declaration of Independence. To those listening with care, it was both a shock to hear and shockingly obvious.

Frederick Douglass had not traveled to Gettysburg that November; thus he wasn't physically present to hear Lincoln speak. But he did not

*The war took a toll on the president; as it wore on he began to look older and more gaunt.*

need to be there nor to read between the lines of Lincoln's concisely constructed three paragraphs to grasp the profound message. To him, it was distinctly familiar: Lincoln made the same constitutional argument that Douglass had been putting forth for years.

The year 1863 thus saw a major upturn in the Union's fortunes. On a much smaller scale, it was also a time when a new relationship began to emerge, as Lincoln and Douglass became men of shared purpose.

# FOURTEEN

# THE MISSION OF THE WAR

Every Slave who Escapes from the Rebel States is a loss to
the Rebellion and a gain to the Loyal Cause.

—FREDERICK DOUGLASS TO ABRAHAM LINCOLN,
AUGUST 29, 1864

Frederick Douglass never received his officer commission. He
got no explanation, though he guessed that Secretary of War
Stanton had had second thoughts over the "radical and ag-
gressive" idea of making a Black man an officer. Angry and disappointed
at the broken promise, Douglass decided not to report to Vicksburg,
Mississippi. As he explained later, "I knew too much of camp life and
the value of shoulder straps in the army to go into the service without
some visible mark of my rank."[1]

With the fight slowed to a halt by winter weather, Douglass criss-
crossed the North in late 1863 and early 1864, delivering lectures. Freed
of his newspaper commitments, he spoke in such distant places as Peoria,
Illinois, and Portland, Maine. "I am, this winter," he acknowledged in a
letter, "doing more with my voice than with my pen."[2] He gave variations

of the same speech in Rochester, Philadelphia, New York, Boston, Baltimore, and Washington. He titled the talk "The Mission of the War."

That speech and Lincoln's Gettysburg Address grew from the same central idea: To Douglass, the Gettysburg address was another "declaration that thereafter the war was to be conducted on a new principle."[3] But in the two hours he spent educating, entertaining, and challenging his audiences, he carried the argument beyond the groundwork he'd shared with Lincoln.

He spoke first of the war, which he described as "a rebellion which even at this unfinished stage of it counts the number of its slain not by thousands nor by tens of thousands, but by hundreds of thousands." After counting out the terrible price the nation was paying, he asked why: "For what all this desolation, ruin, shame suffering and sorrow?" Then he answered his own question: "We all know it is *slavery*."[4]

He picked up Lincoln's theme of "a broken Constitution and a dead Union" and described the alternative. "What we now want is a country—a free country—a country not saddened by the footprints of a single slave—and nowhere cursed by the presence of a slaveholder." Lincoln had spoken of a "new birth of freedom" in his Gettysburg Address; Douglass wanted a "national regeneration" that would lead to a "new order." Theirs was an overlapping vision.

Among his stops on the tour was New York's Cooper Union, still the nation's most prestigious lecture hall. His audience was the Women's Loyal League, a group that advocated a constitutional amendment to end slavery. The crowd cheered, applauded, and laughed; once he was interrupted when the women, along with the handful of men present, "[sprang] to their feet, swinging their hats, and shouting 'Hear, hear.'"[5]

Douglass admitted to the ladies that his earlier reservations about President Lincoln had yet to be erased. He still did not entirely trust the president and reminded his listeners that "Mr. Lincoln wants Union." But he made abundantly clear what Frederick Douglass wanted.

"I end where I began—no war but an Abolition war; no peace but an Abolition peace; liberty for all, chains for none; the black man a soldier in war, a laborer in peace; a voter at the South as well as at the North; America his permanent home, and all Americans his fellow countrymen." He wanted to gain for his brothers the full rights of other Americans: If they were good enough to fight, should they not have the right to vote? The Women's Loyal League agreed, greeting his call for Black suffrage with "Great Applause."[6]

Once again, the outspoken Douglass was out ahead of Lincoln. If real equality could be accomplished, he concluded, "our glory as a nation will be complete, our peace will flow like a river, and our foundation will be the everlasting rocks."*

*This cartoon—labeled "Long Abraham Lincoln a Little Longer"—was published in* Harper's Weekly *shortly after Lincoln won a second term in office.*

# A VISIT TO THE FRONT

One June day in 1864, Abraham Lincoln boarded a river steamer headed for City Point, Virginia. He felt like he carried a great albatross on his

---

* In his thoughtful analysis of this speech and, in particular, its conclusion, biographer David Blight points out that Douglass anticipated Martin Luther King Jr.'s "I Have a Dream" speech ninety-nine years later. Blight, *Frederick Douglass* (2018), p. 421.

shoulders, the weight of a war that, at the start, many believed would last no more than ninety days. Now, after more than three years of fighting, no end was in sight.

In March, Lincoln had ordered his most successful general, Ulysses S. Grant, to come east. Grant arrived at the White House for their first meeting dressed in his rumpled traveling uniform, but Lincoln took an immediate liking to the man. Grant was all business, unpretentious, with a leadership style that won his soldiers' admiration. The two westerners shared similar origins, and the commander in chief respected both the general's willingness to speak his mind and his tenacious fighting style. Lincoln put him in charge, promoting Grant to the military's highest rank, general-in-chief of the United States.

Three months later, on Tuesday, June 21, 1864, Lincoln wondered at the wisdom of his choice. As the steamboat carrying the president approached City Point, Grant's campaign to take Richmond had fallen short, just as his predecessors' attempts had. Grant's army sustained major setbacks fighting its way toward the Confederate capital, first at the Battle of the Wilderness, then at Spotsylvania Court House. More recently, the outcome at the Battle of Cold Harbor ended badly. With no victories and almost fifty thousand casualties in three battles, Lincoln decided he needed to talk with his head general.

More than the war burdened Lincoln. A presidential election loomed less than five months away. No president since Andrew Jackson had served a second term, but Lincoln felt his work was far from complete. After a tough political fight, Lincoln had managed to gain the Republican Party nomination a few days before, so his name would appear on the November ballot, along with a new vice presidential candidate. Andrew Johnson, a former senator from Tennessee, was a compromise choice as a Democrat and a Southerner; he earned Lincoln's respect after sticking with the Union when his state seceded, and Lincoln appointed him Tennessee's military governor. Many Republicans thought that as a border man Johnson would strengthen the ticket, but with so many Americans weary of the war, the outcome of the election was far from a sure thing.

From the upper deck of the steamer, General Grant's headquarters came into view. The encampment consisted of tents for the general and his officers on a high bluff overlooking the James River. A long wooden staircase descended the steep stope to the wharves, warehouses, and hospitals, where Lincoln could see Grant and his aides making their way to the water's edge to greet him. Once the hawsers held the ship fast, the military men came aboard. Lincoln reached out "his long angular arm [and] wrung General Grant's hand vigorously" and greeted each of his officers.[7] "There was a kindliness in his tone and a hearty manner

*This pencil sketch of Lincoln, son "Tad," and General Grant was drawn by Winslow Homer, then working as an illustrator. After the war, Homer became one of America's most admired painters.*

of expression," one of them remembered, "which went far to captivate all who met him."

Lincoln came by choice, looking to escape the pressures of Washington, but also to consult with his army brain trust; as one general observed, "I am of the opinion that he considered himself a good judge of the time when operations should commence."[8] The president and generals talked awhile in one of the ship's cabins then went ashore. Lincoln mounted a horse, a large bay belonging to Grant named Cincinnati, and accompanied by Grant, he rode out to visit the army of more than one hundred thousand troops. He made an odd sight in his tall silk hat and frock coat, an outfit better suited to Pennsylvania Avenue than a dusty army encampment. "But the soldiers loudly cheered Uncle Abe," his unusual figure unmistakable. "As he had no straps," reported a Grant aide-de-camp, "his trousers gradually worked up above his ankles, and gave him the appearance of a country farmer riding into town wearing his Sunday clothes."

In particular, Lincoln wished to see the Black units of the Eighteenth Corps, and they welcomed him as their liberator. "They cheered, laughed, cried, sang hymns of praise, and shouted . . . 'God bless Master Lincoln!' and 'Lord save Father Abraham.'" Lincoln himself was moved to tears, according to one of Grant's adjutants. "The scene was affecting in the extreme, and no one could have witnessed it unmoved."

The president remained with his army for two days, sleeping on the ship and spending his daylight hours reviewing the troops and studying the operations of the army. The visit cemented his working relationship with Grant. Lincoln found his general-in-chief's certainty that he would capture Richmond reassuring, and in the opinion of Secretary of Navy Gideon Welles, who saw Lincoln on his return, "His journey has done him good, physically, and strengthened him mentally and inspired confidence in the General and army."[9]

Lincoln wanted to win the election and, more important, the war.

With his view of the war as a fight for equality, he needed to do both to deliver the freedom he promised to the enslaved and, in particular, to Black volunteers, now a crucial part of the Union army and numbering more than a hundred and thirty thousand men.

A few weeks earlier he was asked by a Kentucky newspaperman to explain his thinking about slavery and Black soldiers. "I am naturally anti-slavery," Lincoln replied. "If slavery is not wrong, nothing is wrong." He told the correspondent that after his earlier reluctance, he accepted Black fighters because he saw it as his only good choice. On the one hand, he could "surrender . . . the Union, and with it, the Constitution"—clearly an unacceptable option—or he could draw upon "the colored element."[10]

A year into the experiment, with so many Black men having proved themselves in battle, he expressed only confidence that they were a "resource which, if vigorously applied now, will soon close the contest."[11] Grant agreed, confiding in Lincoln his belief that "arming the negro . . . is the heavyest blow yet given the Confederacy." Their shared confidence served their belief, as Grant put it, "that slavery must be destroyed," to erase the "stain to the Union."[12]

# THE DARKEST OF DARK DAYS

The war news in July got worse. Hoping to distract Grant from his siege at Richmond, CSA general Jubal Early marched across Maryland and brought the war within earshot of the Capitol. Lincoln rode out in mid-July, curious to see the enemy with his own eyes. Once again a conspicuous figure in his frock coat and tall hat, he climbed atop a parapet at Fort Stevens, located within the Washington city limits and a few hundred yards from the Confederate encampment. Only after a man standing nearby took a bullet in the leg from a Rebel sharpshooter did Lincoln remove himself from the line of fire. The next day Early and his men

*According to legend, when Lincoln stood exposed on the rampart at*
*Fort Stevens, in July 1864, future Supreme Court justice Oliver Wendell*
*Holmes Jr. yelled, in what is likely an apocryphal version of the story,*
*"Get down, you damn fool, before you get shot!"*
COURTESY DC PUBLIC LIBRARY, THE PEOPLE'S ARCHIVE

retreated back toward Confederate lines, but the intimidating message was clear: Lee's army was alive and well and not far away.

As July ended, Grant's siege in central Virginia met with a spectacular failure at the Battle of the Crater. After a month of secretly tunneling beneath a Confederate fortification, Union engineers set off an immense explosion, blowing a hole in the perimeter defense at the city of Petersburg, a few miles south of Richmond. A last-minute decision not to lead the follow-up attack with a division of United States Colored Troops meant that the White soldiers on point were poorly briefed. Most of a Rebel regiment died instantly in the blast, but the defenders recovered quickly; they were soon slaughtering Union men who, slow to attack, wandered into the crater. Confederate general William Mahone joked it was "a turkey shoot." General Grant called it "the saddest affair I have seen in this war."[13]

A new strategy emerged in a conversation Lincoln had with a minister named John Eaton, who arrived in Washington on August 10, 1864. Though a chaplain in an Ohio regiment, the Dartmouth-educated Eaton was tasked with establishing camps for freed Blacks in the lower Mississippi Valley. Nearly two years into the job, he supervised more than one hundred thousand people. Many of the fugitives in his care arrived barefoot and dressed in rags, traumatized, illiterate, and with few skills. Some were sick and dying. But Eaton, an ardent abolitionist before the war, found his calling in guiding the transformation of the so-called "contrabands" to free citizens. At Davis Bend, an island plantation confiscated from Jefferson Davis's family, his "Negro Paradise" produced food and goods for the Union army. Theirs was a new community of independent farmers, one based on freedom, not bondage. According to some reports, it was now the most productive plantation in the region.

On arriving in Washington, Eaton went directly to the White House. Lincoln, who was thinking long and hard about the postwar fate of millions of Blacks formerly in bondage, knew of Eaton's Mississippi project and wanted to know more. The minister was struck by how much the president already knew and his keen understanding of what the changed circumstances meant to Black men being compensated for their labor, to Black women who felt safer than they ever had, and to their children, many of whom were attending school for the first time.

Pleased by Eaton's report, Lincoln shifted the conversation to soldiering as a "means by which the Negro could be secured in his freedom, and at the same time prove a source of strength to the Union." When Reverend Eaton told Lincoln that, on his way east just days before, he'd talked at length with Frederick Douglass after a lecture in Toledo, Ohio, an idea struck the president. As Eaton recalled the moment, "The greatest man of his time asked me, with that curious modesty characteristic of him, if I thought Mr. Douglass could be induced to come to see him."[14]

With Reverend Eaton as the connection, Lincoln invited Douglass to the White House for what would be their second meeting. He wished to discuss what he called the "grapevine telegraph."

## THE GRAPEVINE TELEGRAPH

On Lincoln's orders, a carriage met Frederick Douglass at Washington's Baltimore & Ohio rail station nine days later. After arriving safely at the White House, Douglass learned that the president was already in a meeting, so he settled into a seat in the reception room, awaiting his turn.

Douglass began to read, but his mere presence was out of the ordinary; more than just another dark-skinned servant in the nation's largest house, he was a Black man waiting to meet with the president, man-to-man. Yet Douglass felt surprisingly at home—until Joseph Mills, a Wisconsin Republican, entered the room.

Unable to process what he saw, Mills froze. He couldn't take his eyes off Douglass.

Minding his own business in a corner chair, Douglass sensed the weight of the man's stare and looked up. Caught in the act, fixed by Douglass's return gaze, Mills felt obliged to address him. He inquired who he was.

"I am Frederick Douglass," was the solemn reply.[15]

Out of shock or outrage, Mills, a man to whom words like "darkey" and "Sambo" came easily, summarized his exchange with Douglass in his diary. He mentioned his waiting-room conversation to Lincoln when he later met with the president, and jokingly raised the subject of "miscegenation," a recently coined label for racial intermarriage, which was seen by racist Whites as a danger to racial purity.*

---

\* The word first appeared in a pamphlet titled *Miscegenation: The Theory of the Blending of the Races, Applied to the American White Man and Negro* (1864). The work

Lincoln's reaction to his conversation with Mills was not recorded, and for Douglass, too, the brief encounter was unimportant and got no mention in his subsequent writings or correspondence. Most likely the moment simply blurred with countless others in Douglass's experience when he looked into the eyes of a White man and saw the disregard of someone who thought him less than a man.

As he waited, Douglass did not know the purpose of his summons. He was, however, acutely aware of his recent harsh criticism of President Lincoln. Again and again Douglass had told audiences that the commander in chief was still not doing enough to protect Black soldiers. The shocking aftermath of the Battle at Fort Pillow was a telling example.

Back in April, a Rebel force commanded by General Nathan Bedford Forrest overwhelmed a Union earthworks just upriver from Memphis, Tennessee. In the aftermath of the fight at Fort Pillow, the victors massacred more than two hundred Union soldiers, killing mostly Black troops but also Whites who courageously fought at their side. According to survivor accounts, Forrest's men executed wounded soldiers in cold blood, murdered Black soldiers who held their hands in the air, and shot those fleeing for their lives and freedom in the back. They even buried some wounded men alive. General Forrest, who after the war helped found the Ku Klux Klan, boasted that the bloodletting dyed the Mississippi River red for a distance of two hundred yards. Lincoln's failure to retaliate after Fort Pillow planted new doubts in Douglass's mind concerning the president's commitment to his Black soldiers.

On entering Lincoln's office a few minutes later, Douglass noticed the toll the presidency had taken in the twelve months since their last meeting. Lincoln looked pale, his eyes sunken and dark below his fur-

---

of two New York newspapermen, it was a hoax, part of a political disinformation campaign to advance the cause of those opposed to racial equality. The term would have surprising staying power both in the United States and abroad, with usage up to the present day by contemporary White supremacists.

rowed brow. This was a bewildering moment for the nation but particularly so for Lincoln, and with surprising candor, he got right to business. Douglass quickly learned that the causes of the president's "alarmed condition" were the gloomy war prospects and the November election.[16]

The most powerful newspaper editor in the country, Horace Greeley, now urged Lincoln to negotiate with the Rebels. That very morning, a Washington paper, the *Daily National Intelligencer*, featured the headline "How to Make Peace." George McClellan, formerly Lincoln's head general, was emerging as Lincoln's likely Democratic opponent in November, and the president worried that in the current climate, with the public clamoring for peace, McClellan, who wanted to negotiate with the Rebels, might win. If he did, Lincoln told Douglass ominously, a peace might be forced on the country that left slavery in place. Emancipation was at risk since a Lincoln loss might translate to no constitutional amendment ending slavery. With only about one in twenty of the enslaved in the South freed, that meant the war would have accomplished little.

Lincoln produced a letter from his desk. Faced with the public accusation that he valued abolition more than peace, he had drafted a response. He handed the handwritten sheet to Douglass. It would be another public letter of the kind that, over the course of his presidency, he published periodically to explain his positions.

As he read it, Douglass realized Lincoln proposed uncoupling emancipation and peace, promising not to make the first a precondition for the second. It was a political compromise, one that Douglass himself could never accept. But he could also see that Lincoln was taking him into his confidence. Lincoln looked to him, a Black man, for help as he shaped a matter of policy. Asking Douglass for his counsel seemed an extraordinary compliment, an unprecedented gesture of profound respect.

When Douglass looked up from the document, Lincoln asked, "Shall I send forth this letter?"

Douglass did not mince words; the question demanded a truthful answer.

"Certainly not," he replied.

Lincoln asked why. Again, Douglass spoke directly.

"It would give a broader meaning than you intend to convey; it would be taken as a complete surrender of your anti-slavery politics, and do you serious damage."

Having asked for Douglass's opinion, he got it in no uncertain terms. Lincoln shifted the discussion.

"The slaves are not coming so rapidly and so numerously to us as I had hoped."

Douglass understood both why this was so and why Lincoln did not see it. The president was a White man who, despite growing up poor and in an isolated place, never had blinders imposed on what he saw or learned. Douglass's experience differed; he knew more fugitives didn't come running to the cause simply because they did not know that they were welcome in the U.S. Navy and Army. In the Cotton Kingdom, as during Douglass's childhood in rural Maryland, slaveholders kept enslaved persons ignorant of events and circumstances beyond the boundaries of their plantations. He laid it out for Lincoln, and after a moment's consideration, Lincoln began again.

"Well," he told Douglass, "I want you to set about devising some means of . . . bringing them into our lines." The idea was to organize "a band of scouts, composed of colored men . . . to go into the rebel States, beyond the lines of our armies, and carry the news of emancipation, and urge the slaves to come within our boundaries."[17]

Lincoln asked for *his* help; as if that wasn't extraordinary enough, Douglass sensed a feeling of déjà vu in the air. Lincoln's proposal was a reworking of the "Subterranean Pass-Way" that John Brown had laid out in Douglass's Rochester parlor half a dozen years before. Back then, Douglass decided at the last minute not to go along with what had become a dangerous military action, the raid on Harper's Ferry. Now, however, the man asking Frederick Douglass to take part in a secret, pass-the-word plan was the nation's chief executive.

Douglass was more than a little surprised that Lincoln was embracing a radical idea well beyond what he expected of the usually cautious president. But he agreed to think on the matter and report back.

One of Lincoln's secretaries appeared, announcing the arrival of Connecticut's governor. William Buckingham was a strong Union supporter and personal friend of the president. Douglass immediately stood, saying, "I must not stay to prevent your interview with Governor Buckingham."

Lincoln wouldn't have it. "Tell Governor Buckingham to wait," he instructed his young aide, "for I want to have a long talk with my friend Frederick Douglass."

"Mr. Lincoln, I will retire," Douglass offered again. Once again, Lincoln insisted he stay.

Their conversation last for hours. Despite stark differences, the two men's backgrounds dovetailed. Once children of no importance, they had found vastly different routes to prominence. Men of powerful intellect, each possessed a gift for words and deep empathy for other men. A friendship, that inexplicable bonding of shared instincts, truly took shape in the White House that day.

When a secretary interrupted once more to remind Lincoln that the governor awaited, he again asked that Buckingham be told to wait. Douglass read this gesture as a huge compliment, "the first time in the history of the Republic when its chief magistrate had found an occasion or shown a disposition to exercise such an act of impartiality between persons so widely different in their positions and supposed claims upon his attention." Nor did Governor Buckingham, who was admitted as Douglass was ready to depart, take the least offense at being asked to wait. Douglass felt embraced by Lincoln's magnanimity.

. . .

IN THE DAYS and weeks that followed, Lincoln took Douglass's advice regarding his public letter: He did not publish it, in part because his new, if informal, adviser on slavery affairs, Frederick Douglass, told him not to.

As for Douglass, he left his meeting with Lincoln excited at the new task, and he promptly consulted with "several trustworthy and Patriotic Colored men" regarding a recruitment network. Ten days later, he wrote as he'd promised to do, sketching a plan for spreading the word in the South. He proposed finding two dozen agents who would identify local subagents to persuade enslaved men to join the "Loyal Cause." He suggested a rate of pay (two dollars a day) and that a general agent (presumably himself, though he did not say so) take charge of the scheme. The plan was preliminary, he said, while assuring Lincoln that "All with whom I have thus far spoke on the subject, concur in the wisdom and benevolence of the Idea."[18] Before Lincoln could read the letter from Rochester, however, the momentum of the war shifted.

In Chicago, the Democratic convention at the end of August chose George McClellan as its nominee for president. But the party's platform, which argued the war was a failure and the time had come to seek peace—mostly likely peace with slavery—quickly seemed out of step with the pace of events: On September 2, Union soldiers marched into Atlanta. In Washington, Lincoln and his generals read with elation the telegram from General William Tecumseh Sherman that said it all: "Atlanta is ours and fairly won."[19] The war seemed suddenly winnable and Union spirits rose.

The shift in the tides of war lifted Lincoln's electoral fortunes, carrying him, on November 8, 1864, to another term in office, when he soundly defeated McClellan, with an Electoral College vote of 212 to

21.* Douglass had become a firm supporter of Lincoln, telling John Eaton, "I am satisfied now that he is doing all that circumstances will permit him to do." But he chose to stay relatively quiet during the campaign, aware that some voters might be less likely to vote for Lincoln if they saw the candidate too closely allied to a controversial Black man.

# A HOMECOMING

For Frederick Douglass, as for Lincoln, November 1864 would be memorable. On the first day of the month, the state of Maryland formally abolished slavery within its borders, and Douglass decided to go to his childhood home for the first time in more than a quarter century.

Among the first to welcome him in Baltimore was his sister Eliza Bailey Mitchell. They had been unable to communicate since his departure, since slave correspondence was forbidden and, in any case, she was unlettered. Even so, Douglass found, she had made her way in the world. "Mammy Liza" and her husband, Peter Mitchell, had purchased her freedom—for one hundred dollars—and she birthed nine children. From afar she followed her brother's rise to fame and even named a daughter, Mary Douglass Mitchell, after him. Hearing of his well-publicized return to Maryland, she made the sixty-mile journey from Talbot County for a reunion with Fred, her elder by four years.

Arm in arm, brother and sister walked down the aisle on November 19 at what had once been Douglass's spiritual home, Baltimore's Bethel African Methodist Church, in his old Fells Point neighborhood. Other

---

* In the Fourth Ward in Tennessee, Blacks held an election; though their ballots would not be counted in the official results, their tally is worth noting. Lincoln's ticket garnered 3,193 votes to McClellan's 1. Quarles, *Lincoln and the Negro* (1962), p. 217.

Black Marylanders welcomed their famous son at the first of a series of lectures he gave during his two-week visit to Maryland. The church was packed with both African American and White citizens. In itself that was a revelation to Douglass, since the Baltimore he knew was a place where the divisions between the races had been rigid. Some of the faces looking up at him he recognized, now aged but familiar; others were strangers who came to hear the famous orator.

Speaking from the pulpit, surrounded by American flags, Douglass delivered an address unlike the many speeches for which he had become famous. He exhibited neither anger nor bitterness, but told his audience he came "not to condemn the past but to commend and rejoice over the present."[20] He offered not an indictment of slavery and slaveholders; instead, he spoke of himself in a personal way, something he

*When Frederick Douglass returned to his childhood place in November 1864, he asked to visit the Lloyd family graveyard. "Everything about it [was] impressive," he wrote, "and suggestive of the transient character of human life and glory."*

had rarely done in recent years. He had departed, he told them, "in the full fresh bloom of early manhood [when] . . . not one lock of all my hair was tinged by time or sorrow." Now he returned older and wiser, with "the early frost of winter . . . beginning to thicken visibly on my head."

He told them his life was bookended by this place. "My life has been distinguished by two important events, dated about twenty-six years apart. One was my running away from Maryland, and the other is returning to Maryland to-night." He left, he explained, "not because I loved Maryland less, but freedom more."

He talked for three hours, but his audience remained riveted to the son of Maryland who returned to walk among them. "Not a man or woman left the church," reported one Maryland newspaper, "[nor] evinced the faintest indications of weariness."[21]

He made his pitch to the White citizens present to permit their Black neighbors to vote. "If the negro knows enough to pay taxes, he knows enough to vote." But he finished his speech with the best advice he could muster for a room packed with people who had been enslaved.

> You are in one sense free. But you must not think that freedom means absence from work. Bear that in mind. I would impress it upon your minds, that if you would be prosperous, you must be industrious. . . . The black man is just as capable of being great as the white. All he needs is an effort—a persistent, untiring effort. You have now the opportunity, and I trust you will improve it.

The world as Douglass knew it in his boyhood was changing, though slowly, since another six years would pass before Maryland permitted African Americans to vote. But Douglass, along with his friend Lincoln, was helping to change it.

FIFTEEN

# MY FRIEND DOUGLASS

One eighth of the whole population were colored slaves, not distributed generally over the Union, but localized in the Southern part of it. These slaves constituted a peculiar and powerful interest. All knew that this interest was, somehow, the cause of the war.

—ABRAHAM LINCOLN, SECOND INAUGURAL ADDRESS, MARCH 4, 1865

Abraham Lincoln could neither win the war nor abolish slavery by himself. But after emerging as the clear victor in the November 1864 election, he rode the momentum of the moment, driving the country in the direction he wanted.

On the battlefront, General Sherman made his contribution. As the year approached its end, his army succeeded in dividing the Confederacy at its waistline, completing the "March to the Sea" across Georgia. From his new headquarters in a fine coastal mansion, he wrote to Lincoln, "I beg to present you as a Christmas gift, the city of Savannah."[1] In the new year, Sherman would continue the march, moving north to cinch the noose around the shrinking Confederacy. Rebel soldiers, seeing their cause was doomed, began deserting in droves.

Lincoln's policy of soft persuasion in convincing the border states to free those in bondage was slowly producing results. When Unionist counties in northwest Virginia became West Virginia, in 1863, the new state's constitution provided for emancipation. After Maryland freed its enslaved citizens in November 1864, Missouri followed suit, in January 1865; the recaptured Rebel states of Arkansas and Louisiana were also slave-free. But Kentucky and Delaware lagged and some three million men, women, and children in Rebel territory remained enslaved. A permanent national solution was necessary.

Lincoln threw his full support behind the Thirteenth Amendment, a measure that would prohibit slavery anywhere in the United States and its territories. Though passed by the Senate in the spring of 1864 and incorporated into the Republican platform for the November election, the amendment still awaited approval in the House of Representatives. The climactic vote took place on January 31, 1865.

The House chamber was packed. Dozens of senators came to watch, as did five Supreme Court justices. The press gallery was invaded by a mob of well-dressed women, some of whom had launched a petition drive for universal emancipation two years earlier. Black citizens came in force, too, and one spectator remarked, "It was quite a pepper and salt mixture."[2] Although Lincoln did not attend—he waited for news, nervous and attentive, at the White House—his intense lobbying and dealmaking looked to have broken the earlier impasse.*

Douglass, too, was elsewhere, delivering a lecture in upstate New

---

* The process of passing the Thirteenth Amendment is memorably dramatized in Steven Spielberg's movie *Lincoln* (2012).

York, but his son Charles, no longer a soldier but working at the Freedmen's Hospital in Washington, witnessed the calling of the roll. The result of the three o'clock vote was not a foregone conclusion since the measure twice before failed to reach the two-thirds vote required for passage. Republicans still worried about the wavering Democrats they needed to reach the two-thirds threshold, but the result—119 yeas to 56 nays—approved the amendment with two votes to spare.

When Speaker of the House Schuyler Colfax announced the official tally, "there was a pause of utter silence, as if the voices of the dense mass of spectators were choked by strong emotion."[3] Then followed an eruption of cheers, applause, and foot stomping. The deafening bedlam

SCENE IN THE HOUSE ON THE PASSAGE OF THE PROPOSITION TO AMEND THE CONSTITUTION, January 31, 1865.

*The passage of the Thirteenth Amendment, as*
*portrayed here in* Harper's Weekly, *was cause*
*for a raucous celebration on the floor of*
*the House of Representatives.*

ended only when the shouts of an Illinois congressman for adjournment were seconded. The motion quickly carried, and a mass exodus took the celebration to the streets.

"I wish you could have been there," Douglass's youngest son wrote to his father. "Such rejoicing I never before witnessed, cannon firing, people hugging and shaking hands (white people I mean), flags flying all over the city."[4]

When a large procession of celebrants accompanied by a marching band arrived that evening at the executive mansion, Lincoln made an appearance in one of the tall windows over the entrance portico to give a brief speech. Looking down upon the faces lit by the flickering light of the torches they carried, he agreed that this was indeed a suitable moment to celebrate this "indispensable adjunct to the winding up of the great difficulty." Slavery caused the war; now they were about to abolish it. He congratulated everyone, himself and the crowd included, along with "the country and the whole world on this moral victory."[5]

## "TEARFUL SKIES"[6]

One month later, on March 4, 1865, inauguration day dawned wet and windy. General Sherman's army was marching north through the Carolinas, and few doubted the war was rapidly coming to a close. But the work of freeing those who were enslaved wasn't complete; eighteen states had quickly ratified the Thirteenth Amendment in February; nine more were needed for it to become valid.* Still, there was much to celebrate with Lincoln about to take the oath of office for the second

---

* Lincoln would not live to see ratification. The Thirteenth Amendment reached the constitutionally required threshold of three-fourths of the states only after Georgia passed the measure nine months later, on December 6, 1865.

time. Thousands of spectators came to town. The hotels were full, with guests sleeping on cots in hotel hallways. A large crowd of some thirty thousand people began to assemble at the Capitol.

When Lincoln climbed aboard his carriage for the midmorning ride from the White House, he saw a bedraggled crowd lining Pennsylvania Avenue, their lace, velvet, and woolens dripping wet from a hard rain. The spectators watched as for the first time African American soldiers marched with the other troops, bands, and floats in the inaugural parade, with four companies of the Fifty-Fourth Regiment of the United States Colored Troops joining the presidential escort.

Roughly half of those in attendance at Lincoln's second inaugural were Black; perhaps foremost among them was Frederick Douglass, who had arrived in the city a few days before. When he caught sight of the president's carriage and its four horses, he worked his way as close to the president's barouche as he could. He would recall years later that on inauguration day he had felt a "vague presentiment" that there might be "murder in the air."[7] His memory may well have been enhanced by a knowledge of later events, but the fear was by no means his alone. In response to rumors of a conspiracy to take the president's life, the secretary of war increased security in the city, detailing extra guards to protect Lincoln and deploying detectives to observe the many Rebel deserters in Washington.

Inside the Capitol, out of sight of the milling throng outdoors, Lincoln watched as a red-faced Vice President Andrew Johnson took the oath of office in the Senate Chamber. Smelling strongly of whiskey, Johnson delivered a rambling speech. Meanwhile, Douglass found himself a prime spot outside from which to view Lincoln's swearing in.

When the president stepped onto the east portico, "a tremendous shout, prolonged and loud, arose from the surging ocean of humanity around the Capitol building."[8] As the noise of the crowd faded, Douglass was watching when Lincoln, who stood beside his tipsy vice president, pointed at him. Lincoln was clearly pleased to observe that his friend was in attendance, but Douglass, near enough to read Johnson's expression, could also clearly see the "contempt and aversion" that rippled across Johnson's features. When the new vice president registered that Douglass returned his gaze, he quickly erased his scowl to assume a more neutral expression.

"I got a peep into his soul," Douglass thought. "There are moments in the lives of most men when the doors of their souls are open, and unconsciously to themselves, their true characters may be read by the observant eye. It was at such an instant I caught a glimpse of the real nature of this man." As subsequent developments would prove, Douglass's insight at that moment was accurate. "I felt that, whatever else this man might be," Douglass said, "he was no friend to my people."[9]

Lincoln delivered his second inaugural speech from the east portico of the Capitol. In this image, he sits just left of center, his white shirt visible. Much more difficult to discern are John Wilkes Booth, in the balcony above, and Frederick Douglass, in the crowd below.

Another man watching the ceremony with keen interest was a well-known actor named John Wilkes Booth. Given a ticket to a balcony seat by a woman he was courting—she happened to be a senator's daughter—he would be no more than a witness, just as he was at the execution of John Brown five years before. His performance on the national stage came soon enough.

# 703 WORDS

Tall and gaunt, Lincoln stepped forward just as the sun penetrated the leaden gray clouds for the first time that day. In an extraordinary meteorological coincidence, the actor at center stage stood bathed in brilliant sunlight.

He held not a sheaf of papers but a single sheet, and from his close vantage, Douglass could see this would not be a long speech.

In the four paragraphs of what would be the shortest inaugural address ever delivered by an American president, Lincoln chose not to be triumphalist.[10] He could have celebrated the victory that now seemed assured, but instead Lincoln reminded the crowd this was a war that no one wanted. Rather than claiming victory in what he called "the great contest," he acknowledged only that "the progress of our arms" was "encouraging to all." He wished instead to talk about other matters.

He looked back four years in time to his first inauguration when the country was not yet at war with itself. The national division had been enormous, Lincoln noted, between those who "would *make* war rather than let the nation survive" and those who "would *accept* war rather than let it perish." With sadness he noted his negotiating attempts had failed and then "the war came."

For his listeners, this speech already defied the conventions of the day. People expected orators to present them with a long-form rhetorical argument, and in the past Lincoln typically delivered performances that persuaded, cajoled, and entertained. But as at Gettysburg sixteen months earlier, Lincoln took a different approach, one rich in religious reverence rather than politics.

Slavery, he said bluntly, was "the cause of the war." It might seem "strange that any men should dare to ask a just God's assistance in wringing their bread from the sweat of other men's faces," Lincoln observed, for that *was* what slavery amounted to. But he again shifted his tack: On this national day, he wished not to place blame or seek retribution; "let us judge not, that we be not judged." Instead, he raised the promise of peace and appealed to a higher power to bring about an end to the war. He looked not to reason but to conscience and faith, pointing out that both sides "read the same Bible and pray to the same God."

"Fervently do we pray," he said, "that this mighty scourge of war may speedily pass away." The bloodletting of the terrible war was "true and righteous," the high price paid for ending enslavement. Yet there was, Lincoln believed, a divine balance in the war's events.

Neither Lincoln nor Frederick Douglass, who stood listening intently, put great stock in church rituals. But each held a deep faith in the Almighty's capacity for goodness and justice. Douglass recognized that, rather than reading a state paper, Lincoln was, in effect, delivering a sermon. Hearing the president acknowledge slavery as the war's cause was, for Douglass, both a notion he had insisted upon for years and a particular balm coming from Lincoln as he spoke forthrightly to the nation and the world.

Lincoln wrapped up. With the dignity and economy of lines from Shakespeare, his final, intricate sentence rang out over the crowd. It was a plea for the war's end, one full of phrases destined to enter the American vernacular.

With malice toward none; with charity for all; with firmness in the right, as God gives us to see the right, let us strive on to finish the work we are in; to bind up the nation's wounds; to care for him who shall have borne the battle, and for his widow, and his orphan—to do all which may achieve and cherish a just and a lasting peace, among ourselves, and with all nations.

He was done. After listening for a bit more than six minutes, the crowd, standing ankle-deep in mud, responded with a roar of applause. To Frederick Douglass, as perhaps never before, Lincoln spoke as prophet, delivering a radical speech that blended prayer and sermon, one that equated the blood spilled by the swords of war with the bleeding suffered by the enslaved at the hands of slaveholders. Having linked slavery and war as cause and effect, Lincoln asked for reconciliation.

He turned to the chief justice of the Supreme Court to take the oath of office. After he agreed to its terms with the words "So help me God," a cannon salute boomed. Abraham Lincoln's second term in office, abbreviated though it would be, officially began.

# A FINAL MEETING

At the urging of Black friends, Frederick Douglass went to the White House that evening. Inspired by Lincoln's speech, he felt himself "a man among men" and ignored the taboo that forbade mingling with Whites at a presidential reception. He decided that "a colored man [might] offer his congratulations to the president."[11]

After waiting in a long line with thousands of other citizens, Douglass reached the entrance of the executive mansion. Then two guards suddenly interrupted the flow of people, taking Douglass firmly by the arms.

"No persons of color," they warned.

Unwilling to go quietly, Douglass objected. He insisted that President Lincoln issued no such order. The two burly men in blue uniforms relented—or they seemed to—and "with an air of politeness" permitted him to enter. Once inside, however, they marched him directly to a tall window adapted as an exit.

Douglass halted. "You have deceived me," he said. "I shall not go out of this building till I see President Lincoln." Before the standoff could escalate, Douglass recognized a passerby allowed to enter. "Be so kind as to say to Mr. Lincoln that Frederick Douglass is detained by officers at the door." The man hurried away, and the message, promptly delivered, meant Douglass soon got his wish.

"I walked into the spacious East Room, amid a scene of elegance such as in this country I had never witnessed before." The Marine Band played as women in silk gowns, generals in their uniforms, and members of the cabinet conversed.

Douglass spotted Lincoln in a receiving line, shaking hands and accepting congratulations, towering "like a mountain pine high above all others." Lincoln saw Douglass, too, and in a loud voice that carried over the noise in the room, he called out, "And here comes my friend, Frederick Douglass." Many eyes turned to see the broad-shouldered man, his hair streaked with silver, maneuvering his way through the elegantly dressed guests.

When he approached, Lincoln greeted him, taking Douglass's hand between his two. "Douglass, I saw you in the crowd to-day, listening to my inaugural address. How did you like it?" As one young Union officer noted in his diary that night, "The reception of Douglass was the most cordial of any I saw."[12]

With a long line of well-wishers waiting to greet the president, Douglass respectfully demurred. "Mr. Lincoln, I must not detain you with my poor opinion, when there are thousands wanting to shake hands with you." But in this very public moment, the president wanted more from his new friend.

"You must stop a little Douglass; there is no one in the country whose opinion I value more than yours."

Given no choice, Douglass obliged. Rarely a man of few words, he spoke from the heart as he gave Lincoln what he asked for.

"Mr. Lincoln, that was a sacred effort."

Some of those surrounding the two men smiled; others frowned. A few looked astonished that such an exchange could even happen, since few politicians would have dared welcome Douglass out of fear that mere association with his name would prove toxic in his next campaign. But Lincoln was delighted with Douglass's words: This listener, at least, grasped his essential point.

"I am glad you liked it," he replied. Douglass, deeply honored by Lincoln's attentions but caught by the tide of the crowd, moved on.

Not everyone admired or even understood the speech. The *New York World* thought it an "odious libel" to compare the carnage of the war with the beatings of Negroes and complained that Lincoln had substituted "religion for statesmanship." Other editors found it perplexing that Lincoln didn't celebrate the coming victory. Horace Greeley thought it lacked "generosity." *The Daily Ohio Statesman* described the address "as chilly and dreary as the day on which it was delivered."[13]

Lincoln appeared not to mind, acknowledging that he had anticipated that not everyone would like it, though he thought it would "wear as well as—perhaps better than—anything I have produced."[14] Over time, people would indeed come to agree with his offhanded assessment—"Lots of wisdom in that document, I suspect"—and with Douglass's admiration for it.[15]

Lincoln and Douglass's brief exchange on March 4, 1865, would be their last.

*In this hand-tinted lithograph, titled* Lincoln's Last Reception, *the Lincolns greet members of his cabinet, Union generals, and other visitors at a White House reception in the spring of 1865.*

# SIXTEEN

# APRIL IS THE CRUELEST MONTH

[Douglass is] one of the most meritorious men in America.

—ABRAHAM LINCOLN

With the war ending, Lincoln's spirits rose. In late March 1865, he decided to return to Grant's headquarters at City Point, Virginia, and for more than a week he occupied a cabin on the steamboat *River Queen*. He descended her gangplank daily to visit the wounded, mingle with the troops, and confer with Grant and even General Sherman, who made a turnaround visit from his campaign in North Carolina. Lincoln wanted to be near when Richmond finally fell.

Then it happened. On Sunday, April 2, Jefferson Davis and his government abandoned their capital on a midnight train, headed for Danville near the North Carolina border. Before dawn on Monday, explosions shook Richmond when Rebel soldiers lit powder magazines aboard ironclads in the harbor. They fired bridges and warehouses, too, and soon the flames spread from the waterfront, climbing the hillside into the city. By the time Union troops moved in a few hours later, the conflagration, sweeping from block to block, engulfed much of the Confederate capital. Union troops and military police raced to cordon off the fire, and by nightfall, had it under control.

Overall victory in the Civil War now seemed imminent, and Lincoln could contain himself no longer. "Thank God I have lived to see this!" he told Admiral David Porter. "It seems to me I have been dreaming a horrid dream for years, and now the nightmare is gone. I want to see Richmond."[1]

Against the advice of the secretary of war, on Tuesday morning, April 4, 1865, the *River Queen* slipped her moorings and steamed up the James River, accompanied by Porter's flagship, the USS *Malvern*; a gunboat named the *Bat*; a transport; and a tug. The flotilla, however, halted a few miles south of its destination, its path blocked by several rows of heavy pilings the Rebels had driven into the riverbed.

Lincoln would not be deterred. Together with son Tad, who was celebrating his twelfth birthday, three junior officers, and Admiral Porter, Lincoln clambered into a twelve-oar barge. The much smaller craft then safely maneuvered through a narrow channel between the piles. Lincoln's arrival in Richmond would not be a grand affair with flags flying and cannons firing in salute to the commander in chief. But Lincoln didn't mind. "It is well to be humble," he told Admiral Porter.

With twelve marines pulling against the current, the small, solitary craft reached Rockett's Landing, roughly a mile south of central Richmond, about 11:00 A.M.[2] Lincoln knew this visit to Richmond had its perils. He entered what, for four years, had been enemy territory, a city where people spoke his name as if it were a curse. The Union general now in charge at Richmond had no idea he was coming, so no escort awaited the barge to convoy Lincoln to U.S. Army headquarters, more than a mile away.

A group of a dozen Black laborers were working nearby when Lincoln stepped ashore. The day was warm and sunny, and the elderly leader of the crew shaded his eyes to peer at the new arrivals. He immediately recognized the gangly figure of Lincoln wearing his stovepipe hat. Glimpses they had seen of woodcuts and caricatures told them this was "the Great Emancipator."*

"Bless the Lord, here is the great messiah!" the man called, as he and his coworkers dropped their shovels. They ran to meet Lincoln, and the leader fell to his knees, crying "Glory, Hallelujah!"

"It was a touching sight," Porter reported in a memoir twenty years later, "that aged negro kneeling at the feet of the tall, gaunt-looking man who seemed in himself to be bearing the grief of the nation."[3]

Lincoln was plainly embarrassed.

"Don't kneel to me," Lincoln instructed the men. "That is not right. You must kneel to God only, and thank him for the liberty you will hereafter enjoy."

Surrounding the president, the formerly enslaved men broke into song, serenading Lincoln with a hymn of thanks. In the quiet city, their voices carried and nearby streets, deserted minutes before, began to come to life. Patrolled by Black troops, Richmond was under martial law, but as word of Lincoln's arrival spread, men came running from the waterfront. Families emerged from nearby buildings. "Some rushed forward to try and touch the man they had talked of and dreamed of for four long years, others stood off a little way and looked on in awe and wonder."

As the crowd closed in, Admiral Porter worried the crush of happy people posed a danger. He ordered the marines into formation, surrounding the president, who held Tad's hand. To shouts of "Bless the

---

* The origin of the title "Great Emancipator" is not clear. The Italian revolutionary Giuseppe Garibaldi used it in a letter to Lincoln in August 1863, although there is also conjecture that it is a coinage devised by Blacks after Lincoln issued the Emancipation Proclamation.

*As Lincoln walked into the
Confederate capital of Richmond
after it fell to Union troops in April
1865, an artist traveling with the
president's entourage captured him
extending his hand to a Black Union
soldier.*

Lord, Father Abraham's Come," the outnumbered phalanx moved toward the Virginia capitol more than a mile away.

They made slow progress as the day grew warmer. They walked past
Libby Prison, where many Union prisoners had been held. From time to
time, Lincoln removed his hat to fan himself. Perspiration dampened
his brow.

The freedmen trailing Lincoln saw him as Frederick Douglass could
not. Douglass had been the exception: He was among the minority of
enslaved people who, through some mix of bravery, resourcefulness,
and opportunity, made their own way to freedom. In contrast, most of
the men, women, and children who surrounded Lincoln had remained
enslaved until just days or even hours before. They had been considered
property, wholly owned chattels. Some would have managed to escape at great personal peril; others would over time have bought their
freedom. If not for the war, the Thirteenth Amendment, and Abraham

Lincoln, most feared a fate of permanent servitude, with a good chance their children would be sold away from them. This man seemed the personification of their freedom.

As one point, having collected his thoughts, Lincoln spoke to the throng. "My poor friends," he said, "you are free—free as air. . . . Liberty is your birthright. God gave it to you as he gave it to others, and it is a sin that you have been deprived of it for so many years." The crowd shouted in joyful approval, but when Lincoln resumed speaking, they fell silent.

"You must try to deserve this priceless boon," Lincoln continued. "Let the world see that you merit it, and are able to maintain it by your good works." The advice might have been spoken by Douglass; it closely resembled his unrehearsed remarks at Baltimore on the emotional day the previous fall when he returned to Maryland after more than two decades in exile. "Don't let your joy carry you into excesses," Lincoln continued. "Learn the laws and obey them; obey God's commandments and thank him for giving you liberty."

With the speech over, the crowd opened to permit Lincoln to pass.

As Lincoln and company got closer to the Virginia capitol, the sidewalks were lined with people. Many Whites were framed in windows and doorways, but the procession became a largely African American parade, with Lincoln leading the dense crowd that trailed in his wake, the president's tall form recognizable to all. They passed the Tredegar Iron Works, where smoke still spiraled into the sky. Finally, after more than an hour, the entourage arrived at Jefferson Davis's residence. Lincoln, looking pale and haggard, disappeared into the tall home.

Once inside, hot and tired, he flopped into an easy chair in Davis's study. One of Davis's enslaved house servants brought him a welcome glass of cool water. After eating lunch, Lincoln toured the remains of the captured city, riding in an open carriage, accompanied by an entourage of Black cavalry.

. . .

FREDERICK DOUGLASS TOOK THE STAGE at Faneuil Hall after the news of Richmond's capture reached the Massachusetts capital. Boston reverberated with celebrations, and Douglass, one among numerous speakers at the famous hall, kept his remarks brief. With shared pride, he pointed out that the Fifth Massachusetts Cavalry, a Black regiment, had been the first to enter Richmond. And he reminded the crowd of the war's purpose.

"I rejoice, fellow-citizens—for now we are *citizens*. . . . What I want, now that the black men are citizens in war, is, that shall be made fully and entirely, all over this land, citizens in peace."[4]

A WEEK LATER, on April 11, General Robert E. Lee met General Ulysses S. Grant at Appomattox Court House, Virginia, to discuss terms and affix his signature to a document of surrender. Robert Todd Lincoln, the president's oldest son, stood by as a Grant adjutant. On returning to his men after the agreement was signed, Grant told them, "The war is over; the rebels are our countrymen again." The words were Grant's, the sentiment Lincoln's.

That evening, when the news reached him in Washington, the president ordered the firing of five hundred cannons at daylight in celebration. Lincoln, Douglass, and the nation regained peace with what, for practical purposes, was the end of the Civil War.*

---

* Three contingents of Rebel soldiers would fight on for a time, but on April 26, May 4, and May 12, Generals Joseph E. Johnston in North Carolina, Richard Taylor in Alabama, and Edmund Kirby Smith in Texas, respectively, surrendered their commands.

*A contemporary woodcut depicting Lee's surrender. "The memorable event,"
reads the caption, "terminated the Great Rebellion." Ulysses S. Grant stands at
left, with the terms of surrender in hand, and Robert E. Lee on the right.
Officers and troops of both armies are arrayed in formation behind them.*

## DEATH OF A PRESIDENT

The Civil War took the lives of nearly three-quarters of a million soldiers, but the death of just one man, shot on Good Friday 1865, reverberated like no other. His killer used neither an army rifle nor one of the
dreaded minié balls that proved so deadly in the war's killing fields at
distances of two hundred yards and more. The murder weapon would
be a single-shot pistol fired at point-blank range.

The man armed with the Philadelphia Derringer spent his adoles-
cence in slaveholding Maryland, his family home across the Chesapeake

Bay from Frederick Douglass's birthplace. The shooter grew up believing slavery was "one of the greatest blessings that God ever bestowed upon a favored nation," and that its goodness extended not only to Whites but to Blacks, whom he regarded as "thick-skulled darkies."[5] The son and brother of world-renowned actors, he established himself as a performer by age twenty, favoring such Shakespearean roles as the murderous king in *Richard III* and Brutus, the trusted confidant who joins the conspiracy to kill Julius Caesar. By April 1865, a month short of his twenty-seventh birthday, he was regarded as the "handsomest man in Washington." His swashbuckling performances possessed "the fire, the dash, [and] the touch of *strangeness*."[6]

That strangeness extended to his private life. Years earlier, Booth temporarily abandoned his acting company in Richmond and patched together a military uniform so he could impersonate a militiaman and stand guard as the Commonwealth of Virginia hanged John Brown; he knew a theatrical moment when he saw one and did not want to be offstage. Known as a prodigious drinker—however many brandies he consumed, he never seemed intoxicated—he was a man whose sexual appetites ran the gamut from prostitutes to the women of Washington high society.

With the war on, he nurtured a deepening well of anger toward the Union in general and Abraham Lincoln in particular. He continued his acting career, finding the theater provided him with, in effect, a free pass to cross Union lines in order to play to both Rebel and Union audiences. Those travels also meant opportunity, and he found common cause with other Rebel sympathizers. Working with Confederate spies and a mix of other conspirators in the North and South, he worked up an elaborate plan to kidnap Lincoln and smuggle him across the Potomac in order to exchange him for Confederate prisoners of war. After Appomattox, however, the kidnapping no longer made sense because of Grant's and Lincoln's generous terms. Lee's soldiers had not been interned in P.O.W. camps but were permitted to keep their sidearms and horses and head for home.

Then, on April 11, 1865, Lincoln delivered a victory speech at the White House. Looking to the future and, in particular, to what would come to be known as Reconstruction, he recognized that changes needed to be made in the South. Having won the war, he wished to win the peace, and he spoke of forming new state governments. Lincoln made clear the right to vote would be granted to Black men who were literate or who'd fought for the Union.

The idea was anathema to John Wilkes Booth. Listening that evening to Lincoln's words amid a sea of umbrellas, he turned to a companion and said, "That is the last speech he will ever make."

The approaching peace did nothing to diminish his dangerous ambition. Booth remained intent upon doing "something that would bring his name forward in history."[7]

*John Wilkes Booth, actor and man-about-town during the war years, posing with gloves and cane in hand.*

# GOOD FRIDAY

Lincoln was in better spirits than he had been in months. He rose early on Good Friday, April 14, 1865, and breakfasted with his son Captain Robert Todd Lincoln. Robert recounted the details of Lee's surrender, a scene he'd witnessed; his father relished the story. Over the course of the morning, the elder Lincoln tended to the nation's business, conversing with the Speaker of the House and convening a cabinet meeting. The good-humored Lincoln seemed restored, and his secretaries later described him as "singularly happy . . . after four years of trouble and tumult he looked forward to four years of comparative quiet and normal work."[8]

In the afternoon, Lincoln abandoned his desk for a carriage ride with Mary. She, too, was struck by his mood and asked about it. "I consider this day, the war, has come to a close," he responded. He told her he was ready to put the death of their son Willie behind them, too. "We must both," he told Mary, "be more cheerful in the future."[9]

The president and first lady expected to attend the theater that evening in the company of Julia and Ulysses Grant. Although the morning papers reported the plan, General Grant, after initially accepting the invitation, begged off; the Grants instead boarded a train for Burlington, New Jersey, to visit their children. Several of Lincoln's advisers counseled him to stay home, arguing that a widely publicized visit to Ford's Theatre might put him at risk in a city full of former Confederates. But after four years of threats that came to nothing, Lincoln wished to go anyway; the theater was a favorite amusement and he looked forward to a healthful dose of laughter. A younger couple of the Lincolns' acquaintance, Major Henry Rathbone and his fiancée, Clara Harris, the daughter of a New York senator, agreed to join the party.

The foursome arrived at about 8:30 P.M., well after the curtain went up on a forgettable farce called *My American Friend*. But the audience didn't mind the interruption. One of the actors, seeing the commotion in the presidential box, ad-libbed a line—"This reminds me of a story, as Mr. Lincoln would say"—and the crowd cheered.[10] The house orchestra played "Hail to the Chief." Lincoln stepped to the velvet balustrade at the front of the box, which looked down on the stage from a height of almost twelve feet. His bow and smile met with a fresh ovation from the nearly full house. Only then did he take a seat in the rocking chair considerately provided by the management for his comfort. The play resumed.

# THE CONSPIRATORS

Word of the Lincolns' night out reached John Wilkes Booth early that afternoon when he went to check his mail at Ford's Theatre.

His larger band of kidnappers had disbanded but Booth, unwilling to accept the outcome of the war, maintained a cell of conspirators. They continued to meet, though when he shifted the terms of engagement— he now wanted to kill the president rather than kidnap him—the crew shrank further. Lincoln's secretaries John Hay and John Nicolay would later call his little circle "a small number of loose fish," but Booth could still call upon the violent intentions of Lewis Powell and George Atzerodt.[11] Powell was an Alabama native and former Confederate soldier wounded and captured at Gettysburg. He was battle-hardened and wanted passionately to the avenge the South. Atzerodt was a disgruntled Prussian immigrant.

On the evening of April 14, Booth summoned them to a meeting at eight o'clock. He issued his instructions: Powell was to proceed to Lafayette Square and the home of William Seward, where the secretary of state lay convalescing from a carriage accident the previous week. With doctors coming and going, Powell might gain access by posing as a deliveryman bringing medicines from an apothecary. The task of ending the life of Vice President Andrew Johnson went to Atzerodt; Booth's plan called for him to go to Kirkwood House, Johnson's hotel, to deliver an official-looking envelope. Booth kept the largest target for himself, and the men agreed that two hours later they would "decapitate the government" by simultaneously killing Seward, Johnson, and Lincoln at 10:14 P.M.

Riding a rented horse, Booth made his way to the familiar confines of Ford's Theatre. He tied up the animal in the alley behind the theater, anticipating a speedy escape, and entered through the stage door. At ten minutes after ten, he made his way from the parquet level of the theater to the dress circle, humming as he went. With most eyes on the performers, he moved quietly toward the State Box. Dressed in a dark suit, hat, and boots with spurs, he carried a small gun—the length from the walnut stock to the mouth of the rifled barrel was less than six inches—and a bowie knife with a long, well-honed blade.

The unreliable Washington policeman assigned to Lincoln was not at his post so only Lincoln's footman stood between killer and quarry. Booth produced a senator's calling card—the name on it was familiar to the guard, though to which senator it belonged is a detail lost to history—and the president's man ushered Booth into a little hallway.* Now only an unlocked door separated him from the double box where the president and his party watched the play. Looking through a peephole, Booth saw Lincoln clearly, with Mrs. Lincoln sitting to the president's right. He was in position.

---

* The best guess as to the senator's identity is John Hale of New Hampshire, since Booth and Hale's daughter Lucy had only recently ended a love affair; when Booth died, he had a photograph of Lucy Hale on his person. For a discussion of this notion and why the name Hale did not surface in the subsequent investigation, see Achorn, *Every Drop of Blood* (2020), pp. 280–82, 284–85, 288.

The executioner did not hesitate long. The audience's guffaws at a guaranteed laugh line was his cue, and Booth stepped forward to fire the derringer at the back of Lincoln's head. For many in the theater, the gunshot went unnoticed beneath the explosion of hilarity.

As Lincoln slumped forward in his chair, Booth dropped his gun and brushed past the president's rocker. Always the actor looking to make a dramatic exit, Booth rested a boot on the box's railing, ready to leap onto the stage below and run for the exit. Major Rathbone, though surprised by the half-heard gunshot and the veil of gun smoke, recovered quickly and went for Booth. But the actor managed to pull his knife from its sheath and swung it at Rathbone, tearing a great gash in the major's left arm.

Then Booth jumped, delivering his chosen line, *"Sic semper tyrannis,"* the Virginia state motto, which translates as "Thus always to tyrants." When one of his spurs caught in the bunting that decorated the box, his

*The moment the shot was fired at Ford's Theatre, as represented in a Currier & Ives print released in the weeks afterward.*

athletic leap became a tumble. Booth crash-landed on the stage, his right leg twisted beneath him, fracturing the smaller bone in his lower leg. Then he was up and, in a limping run, heading for center stage, where he delivered one last line.

Confused whether the unexpected arrival played a part in the play, the stunned audience watched as Booth raised both arms, brandishing the broad and bloodied blade as if he had just killed Caesar. "The south is avenged!" he cried before disappearing into the familiar back passages of the theater, bound for the stage door, his horse, and his escape.[12]

What had happened became clear only when a terrible shriek rang out. "They have shot the president!" screamed Mary Lincoln. "They have shot the president!"

Unconscious but breathing, Lincoln was soon carried to a house across Tenth Street; according to Victorian morality, his memory would have been sullied by dying in an unholy theater on Good Friday. His bearers laid the mortally wounded man diagonally across the bed, since he was taller than the bed was long.

A deathwatch assembled, including members of his cabinet. Senator Charles Sumner arrived with Lincoln's son Robert; Sumner remained at Lincoln's bedside all night, holding the limp hand of the dying president. Mary Lincoln, comforted by her son, wept in a nearby room when Lincoln stopped breathing, at 7:22 A.M. on Saturday, April 15, 1865.

Seward was not in attendance. Lewis Powell had attacked him, though the secretary of state would miraculously survive despite serious stab wounds. Andrew Johnson appeared briefly at Lincoln's deathbed scene; he had escaped the night's violence unscathed because George Atzerodt lost his nerve and made no attempt on the life of the vice president.

Even before Lincoln died, the Black citizens of Washington mourned him. In the dark before dawn, a member of Lincoln's cabinet stepped

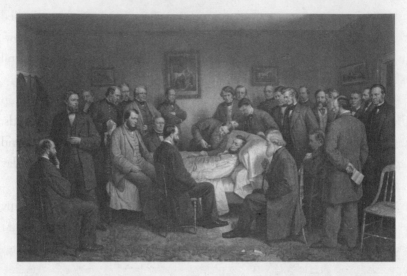

*One of the many commemorative images of the Lincoln deathbed scene published a few years after the assassination. The dying man is surrounded by doctors, members of his cabinet, military men, and others. Eldest son Robert Todd Lincoln leans over his father's pillow, and to his right stands Charles Sumner.*

outside and saw crowds had already begun to fill the streets. "The colored people," the secretary of the navy recorded, ". . . were painfully affected."[13]

When he stopped breathing, one of the several doctors on duty confirmed he was dead. Secretary of War Stanton broke the terrible silence that followed.

"Now he belongs to the ages."[14]

## MOURNING IN ROCHESTER

The dot-dash of the telegraph brought the news to Rochester that the great and good Abraham Lincoln had joined the Union dead.

A mere six weeks earlier, at the White House, Lincoln had hailed "my friend, Frederick Douglass"; in return, Douglass thanked the now-deceased president, offering a heartfelt compliment for his inaugural speech as a "sacred effort."

Theirs had been a budding friendship. It was not a political courtship nor a convenient or collegial collaboration, but a true meeting of minds. Now, after the crack of a pistol shot, Lincoln once more would be found in the East Room, where the two men last spoke. This time Lincoln lay in state.

On the afternoon of Lincoln's death, Frederick Douglass and many other mourning Rochesterians "betook themselves to the City Hall." At 3:00 P.M. a public memorial service convened, and as Douglass later remembered, "though all hearts ached for utterance, few felt like speaking. We were stunned and overwhelmed by a crime and calamity hitherto unknown to our country and our government."[15]

Douglass found a seat in the back of the auditorium; the audience was largely White, and Douglass hadn't been invited to sit on the dais. He listened quietly as the city's mayor, a judge, and an Episcopal rector spoke. However, his presence noted, he soon heard his neighbors chanting, *Douglass! Douglass! Douglass!*

The mayor beckoned him to the stage. The crowd made way.

Hundreds of people had been turned away at the doors, and Douglass, looking out over the overflow house, admitted he was ill prepared to speak. "This is not an occasion for speech making, but for silence," he told the men and women of his city. "I have scarcely been able to say a word to any of those friends who have taken my hand and looked sadly in my eyes to-day."[16]

Grasping the importance of the moment, Douglass searched his mind for "some good that may be born of the tremendous evil."

In what would be one of the most direct and heartfelt speeches of his life, he suggested that Lincoln's death was a reminder to a nation that, until the assassination, had been "in danger of losing a just appreciation of the awful crimes of this rebellion." Perhaps out of relief, people had begun to put the war behind them; in that case, Lincoln's death might be seen as a necessary reminder "to bring us back to that equilibrium which we must maintain if the Republic was to be permanently redeemed."

The crowd applauded.

Speaking without notes but warming to his subject, Douglass recalled shaking Lincoln's "brave, honest hand, and look[ing] into his gentle eye." From memory, he quoted the president's inaugural at length, reminding his listeners that the "scourge of war" should not speedily be forgotten. "Let us not be in too much haste in the work of restoration," he advised. "Let us not be in a hurry to clasp to our bosom that spirit which gave birth to Booth." Most important of all, he urged, "Let us not forget that justice to the negro is safety to the Nation."

Speaking in Rochester that funereal afternoon, Douglass felt a sense of belonging, a stark contrast to the outsider status his nation had shown him as a child and young man. He invited the audience to embrace those who cared about the remade nation. "Know every man by his loyalty, and wherever there is a patriot in the North or South, white or black, helping on the good cause, hail him as a citizen, a kinsman, a clansman, a brother beloved." The crowd showered him with his largest ovation of the afternoon. He hit the note he wanted; it had struck a chord with his listeners.

Writing of the moment years later, Douglass would remember the afternoon of grief, shared by the White and Black alike; their sense of loss had made them "more than countrymen, it made us Kin."[17]

He might have said the same thing of his recently dead kinsman, Abraham Lincoln. "Though Abraham Lincoln dies," said Douglass, "the Republic lives." His profound belief and hope were that, with the war to abolish slavery finally at an end, Lincoln's promise of a "new birth of freedom" was indeed aborning, leading to equality and reconciliation between White and Black.

## EPILOGUE

———◆———

# A BONE-HANDLED CANE

[T]he best man, truest patriot, and wisest statesman of his time and country . . . [Mr. Lincoln's] name should never be spoken but with reverence, gratitude, and affection.

—FREDERICK DOUGLASS ON ABRAHAM LINCOLN

Abraham Lincoln went home to Illinois in a box. After lying in state in the East Room and the Capitol Rotunda, his remains retraced the route that the living Lincoln took four years before as president-elect.

The somber, twenty-mile-per-hour train journey was interrupted by stops in major cities like Baltimore, New York, and Chicago, where processions carried Lincoln's casket along crowd-lined streets to important public buildings, including Philadelphia's Independence Hall, birthplace of the Declaration of Independence. The exhumed remains of son Willie, dead three years earlier, accompanied his father on the train, though surviving sons Robert and Tad remained in Washington. They consoled their bereft mother, who suffered "the wails of a broken heart, the unearthly shrieks, the terrible convulsions, the wild, tempestuous outbursts of grief from the soul."[1]

Millions of Americans paid their respects along the 1,654-mile route traveled by the "Lincoln Special." One stop on the twelve-day journey was Rochester, New York, where the funeral train halted for fifteen minutes on April 27 at 3:20 A.M. The coffin never left the presidential car, but despite the early hour, the tracks were lined with people carrying torches. An artillery salute was fired as "an immense crowd" watched at the depot.[2]

Later that same morning, the War Department released the news that John Wilkes Booth, after eluding capture for twelve days, was dead. The manhunt ended in Port Royal, Virginia, where Booth took refuge in a tobacco barn. He refused to give himself up, and his pursuers, looking to flush him out, set fire to the building. Despite orders to take him alive, a soldier, sighting Booth through a gap in the rough siding, shot the fugitive in the neck. The slug severed Booth's spinal cord. Alive but paralyzed, Lincoln's killer was dragged to safety and died of asphyxia three hours later.

When the funeral train arrived in Springfield, Lincoln's open coffin again lay in state, this time in the Illinois capitol, the great limestone building shrouded "roof to basement in black velvet and silver fringe."[3] Two days later, on May 4, 1865, he was buried at a simple ceremony. Accompanying the prayers and hymns, the words of his Second Inaugural Address were recited over the grave.

## AN OBLONG BOX

A few weeks later, a package arrived at the Douglass home on Rochester's South Avenue. Mary Todd Lincoln had sent the long, oddly shaped box, and inside Douglass found the dead president's favorite walking stick. Noting in an accompanying letter that her late husband considered him a special friend, Mary Lincoln wrote, "I know of no one that would appreciate this more than Fred. Douglass."⁴

Douglass replied, sending the widow Lincoln a note of thanks. "I assure you that this inestimable memento of his excellency will be retained in my possession while I live." He called the maple stick with the well-worn bone handle "an object of sacred interest." Perhaps more important still, he interpreted the gift as an "indication of [Lincoln's] human interest in the welfare of my whole race."⁵

President Andrew Johnson exhibited no such concern. After taking office, he instituted a range of policies that allowed the passage of so-called "Black Codes." These permitted former Confederate states to avoid granting freed men new civil and political rights. The laws also limited freedom of movement, leaving few options other than to return to work for former slaveholders. A brutal battle over such issues broke out between the racist president and congressional Republicans. Douglass, attempting to have his voice heard, bulldozed his way into the White House on February 7, 1866, along with a delegation of other influential Black men.

The unwanted meeting with Johnson did not go well. After listening to a forty-five-minute tirade in which Johnson described himself as "the friend of the colored man," Douglass argued with the president. Their bitter exchange—Douglass refused to kowtow to Johnson—left the president livid. "Those d____d sons of b____s thought they had me in a trap," sputtered Johnson after his visitors departed. "I know that d____d Douglass; he's just like any n____r, & would sooner cut a white man's throat than not."⁶

The remainder of Johnson's term would be consumed by a legislative war with Congress, which, despite the president's opposition, managed to pass the Fourteenth Amendment to the Constitution, in June 1866, guaranteeing "equal protection" of "life, liberty, or property" for all citizens. Congress would also attempt to impeach Johnson, in 1868; though the House of Representatives approved articles of impeachment, the trial in the Senate fell one vote short of the two-thirds majority required to remove him from office. Following Ulysses S. Grant's election as president that November, the Fifteenth Amendment was enacted and ratified, guaranteeing all citizens the right to vote, regardless of "their race, color, or previous condition of servitude."

Newly empowered Black voters asserted themselves in the late 1860s in the South, voting their brethren into local, state, and even national offices. But Frederick Douglass's days as an agitator and firebrand at the ramparts faded; looking back a few years later, he wrote, "The anti-slavery platform had performed its work, and my voice was no longer needed."[7] He moved to Washington, D.C., in 1870, and returned for a time to the newspaper business as owner of the *New National Era*. But he lost interest in the short-lived paper, handing over the reins to Lewis and Frederick Jr., before the publication folded in a cascade of debts a few years later.

In 1872, his family home in Rochester burned, probably as the result of arson. His wife, Anna, who still resided there, escaped safely, and Douglass hurried back to the city that had welcomed him twenty-five years before. On arrival, however, he was turned away from two hotels, treatment that the angry Douglass attributed to "Northern colorphobia." He complained bitterly that even in a liberal Northern city, "that Ku Klux spirit . . . makes anything owned by a colored man a little less respected and secure."[8] Slavery had ended; racial discrimination did not, and the years that followed would see a gradual erosion of the rights only recently granted to African Americans.

Many of the abolitionists he'd collaborated with began to fade into the past. Douglass's first mentor, William Lloyd Garrison, ceased publication of *The Liberator* in 1865; though he involved himself with the women's suffrage movement for some years, he would die in 1879 after a long illness. On the morning of Charles Sumner's death, on March 11, 1874, Frederick Douglass was summoned to his bedside. Still preoccupied with the rights of freedmen, the senator urged Douglass to advance his Civil Rights Act, then pending in Congress. "Don't let that bill fail," he pleaded.[9] A watered-down version did pass, but the Supreme Court struck it down a few years later. Another eight decades would go by before the Civil Rights Act of 1964 was enacted during Lyndon Johnson's presidency. But in 1876 Douglass would have perhaps his proudest moment as a public man.

## THE FREEDMAN'S MEMORIAL

Flags flew at half-mast. Congress had declared April 14, 1876, a public holiday, and dozens of senators and congressmen, Supreme Court justices, and members of the cabinet made the one-mile trip from the Capitol to Lincoln Square. Even President Ulysses S. Grant arrived to take a seat on the temporary platform. Next to the stage, hidden by a drapery of red, white, and blue bunting and American flags, a large but shapeless form rose some twenty feet in the air.

Although the men of the government came to remember a dead president, the scene that unfolded was no routine commemoration of a great man. The honoree would be Abraham Lincoln, but the inspiration for the day's events belonged not to a politician but to a formerly enslaved woman, now elderly, who stood nearby. Upon hearing of Abraham Lincoln's death exactly eleven years before, Charlotte Scott had announced she wished to dedicate her life savings, the modest but hard-earned sum of five dollars, to build a monument to "the best friend of the colored people," the man who authored the Emancipation Proclamation and engineered passage of the Thirteenth Amendment, thereby ending American slavery forever. Scott's spontaneous gesture triggered a campaign among grateful African Americans, many of them former soldiers and freedmen. They contributed their own dollars to fulfill her wish.

The realization of Charlotte Scott's idea was about to be unveiled as the Freedman's Memorial.[10]

The sound of music wafted in as a parade high-stepped into the square. The marchers included National Guardsmen, the Knights of Saint Augustine, and the Sons of Purity—all told, some twenty Negro organizations—accompanied by banners and flags, cornet bands and drum corps. As their colorful uniforms blended into a crowd of some twenty-five thousand, roughly half of whom were Black, the scheduled speakers at the day's event walked from their carriages in the procession to join President Grant and the others on the platform. The most recognizable of the new arrivals was Frederick Douglass. Neither his generous mane of swept-back white hair nor his full beard could obscure the intense flashing eyes that, as in every photograph he ever took, not only engaged those looking at him but seemed to challenge them, too. Douglass had been the inevitable choice to deliver the keynote address.

At two o'clock, the program in Lincoln Square opened with a min-

*Mathew Brady took Douglass's picture, too. This image, made at roughly the time Douglass dedicated the Freedman's Memorial, captures his still-commanding presence, though he has evidently aged, with his mane gone to white.*

ister's invocation, followed by a recitation of the Emancipation Proclamation. The crowd also heard the story of the statue, how Scott's five dollars grew to the seventeen thousand dollars paid to American sculptor Thomas Ball. Then the moment came to unveil Ball's bronze.

General Grant rose from his chair. The silent crowd watched, still and expectant. The president stepped forward, paused, and then without uttering a word, pulled a velvet cord. It released the massive curtain of fabric, which slumped to the ground. In the brief silence that followed, all eyes lifted to gaze upon the towering statue.

A nine-foot-tall Lincoln dominated the composition, his right hand resting on a podium, the fingers grasping a copy of the Emancipation Proclamation. The somber-faced figure looked down, his other arm extended as if in a gesture of benediction over a kneeling man. Naked from the waist up, the well-muscled former bondsman, shackles behind him, appeared to be rising with one knee off the ground. Cast into the base in twelve-inch letters was the word EMANCIPATION.

*The Freedman's Memorial, also known as the Emancipation Memorial and the Emancipation Group.*

The quiet suddenly gave way to a deafening explosion of sound, with spontaneous cries of admiration, a brassy burst of music from the Marine Band, and a booming cannon salute.

Now came Frederick Douglass's turn.

Of all the thousands of speeches he'd delivered over the years, this was the only time he—or, for that matter, any Black man of his century—would command the full and immediate attention of the three branches of the American government.* Douglass promptly recognized the congressional leadership, the chief justice, and "the honored and truest President of the United States," but he just as quickly made clear that today they were guests. The hosts of this gathering, he said, were "we, the colored people, newly emancipated and rejoicing in our blood-bought freedom." Black folk had underwritten this monument of remembrance for the great services rendered by Lincoln to "ourselves, our race, to our country and to the whole world."[11]

Some in the vast audience had arrived thinking that Douglass, now in his fifty-ninth year, was aging into irrelevance. He himself would later admit that, with the end of the war a decade before and abolition won, "I had reached the end of the noblest and best part of my life."[12] But before he faded away, Douglass wanted to get a few things straight.

To the surprise of those who came expecting a celebration of national pride and patriotism, Douglass pointed out that Lincoln, "the Great Emancipator," had not always been his people's best friend. "Truth compels me to admit," Douglass told the crowd, "even here in the presence of the monument we have erected to his memory, Abraham Lincoln was not, in the fullest sense of the word, either our man or our model.

---

* As Douglass's biographer David Blight has pointed out, another 133 years would elapse before a second Black man could lay claim to so distinguished an audience; that was in 2009 when Barack Obama delivered his first inaugural speech.

In his interests, in his association, in his habits of thought, and in his prejudices, he was a white man."

In case he hadn't been clear enough, Douglass spoke separately to the two halves of the audience. "You are the children of Abraham," he said to the powerful men on the stage and the other White listeners. Addressing his Black fellow citizens, Douglass said, "We are at best only his step-children."

Yet he had made his peace with Lincoln's slow rise to the cause of freeing the Black man. "Had he put the abolition of slavery before the salvation of the Union," Douglass acknowledged, Lincoln would have alienated Whites and "rendered resistance to rebellion impossible. Viewed from the genuine abolition ground, Mr. Lincoln seemed tardy, cold, dull, and indifferent; but measuring him by the sentiment of his country, a sentiment he was bound as a statesman to consult, he was swift, zealous, radical, and determined."

Douglass spent an hour delivering his history lesson, praising Lincoln, speaking respectfully of his memory. But he refused to do the sixteenth president the disservice of reducing him, as history had already begun to do, to a saintly and uncomplicated figure who, out of the sheer goodness in his heart, ended slavery. Douglass knew Lincoln as a man of complex and shifting intellect. At first, "his great mission was . . . to save the country from dismemberment and ruin." Only later, Douglass pointed out, had Lincoln devoted himself to the great work of "free[ing] his country from the great crime of slavery."

Douglass cherished his personal relations with Lincoln, but he could not offer a humble hymn of praise. Perhaps more than anyone present, Frederick Douglass—a freedman himself, a writer of great gifts, a fighter for freedom—recognized that monuments are about memory. What he wished to convey above all else to his impressive audience was that Lincoln must be remembered fully.

That day would not be the last of his public life. The next year

President Rutherford B. Hayes rewarded Douglass for his continuing service to the party, appointing him U.S. Marshal of the District of Columbia. It was a first: No Black man had ever been nominated for a position that required Senate approval. Though largely ceremonial, the job cemented Douglass's national standing as Black America's most visible and admired man.

He purchased a handsome brick mansion called Cedar Hill. Located in Southeast Washington, D.C., on a fifteen-acre parcel, it overlooked the Anacostia River and the Capitol beyond. Douglass saw with a mix of satisfaction and irony that the original deed specified the property was "for the use, benefit and enjoyment of white persons only." Lincoln and the Civil War had changed that.[13]

Douglass gave fewer lectures as he became a man of means, with holdings and directorships in banks, insurance, and manufacturing.[14] After Anna died, in 1882, he married Helen Pitts, a White woman who'd worked as his secretary when he served as Recorder of Deeds in the Garfield administration, another political appointment. In contrast to Anna, who never learned to read or write, Helen was a graduate of Mount Holyoke Female Seminary. The couple shared many interests. They welcomed students from Howard University for Sunday tea and traveled widely to Europe and the Middle East. Disapproval of his marriage was widespread among Blacks, Whites, and even his children, but Douglass refused to take the objections seriously. He observed that his first wife "was the color of my mother, and the second, the color of my father."[15]

Douglass worked at a third and expanded version of his autobiography. Published in 1881, *Life and Times of Frederick Douglass* reflected how far its author had come. If it lacked some of the shock value of his earlier slave narratives, it put Douglass's remarkable rise into its historic context as he recounted his relations with John Brown, Mrs. Stowe,

*Douglass, together with his second wife, Helen Pitts Douglass (seated), and sister-in-law Eva Pitts, ca. 1885.*

Gerrit Smith, and other notables. Above all, as he wrote of his life at Cedar Hill, he mused upon his relationship with Abraham Lincoln. In drafting those pages, he cast an occasional glance at a posthumous likeness of Lincoln. "His picture, now before me in my study," Douglass noted in *Life and Times*, "corresponds well with the impression I have of him."[16]

Douglass reengaged in the fight to get the vote for women; back in 1848, he had been one of the few men present at the landmark Seneca Falls convention. On February 20, 1895, he attended a women's rights rally, where he entered the hall arm in arm with his fellow warrior Susan B. Anthony. They were greeted with tumultuous applause.

He returned to Cedar Hill shortly after dark. While dining with Helen, he recounted the events of the exhilarating day, then abruptly rose from his chair. A moment later, he fell to his knees and collapsed to

*"Men called him homely,"
Frederick Douglass wrote after
Lincoln's death, "and homely he
was; but it was manifestly a
human homeliness." He liked
this picture of the dead
president, which was painted
and engraved by William E.
Marshall in 1866, and hung a
copy in his library.*

the floor. Although he outlived his friend Lincoln by almost thirty years, Frederick Douglass, age seventy-seven, was dead.

## LAYING CLAIM TO LINCOLN

Abraham Lincoln got no chance to write an autobiography. The job of chronicling his life was left to friends, colleagues, and newspapermen. An old law partner, his long-time bodyguard, and dozens of others produced an avalanche of reminiscences and biographies that culminated with the exhaustively researched and authorized *Abraham Lincoln: A History*. Written by John Hay and John Nicolay, Lincoln's former secretaries, it appeared in ten volumes in 1890.

The fate of Frederick Douglass was the opposite. During the years that born-in-a-log-cabin "Honest Abe" gained almost mythic status, Douglass began a steep fade into obscurity.

He lived long enough to worry about new inequalities, boldly telling a Washington, D.C., audience late in his life, "I admit that the negro, and especially the plantation negro, . . . is worse off, in many respects, than when he was a slave."[17] But Douglass would die a year before the Supreme Court made this inequality official. In 1896, the landmark case *Plessy v. Ferguson* established the doctrine of "separate but equal," upholding recent "Jim Crow" laws that, in many southern states, disenfranchised Black voters and permitted racial segregation in public places. The result was more than half of a century of separate-but-far-from-equal, since it wasn't until 1954 that the court ruled the doctrine unconstitutional in the momentous *Brown v. Board of Education* decision.

That the memory of Frederick Douglass was suppressed alongside the rights of African American citizens during those years is no surprise.

During those decades, Lincoln's lionization continued, particularly in what became his most memorable biography. Written by a Chicago journalist and poet named Carl Sandburg, *Abraham Lincoln* was published in two parts, with *The Prairie Years* appearing in 1926, followed thirteen years later by *The War Years*. A better writer than historian, Sandburg won a Pulitzer Prize and wide readership for his poetic prose. Lincoln, whom so many loved to hate in his own time, emerged as a man posterity worshipped. Sandburg made him a hero at the center of the American story.

Meanwhile, Douglass was mentioned rarely or not at all in history texts. Then, after World War II, a young scholar named Philip Foner began looking for a commercial publisher or a university press to publish Douglass's papers. But most of the editors he approached had never

*The elderly Frederick Douglass at his home, Cedar Hill, where he would die in 1895. He purchased the desk at which he sits from the estate of his old abolitionist ally Charles Sumner.*

heard of Douglass.[18] Foner eventually persuaded the Marxist press International Publishers to release *The Life and Writings of Frederick Douglass*; its five volumes came off the presses between 1950 and 1955. The books helped launched a rediscovery of Douglass, as did an early biography by pioneering African American studies professor Benjamin Quarles.[19] The return of Douglass's voice to the national conversation fueled the civil rights movement and the activism of the 1950s and '60s, which led to the Civil Rights Acts of 1964 and 1968.

During those years, Lincoln's saintly status lost some of its luster. *Ebony* magazine put the question in stark terms in an article titled "Was Lincoln a White Supremacist?"[20] The discussion that followed resulted in a more measured view of the man.

By the end of the twentieth century, Lincoln came off his pedestal and Douglass rose from obscurity. Today these two good men once again occupy a shared space in the ongoing story of the American experiment.

# THE FOG OF MEMORY

To see Lincoln clearly, the name "Great Emancipator" needed to be retired. To know Douglass, we cannot use the rosy lens that is the "Lost Cause."

To explain: Shortly after the Civil War ended, a Virginia newspaper editor promoted the idea of the Lost Cause. According to this "moonlight and magnolias" view, later perpetuated by the book and movie *Gone with the Wind*, the antebellum South was a genteel culture that, faced with Northern aggression, had no choice but to defend itself. Embedded in this sentimental distortion of history is the acceptance of slavery as a paternalistic good that was of mutual benefit to Whites and the Blacks they enslaved.

More than perhaps anyone else, Douglass understood the utter dishonesty of the Lost Cause perspective on the Civil War. Douglass spent the war years telling people that the Civil War was about slavery. The politicians in the states that withdrew from the Union understood that then; slavery, not states' rights, had been at the center of debate at secession conventions.[21] Ironically, Abraham Lincoln was among the many in the North who needed to be persuaded that slavery was the bleeding heart of the conflict.

Recollecting his younger days floating down the Mississippi, Lincoln once observed, "The pilots on our Western rivers steer from *point to point* as they call it—setting the course of the boat no farther than they can see; and that is all I propose to myself in this great problem."[22] The largely self-taught Lincoln approached many challenges—most of all slavery—in the same way. He was a pragmatic problem-solver confident that solutions, like destinations, would offer themselves with the passage of time.

During Lincoln's boyhood, the inferiority of the Black man was received wisdom, a belief he shared with almost all Whites in the North as well as the South. Then, as a young man, Lincoln's coordinates changed as his values evolved and he accepted that slavery was a clear moral wrong. In manhood he began to imagine a route that, in time, could lead to abolition; and he gradually accepted that Blacks were the equal of Whites and must be made full citizens. Only in the last several years of his life did Lincoln manage to steer the country, once and for all, away from slavery.

Frederick Douglass's personal history was very different. In his youth, he smelled and tasted the blood of slavery; sometimes that blood was his own. He knew from a very young age what he wanted: *freedom*, plain and simple. After he gained freedom for himself, on his own, his goal became to free all of those enslaved in his country. Unlike Lincoln, from youth he possessed a North Star—it was freedom for his people— a constant he could rely upon. His bearings never changed as he made himself famous, on his own terms, and played an immense role in achieving freedom for his people.

In this book we have looked at how Lincoln—lawyer, legislator, careful reader of the nation's founding documents—came face-to-face in the 1850s with the Kansas–Nebraska Act, then *Dred Scott v. Sandford*. We have seen how the politics of slavery rapidly changed, an evolution that accelerated after John Brown's raid, the secession of Southern states following Lincoln's election, and the advent of war. Lincoln did not direct any of these occurrences: As he admitted to a Kentucky newspaperman, "I claim not to have controlled events, but confess plainly that events have controlled me."[23] Still, his actions did shape the course of that war.

He started out thinking the fight was for Union. Although he never abandoned that belief, he slowly moved to the view that the only way to save the Union was to banish slavery, and, later, that enlisting Black men was essential. By the end of the war, the flood of African American volunteers numbered roughly 10 percent of the total soldiers and sailors who fought for the Union, providing a key, even decisive, advantage in the war. The agency of the Black Union soldier would long be overlooked by most historians, just as Douglass was for so many decades. But in his time Lincoln recognized both. He adopted the belief that the Black man should vote and that, in short, Black lives meant as much as White ones did and that the laws of the Union needed to be brought in line with the founding promises of equality.

At the beginning of his public life, Frederick Douglass opened the eyes of audiences to the injustices of slavery. Before the terms were coined, he was a "poster boy" for abolitionism, and later, when he broke from Garrison, he became a "public intellectual." Initially his had been a voice that most White Americans did not want to hear, but in his middle years, many of those same people—most prominently among them, Abraham Lincoln—listened. Douglass possessed a raw and original intellectual power unlike any contemporary, Black or White.

The fault lines of the Civil War era threw Douglass and Lincoln together. When needed the most, these two unlikely people appeared on the scene, as Andrew Jackson had done during the War of 1812, each of them born with nothing. They were underdogs who somehow rose to become national figures at a time of crisis. Like other American saviors, Lincoln and Douglass would transcend their era, standing taller than their contemporaries.

Lincoln did what no other politician of his era could do: free the enslaved. Since Lincoln left us little commentary on their friendship, how large an influence Douglass was on his thinking cannot be proved. Yet it is clear that Douglass was an alter ego to Lincoln, a conscience to the president and their nation, one that nagged and prodded and never bent. Douglass played to Lincoln's better angels, helping guide the president through a dark time toward a brighter, fairer, better one.

Both Douglass and Lincoln, as they worked to change the future of Black Americans, influenced their nation's direction toward a more perfect union. Their immense and shared accomplishment was ending slavery; their next goal, however, to achieve true equality, was left unfinished. In their honor, the work must go on.

# THE MAINTENANCE OF MEMORY

A RACE SET FREE
AND THE COUNTRY AT PEACE
LINCOLN
RESTS FROM HIS LABORS.

—INSCRIPTION ON THE PEDESTAL BENEATH BOSTON'S
EMANCIPATION MEMORIAL, 1879

In 1879, Boston got its own Freedman's Memorial. It was a replica of the original statue that Frederick Douglass dedicated three years before. As it did in Washington's Lincoln Park, the likeness of the sixteenth president stood impossibly tall on its perch, with the same figure of a Black man crouching at Lincoln's feet. The sculpture cast a long shadow across Park Square, a busy intersection barely a block from the Public Garden and Boston Common.

Four score and one year later, however, the monument disappeared on December 29, 2020.

At 8:30 A.M. on that sunny and mild winter day, a tall crane arrived.

After a crew secured the bronze casting, the crane operator swung the entire Emancipation Group, as the sculpture was known to Bostonians, onto the bed of a large truck. A handful of witnesses saw it happen but when the truck departed, there was no fanfare. Just a few among the small crowd of onlookers clapped as the likeness of Abraham Lincoln left Park Square forever.

Many variations of this scene have played out over the course of the last few years. Literally hundreds of statues have been removed from public spaces, some of them violently, as the nation debates racial injustice and rethinks old imagery. Confederate statues dating from the Jim Crow era have been particular targets—more than two hundred have come down—and many people argue their disappearance makes sense because they were installed as much to diminish African Americans as to honor the soldiers and officers portrayed.

But must we remove Lincoln's statues, too? Or Frederick Douglass's? Douglass hasn't been immune to attempts to diminish his memory. In Rochester, New York, his home for many years, a statue of the great abolitionist was crudely torn from its base under the cover of night on July 5, 2020; after dragging it more than fifty feet, the marauders dumped it into a nearby gorge. At the time, Rochester mayor Lovely A. Warren commented, "To have any Frederick Douglass statue damaged in our city of course is disheartening." The location of the statue, near a stop on the Underground Railroad where Douglass and others led runaways to freedom, made the vandalism all the more shocking. "It's a travesty and devastation," said Mayor Warren.[1] In the years since, no perpetrators have been identified and thus no charges filed, but the statue was rapidly replaced, so Douglass's likeness once more gazes over Maplewood Park.

While most statues of both Lincoln and Douglass remain undisturbed, the contrasting fates of the Freedman's Monument and its duplicate do raise a question worth pondering: Why did the one in Washington remain in place while Boston's was removed?

Let's take a closer look.

# HISTORY AS DISPUTED TERRITORY

Discontent with Thomas Ball's sculpture began even before the replica arrived in Boston.

When Douglass dedicated the Freedman's Memorial in Washington, D.C., he praised Lincoln. He was also honest about his friend—as recounted earlier in this book, Lincoln needed many years to accept the equality of the Black man—but Douglass still held Lincoln in high esteem for his late-in-life actions. In the closing words of his speech, on April 14, 1876, Douglass reminded his Black brothers and sisters that Lincoln was their "great and glorious benefactor."[2]

On the other hand, Douglass had very real reservations about the statue. Standing in the shadow of the tall monument on a sunny spring afternoon, he spoke carefully, calling Ball's sculpture a "highly interesting object." To the perceptive listener then—and, given recent events, to us today—Douglass's disappointment is obvious. He may have kept his harsher thoughts to himself at the dedication out of respect for the many former soldiers and enslaved people who had donated hard-earned dollars to pay for the monument. But that didn't mean it had his whole-hearted approval.

Five days later, he went public with a more candid assessment. In a letter published in the *National Republican,* Douglass was explicit:

> Admirable as is the monument by Mr. Ball in Lincoln park, it does not, as it seems to me, tell the whole truth. . . . The mere

act of breaking the Negro's chains was the act of Abraham Lincoln, and is beautifully expressed in this monument. But the . . . negro here, though rising, is still on his knees and nude. What I want to see before I die is a monument representing the negro, not couchant on his knees like a four-footed animal, but erect on his feet like a man.[3]

In Douglass's view, the statue implied African Americans had done nothing to gain their freedom—and he knew firsthand how utterly wrong that was. For decades, men like Douglass had fought a gallant fight to end slavery. In the war alone, a total of 209,145 Black Americans had worn Union uniforms in pursuit of freedom.*

Another man bears mention here. If you drill down a bit, the backstory of the kneeling figure emerges. He wasn't a nameless, generic Black man, but one of the many who put his life on the line as a freedom fighter.

When the war began, Archer Alexander was still in bondage in Missouri, a border state that, though it had not seceded, remained part slave, part free. Alexander knew where his sympathies lay, so when he learned, in February 1863, that the wooden posts beneath a bridge Union soldiers would soon march across had been sawn through, he knew he had to get word to the Union army. He put his life in peril when, under the cover of night, he ran away from his slaveholder, walking a dangerous five-mile route to deliver his valuable intelligence. Afterward, he had no choice but to disappear into anonymity in busy St. Louis, where he lived under a new name until he became a free man with the fall of the Confederacy.[4]

---

* Today, the names of all those soldiers are listed on panels on the African American Civil War Memorial, a sculpture dedicated much later, in 1998, at Vermont and U Streets, in the nation's capital.

By any measure, Alexander was a hero, but we know little else about him except for one key fact: When Bell got the commission for the Freedman's Monument, the chairman of the group charged with erecting it gave the sculptor photographs of Archer Alexander to use as a model for his kneeling figure. Thus, the kneeling figure in the sculpture was "[in] both face and figure . . . as correct as that of Mr. Lincoln himself."[5]

Alexander almost certainly saved the lives of many Union soldiers, yet he appeared to be without agency, a naked and unidentified Black man at the feet of his White savior. His portrayal, which dismayed Douglass, led to the calls in our time for the removal of both the Boston and Washington statues.

## TO REMOVE OR NOT TO REMOVE?

In June 2020, the City of Boston launched a public review of the Emancipation Group in Park Square. The Boston Arts Commission listened to a total of five hours of live testimony. After the second hearing, artist Ekua Holmes, a vice chair of the commission, remarked,

> Public art is storytelling at the street level. As such, the imagery should strike the heart and engage the mind. What I heard today is that it hurts to look at this piece, and in the Boston landscape we should not have works that bring shame to any group of people.[6]

That same month, the Freedman's Memorial became the target of nightly protests. Washington, D.C., Mayor Muriel Bowser took the precaution of dispatching city workers, dressed in orange vests, to encircle the memorial with a metal fence and concrete barriers. At a press conference, she argued that the city should determine the fate of the monument, that she was unwilling to risk "hav[ing] a mob decide they want to pull it down."[7]

Back in Boston, a petition demanding the statue's removal landed with a thud at the Arts Commission offices; circulated by artist Tory Bullock, it bore the signatures of 12,000 people. A survey conducted by the city garnered 645 responses. More than 160 letters were read and considered, the overwhelming majority of which favored removal. Then on June 30, 2020, the Boston Arts Commission voted: It ruled—unanimously—that the statue had to go. The commission issued a statement that read, in part, "The decision for removal acknowledge[s] the statue's role in perpetuating harmful prejudices and obscuring the role of Black Americans in shaping the nation's freedoms."[8]

Meanwhile, the debate concerning the Freedman's Memorial in Washington continued. Evelyn Brooks Higginbotham, chair of the history department at Harvard University, weighed in. "Even though the image is problematic . . . African Americans themselves paid for this monument and it was their way of saying slavery had ended."[9] Eleanor Holmes Norton, D.C.'s congressional representative, countered that it should be relocated to a museum because "the statue fails to note in any way how enslaved African Americans pushed for their own emancipation."

Former congressman Jesse Jackson Jr. observed, "We can't tear down everything. . . . How much sense does that make?"[10]

Historian David Blight, whose biography of Frederick Douglass won the 2019 Pulitzer Prize for History, was blunt in a *Washington Post* op-ed: "Do not tear this monument down." Instead, he suggested commissioning a second statue portraying Douglass delivering his dedication speech, concluding, "So much new learning can take place by the presence of both past and present."[11]

A great-great-great grandson of Douglass also called for the memorial to stay, and at least for now, it appears, the Freedman's Memorial isn't going anywhere. Because its site, Lincoln Park, is federal land under the jurisdiction of the Department of Interior, an act of Congress might be required to remove it—the legality isn't crystal clear—and, in any case, the anger and outrage seem to have cooled. Only time will tell, of course, what the next chapter in the controversy will be, though most likely an announcement will be forthcoming in Boston of a new home for the Emancipation Group in a less in-your-face setting than Park Square.

I WROTE *The President and the Freedom Fighter* to start conversations about Lincoln and Douglass, two indispensable Americans. Over the last year, the book's publication has given me the privilege to greet thousands of people eager to read the book, and I am grateful for their enthusiasm. I am also encouraged that they are hungry to look honestly and open-mindedly at the past, to revisit and relive its lessons.

I find it puzzling that two identical statues met opposite fates but, in my opinion, tearing down statues is not the right answer. When such removals become okay, many more monuments will be ripped down without permission or damaged in the middle of the night to elude scrutiny, as was done with the statue of Douglass in Rochester.

Since when does our past have to be perfect? We're certainly not. As a society, how do we know where to go and how to progress if we don't know exactly where we have been? Above all, I believe deeply that the swirl of public conversations—about hatred, healing, and heritage, all elements in play here—will make us better able to think in an open-minded way about how to continue making the United States the best it can be.

—*Brian Kilmeade, May 2021*

# ACKNOWLEDGMENTS

So many people made valuable contributions to the idea, execution, and promotion of this book that it's hard to fit them all into just one section, but I will try. First off, a salute to Fox Nation's great executives Jason Klarman, John Finley, and Jennifer Hegseth for letting me crisscross the country telling great stories about America's history for the series *What Made America Great*. Doing so allows me to talk to the best and brightest who are keeping our past alive, which is how the idea for *The President and the Freedom Fighter* first took root. I wanted to tell a Civil War story that didn't further divide the nation while confronting the horrific era of slavery, and I hope you, the reader, feel we did just that. The fact that I will be able to talk about this story on Fox News and in a Fox Nation TV special is invaluable, and all in thanks to Executive Chairman and CEO of Fox Corporation Lachlan Murdoch, CEO of Fox News Suzanne Scott, and President and Executive Editor Jay Wallace. As far as the actual shooting, editing, and writing of the special goes, Fox Senior Producer Carrie Flatley produced every detail, neither too big nor too small, in every shoot. In fact, it was she who helped me come up with the concept of interweaving Douglass's and Lincoln's stories into a single narrative. Dan Cohen helped tell the story of two people in just one hour. Bud Knapp, Monica Mari, and Mary Drabich are also indispensable.

In helping to hone the concept of the project into a fast-moving, reader-friendly book, credit goes to the best publishing president in the country, Adrian Zackheim. He not only oversaw the entire book process, but he became so intrigued by this story that he visited the physical sites where it all took place over 150 years ago. Adrian's greatest move was to keep Bria Sandford on as Supreme Allied Commander and Editor of All Things Brian. Without her clear, steady hand, intelligence, and ability to spackle together my sometimes fractured thoughts, this book would not have happened, especially with the challenges brought on by this pandemic.

The team at Sentinel that promotes the book, makes sure it arrives at and is actually *seen* in bookstores, and lines up a twelve-week tour around my TV and radio schedule is simply first class. They are led by Tara Gilbride, Regina Andreoni in marketing, and lead publicist Marisol Salaman, who never leaves a loose end loose; who, to my knowledge, has never made a mistake; and who sets every book up for success. With new addition DeQuan Foster, they are even better! The book production team has always been fantastic and had to pull out all the stops to get this book printed in time coming out of a pandemic. Paul and Amanda Guest, who head up social media promotion, do a remarkable job of getting word out through very creative and resourceful digital campaigns.

Providing the fuel that ignites, supports, and sustains this book in the public's mind is the *Fox and Friends* team. They make every book launch feel like graduation, prom, and wedding combined! Led by Vice President Gavin Hadden, along with the steady hand of Lauren Petterson, the team allows me to tell these American stories on our show and let the most patriotic audience in TV know that there is yet another reason to believe that our nation is indeed great. Executive Producer Tami Radabaugh and senior producers Kelly Nish and Sara Sonnack always find a way to skillfully fold in book mentions and appearances in order to allow these passion projects to experience such success, and their support goes way beyond the broadcast. A. J. "Mr. Everything" Hall is always finding new ways to condense and edit the book into smaller chunks that let our audience know what they can expect when they dive into the chapters. Also infusing brilliance into those packages is Megan Macdonald. Jayleen Murray has been a big plus for all three *Fox and Friends* anchors, and whether it's through uploading videos or coordinating events, she astounds us with her energy, workload, and productivity. Of course, in front of the camera I am truly moved by the stalwart support of my co-anchors Ainsley Earhardt and Steve Doocy, along with Jillian Mele and Janice Dean. I will also never forget the weekend team: Pete Hegseth, Will Cain, Rachel Campos Duffy, and Lawrence Jones. The support of the other stellar Fox shows is so vital and appreciated. They always find room in their rundown for an appearance, which gives us a coveted opportunity to reach other Fox fans days, nights, and weekends.

No one does more with and for me on a daily basis than Coordinating Producer Alyson Mansfield. While her main job is executive producer of *The Brian Kilmeade Show* on Fox Radio, she also books all my TV and radio responsibilities with book tours, fill-in hosting requests, Fox Nation shoots, and live stage shows. Behind the scenes, but shining through on a daily basis, is Eric Albeen. His creativity astounds me and his adjustments for my many road shows, and for my pre-tapes so that I can go on the road early—an extra burden he never complains about (at least to me)—is truly appreciated. Pete Caterina's boundless energy and willingness to book and adjust for the tours have been invaluable to the success of the show and this project. Radio executives Reynard Erney, John Sylvester, and Maria Donovan have also been huge assets to the books, the show, and me. They always go out of their way to promote and support, along with Willie Sanchez, Tamara Karcev, and Dave Manning. I will always be in awe of the separate support of my radio affiliates who spread the word in their markets out of goodwill and respect. I don't take it for granted. One of the most special things about our book tours is getting to meet all the listeners and station staff in the separate markets and letting them know how much they matter to all of us—so thank you!

Finally, I'd like to thank UTA super-agents Adam Leibner, Jerry Silbowitz, and Byrd Leavell for making all of the moving parts work in sync on a daily basis, and Jay Sures for forming the best agency in the country and putting me on the roster.

# NOTES

## PREAMBLE

1. Declaration of Independence, original of rough draft, in *The Papers of Thomas Jefferson*, vol. 1, Julian P. Boyd, ed. (Princeton, NJ: Princeton University Press, 1950), pp. 243–47.
2. *Notes of Debates in the Federal Convention of 1787*. Madison did not publish that journal until decades later, however, by which time he had made many emendations and corrections. See especially Mary Sarah Bilder, *Madison's Hand: Revising the Constitutional Convention* (Cambridge, MA: Harvard University Press, 2015). https://slavery.princeton.edu/stories/james-madison.
3. "Address to the Republic," November 9, 1789.

## CHAPTER I: FROM THE BOTTOM UP

1. Henry Onstot, quoted in Wilson, *Honor's Voice* (1998), p. 53.
2. Caleb Carman to William H. Herndon, November 30, 1866.
3. Lamon, *The Life of Lincoln* (1872). The flatboat story also appears in *Herndon's Lincoln* (1890) and other early biographies.
4. Much of this section is based upon the notes Lincoln prepared for a campaign biography at the request of the *Chicago Press and Tribune*. The several thousand words he put on paper would be the closest he ever came to writing an autobiography. "Autobiography Written for John L. Scripps," June 1860. *Collected Works of Abraham Lincoln*, vol. 4 (1953), pp. 61–67.

5. Donald, *Lincoln* (1995), p. 28.
6. Lincoln, "Autobiography Written for John L. Scripps" (1860), p. 62.
7. Sarah Bush Lincoln interview with William H. Herndon, September 8, 1865.
8. John Hanks interview with William H. Herndon-1865–1866.
9. Wilson, *Honor's Voice* (1998), p. 57.
10. Lincoln, "Autobiography Written for John L. Scripps" (1860), p. 63.
11. Douglass, *Narrative of the Life of Frederick Douglass, an American Slave* (1845), p. 6.
12. Douglass, *My Bondage and My Freedom* (1855), p. 77.
13. Douglass, *My Bondage* (1855), p. 135.
14. Douglass, *My Bondage* (1855), p. 143.
15. Douglass, *Narrative* (1845), p. 32.
16. Douglass, *My Bondage* (1855), p. 147.
17. Douglass, *Narrative* (1845), p. 31.
18. Douglass, *My Bondage* (1855), p. 146.
19. Douglass, *My Bondage* (1855), p. 146.
20. Douglass, *Narrative* (1845), p. 38.
21. *The Liberator*, July 4, 1854.
22. Adams, *Memoirs* (1876), December 24, 1832.

## CHAPTER 2: A FIGHTING CHANCE

1. Herndon and Weik, *Herndon's Lincoln* (1890), p. 1.
2. Mentor Graham interview with William H. Herndon, October 10, 1866.
3. Henry McHenry to William H. Herndon, October 10, 1866.
4. Robert B. Rutledge to William H. Herndon, ca. November 1, 1866.
5. James Short to William H. Herndon, July 7, 1865.
6. Robert B. Rutledge to William H. Herndon, ca. November 1, 1866.
7. James Short to William H. Herndon, July 7, 1865.
8. Robert B. Rutledge to William H. Herndon, ca. November 1, 1866.
9. Henry McHenry, quoted in Wilson, *Honor's Voice* (1998), p. 31.
10. Nicolay and Hay, *Abraham Lincoln* (1890), vol. 1, p. 81.
11. Jason Duncan to William H. Herndon, late 1866, early 1867.
12. Mentor Graham interview with William H. Herndon, May 29, 1865.
13. AL, Communication to the People of Sangamon County, March 9, 1832.
14. AL, Communication to the People of Sangamon County, March 9, 1832.
15. Elizabeth Edwards interview with William H. Herndon, January 10, 1866.
16. Robert L. Wilson to William H. Herndon, February 10, 1866.
17. W. G. Greene to William H. Herndon, May 29, 1865.
18. James McGrady Rutledge, quoted in Wilson, *Honor's Voice* (1998), p. 103.
19. Herndon and Weik, *Herndon's Lincoln* (1890), p. 126.
20. Herndon and Weik, *Herndon's Lincoln* (1890), p. 162.
21. Lincoln, "Autobiography Written for John L. Scripps" (1860), p. 61.

22. Protest in the Illinois Legislature on Slavery, March 3, 1837.
23. Lincoln, "Autobiography Written for John L. Scripps" (1860), p. 65.
24. Herndon and Weik, *Herndon's Lincoln* (1890), p. 375.
25. Douglass, *My Bondage* (1855), p. 203.
26. Douglass, *Narrative* (1845), p. 66.
27. Douglass, *Narrative* (1845), p. 63.
28. Douglass, *Narrative* (1845), p. 65.
29. Douglass, *My Bondage* (1855), p. 228.
30. Douglass, *My Bondage* (1855), p. 246.
31. Douglass, *My Bondage* (1855), p. 246.
32. Douglass, *My Bondage* (1855), p. 275.
33. "Dialogue Between a Master and Slave," in Bingham, *The Columbian Orator* (1797).
34. Douglass, *My Bondage* (1855), p. 159.
35. Douglass, *My Bondage* (1855), p. 158.
36. Douglass, *My Bondage* (1855), p. 303.
37. Preston, *Young Frederick Douglass* (2018), p. 177.
38. Douglass, *My Bondage* (1855), p. 314.
39. Douglass, *Life and Times* (1881), p. 198.
40. Douglass, *Life and Times* (1881), p. 200.
41. Douglass, *Life and Times* (1881), p. 200.
42. Douglass, *My Bondage* (1855), p. 340.

CHAPTER 3: SELF-MADE MEN

1. Douglass, *Narrative* (1845), p. 116.
2. Douglass, *Life and Times* (1881), p. 210.
3. Douglass, *My Bondage* (1855), p. 356.
4. Douglass, *My Bondage* (1855), p. 357.
5. *The Liberator*, January 1, 1831.
6. *The Liberator*, August 20, 1841.
7. Douglass, *Narrative* (1845), p. 117.
8. Accounts of Douglass's speech vary considerably. See Garrison, preface to Douglass, *Narrative* (1835), pp. iv–vi; McFeely, *Frederick Douglass* (1990), pp. 86–90; Blight, *Frederick Douglass* (2018), pp. 98–100; Lampe, *Frederick Douglass* (1998), pp. 59–63; Douglass, *Narrative* (1845), p. 117.
9. Douglass, *My Bondage* (1855), p. 358.
10. May, *Some Reflections of Our Antislavery Conflict* (1869), p. 122.
11. Garrison, preface to Douglass, *Narrative* (1835), p. iv.
12. Garrison, preface to Douglass, *Narrative* (1835), p. v.
13. Garrison, preface to Douglass, *Narrative* (1845), p. vi.
14. AL, "The Perpetuation of Our Legal Institutions," January 27, 1838.

15. Helm, *The True Story of Mary, Wife of Lincoln* (Los Angeles, CA: McCall Publishing Co., 1928), p. 41.
16. Speed, *Reminiscences* (1896), p. 34.

CHAPTER 4: ON THE ROAD

1. Douglass, *My Bondage* (1855), p. 359.
2. *The Liberator,* October 15, 1841.
3. "Like two very brothers," Douglass would later write to White, "[we] were ready to dare—do, and even die for each other." FD to William White, July 30, 1846.
4. Several versions of the events at Pendleton appeared in contemporary slavery publications, including one in *The Liberator,* October 13, 1843. See also Douglass, *Life and Times* (1882), p. 234.
5. FD to Richard Josiah Hinton, quoted in Lampe, *Frederick Douglass* (1998), p. 189.
6. *The Liberator,* August 30, 1844.
7. Foner, *The Life and Writings of Frederick Douglass,* vol. 1 (1950), p. 60.
8. *Pennsylvania Freeman,* March 6, 1846.
9. Douglass, *Life and Times* (1881), p. 262.
10. McFeely, *Frederick Douglass* (1990), p. 144.
11. FD to Ellen Richardson, April 29, 1847.
12. *Sheffield Mercury,* September 11, 1846.
13. *The North Star,* December 22, 1848.
14. *The Liberator,* July 23, 1847.
15. Douglass, *Life and Times* (1881), p. 270.
16. *The North Star,* December 3, 1847.
17. Findley, *A. Lincoln,* (1979), p. 130.
18. Abraham Lincoln, speech in House of Representatives, January 12, 1848.
19. AL to Joshua F. Speed, August 24, 1855.
20. Abraham Lincoln, "Peoria Speech," Illinois, October 16, 1854.
21. AL to Joshua F. Speed, August 24, 1855.
22. Beveridge, *Abraham Lincoln: 1809–1858,* vol. 1 (1928), p. 482.
23. Lincoln, "Autobiography Written for John L. Scripps" (1860), p. 67.
24. Gerrit Smith to FD, December 8, 1847.
25. Gerrit Smith to Elizabeth Livingston Smith, July 16, 1815.
26. Gerrit Smith obituary, *New York Times,* December 29, 1874.
27. Foner, *The Life and Writings of Frederick Douglass,* vol. 2 (1950), p. 54.

CHAPTER 5: WHERE THERE IS SMOKE

1. Harriet Beecher Stowe to FD, July 9, 1851.
2. Douglass, "Resistance to Blood-Houndism," January 8, 1851.
3. Hochman, "'Uncle Tom's Cabin' in the 'National Era'" (2004), p. 144.

4. Hedrick, *Harriet Beecher Stowe: A Life* (1994), p. 235.
5. Harriet Beecher Stowe to William Lloyd Garrison, December 19, 1853.
6. Douglass, *Life and Times* (1881), p. 289.
7. In 1860, he recalled (in the third person) that in the early 1850s "his profession had almost superseded the thought of politics in his mind." Lincoln, "Autobiography Written for John L. Scripps" (1860), p. 67.
8. Lincoln, "Notes for a Law Lecture" (ca. 1850).
9. Unless otherwise noted, Lincoln's words in this passage are drawn from his "Peoria Speech," October 16, 1854.
10. See Burlingame, *The Inner World of Abraham Lincoln* (1994), p. 27. Chapter 2, "'I Used to Be a Slave'" offers a cogent look at Lincoln's thinking regarding slavery.
11. Browne, *Abraham Lincoln and the Men of His Time*, vol. 1 (1907), p. 285.
12. Beveridge, *Abraham Lincoln: 1809–1858*, vol. 3 (1928), p. 238.
13. William H. Pierce, quoted in Lehrman, *Lincoln at Peoria* (2008), p. 57.
14. Horace White, "Address before Illinois State Historical Society," January 1908.
15. Here and after, Charles Sumner, "The Crimes Against Slavery," May 19–20, 1856.
16. Here and after, see "Alleged Assault Upon Senator Sumner." Senate Report no. 182, 34th Congress, Session 1, June 2, 1856; and Senate Report no. 191, 34th Congress, Session 1, May 28, 1856. See especially the testimony of Sumner and Brooks. See also Donald, *Charles Sumner and the Coming of the Civil War* (1960), pp. 278–311.
17. Donald, *Charles Sumner and the Coming of the Civil War* (1960), p. 301.
18. Donald, *Charles Sumner and the Coming of the Civil War* (1960), p. 305.
19. Salmon Brown, quoted in Reynolds, *John Brown, Abolitionist* (2005), p. 158.

## CHAPTER 6: A SUBTERRANEAN PASSWAY

1. Douglass, *Life and Times* (1881), p. 278.
2. Douglass, *Life and Times* (1881), p. 280.
3. *The North Star*, February 18, 1848.
4. John Brown to Henry L. Stearns, July 15, 1857.
5. Lyman Epps Jr., quoted in Reynolds, *John Brown, Abolitionist* (2005), p. 127.
6. *Dred Scott v. John F. A. Sandford*, March 6, 1857.
7. Douglass, *Life and Times* (1881), pp. 323–24.
8. Douglass, *Life and Times* (1881), p. 325.
9. A. J. Philips to W. P. Smith, October 17, 1859.
10. *New-York Times*, October 18, 1859.
11. Reynolds, *John Brown, Abolitionist* (2005), p. 320.
12. Horwitz, *Midnight Rising* (2011), p. 176.
13. Villard, *John Brown, 1800–1859* (1909), p. 453.
14. Alexander R. Boteler, "Recollections of the John Brown Raid," *Century Magazine*, July 1883, p. 409.

15. Israel Green, quoted in Horwitz, *Midnight Rising* (2011), p. 180.
16. Brown interview with Mason, Vallandingham, and others, conducted on October 18, 1859, published in the *New York Herald*, October 21, 1859.
17. Douglass, *Life and Times* (1881), p. 311.
18. *Frederick Douglass' Paper*, November 11, 1859.
19. *Frederick Douglass' Paper*, December 16, 1859.
20. Henry David Thoreau, "A Plea for Captain John Brown," October 30, 1859.
21. In his poem "The Portent," Herman Melville wrote, "[T]he streaming bear is shown / (Weird John Brown), / The Meteor of the War." *Battle-Pieces and Aspects of the Civil War*, 1866.

CHAPTER 7: THE DIVIDED HOUSE

1. James A. Briggs to AL, October 12, 1859. The telegram arrived while Lincoln was out of town; he read it on his return on October 15.
2. AL, speech to Republican State Convention, Springfield, IL, June 16, 1856.
3. Donald, *Lincoln* (1995), p. 209.
4. Lincoln-Douglas debate, Springfield, Illinois, July 17, 1858.
5. Lincoln-Douglas debate, Alton, Illinois, October 15, 1858.
6. William Henry Seward, March 11, 1850.
7. *American Journal of Photography*, cited in Holzer, *Lincoln at Cooper Union* (2004), p. 88.
8. Richard C. McCormick, "Lincoln's Visit to New York in 1860," *New-York Post*, May 3, 1865. Reprinted in Wilson, ed. *Intimate Memories* (1945), pp. 250–55.
9. Meredith, *Mr. Lincoln's Camera Man: Mathew B. Brady* (1974), p. 57.
10. Meredith, *Mr. Lincoln's Camera Man: Mathew B. Brady* (1974), p. 59.
11. Ward Lamon's description, from his *Life of Lincoln* (1872, 2012), p. 384.
12. Meredith, *Mr. Lincoln's Camera Man: Mathew B. Brady* (1974), p. 59.
13. Holzer, *Lincoln at Cooper Union* (2004), p. 107.
14. McCormick, "Lincoln's Visit to New York in 1860," *New-York Post*, May 3, 1865.
15. AL, Cooper Union speech, February 27, 1860.
16. AL, Cooper Union speech, February 27, 1860.
17. McCormick, "Lincoln's Visit to New York in 1860," *New-York Post*, May 3, 1865.
18. AL to Lyman Trumbull, April 29, 1860.
19. FD, "The Trials and Triumphs of Self-Made Men," Halifax, England, January 4, 1860.
20. Kendrick and Kendrick, *Douglas and Lincoln* (2008), p. 46; FD, "To My British Anti-Slavery Friends," *Douglass' Monthly*, June 1860.
21. Annie Douglass to FD, December 7, 1859.
22. Douglass, *Life and Times* (1881), p. 328.
23. FD, "To My British Anti-Slavery Friends," *Douglass' Monthly*, June 1860.
24. Kendrick and Kendrick, *Douglas and Lincoln* (2008), p. 46.

25. Temple, "Lincoln's Fence Rails" (1954), p. 22.
26. Temple, "Lincoln's Fence Rails" (1954), p. 26.
27. John Farnsworth to Elihu B. Washburne, May 18, 1860.
28. Donald, *Lincoln* (1995), p. 251.

## CHAPTER 8: THE ELECTION OF 1860

1. AL to Harvey G. Eastman, April 7, 1860.
2. *Illinois State Journal*, May 7, 1860.
3. Donald, *Lincoln* (1995), p. 254.
4. Quote in Donald, *Lincoln* (1995), p. 256.
5. AL to Samuel Haycraft, November 10, 1860.
6. AL to Lyman Trumbull, December 10, 1860.
7. *Douglass' Monthly*, June 1860.
8. FD to Gerrit Smith, July 2, 1860.
9. *Douglass' Monthly*, September 1860.
10. *Douglass' Monthly*, June 1860.
11. Headnote to "Speech on John Brown" in Foner and Taylor, eds. *Frederick Douglass, Selected Speeches and Writings* (1999), p. 417.
12. Tremont Temple Resolution, *Harper's Weekly*, December 15, 1860.
13. Tremont Temple Resolution, *Harper's Weekly*, December 15, 1860.
14. Kendrick and Kendrick, *Douglas and Lincoln* (2008), pp. 66–67.

## CHAPTER 9: MR. LINCOLN'S WAR

1. Lamon, *Life of Lincoln* (1872, 2012), p. 306. See also Searcher, *Lincoln's Journey to Greatness* (1960).
2. AL address at Springfield, February 11, 1861.
3. AL to Alexander Stephens, December 22, 1861.
4. *Douglass' Monthly*, March 1861.
5. Rutherford B. Hayes to Laura Platt, February 13, 1861.
6. AL, speech at Cincinnati, February 12, 1861.
7. AL, speech at Cleveland, February 15, 1861.
8. Grace Bedell to AL, October 15, 1860; AL to Grace Bedell, October 19, 1861.
9. Searcher, *Lincoln's Journey to Greatness* (1960), p. 116.
10. Here and after, unless otherwise specified, the account of the Baltimore conspiracy is Lincoln's own version, as recounted by Benson Lossing in his book *The Pictorial History of the Civil War*, vol. 1 (1868), pp. 279–82. See also Waller, *Lincoln's Spies* (2019), pp. 4–7.
11. AL, speech at Philadelphia, February 22, 1861.
12. *Harper's Weekly*, March 9, 1861.
13. *Douglass' Monthly*, April 1861.

14. AL, First Inaugural Address, March 4, 1861.
15. *Douglass' Monthly,* April 1861.
16. *Douglass' Monthly,* May 1861.
17. For a more detailed and highly readable account of the fall of Fort Sumter, see McPherson, *Battle Cry of Freedom* (1988), pp. 264–75.
18. Detzer, *Allegiance* (2001), p. 264.
19. Quoted in McPherson, *Battle Cry of Freedom* (1989), p. 274.
20. John Ellis, quoted in Nicolay and Hay, *Abraham Lincoln* (1890), vol. 4, p. 90.
21. *Douglass' Monthly*, May 1861.
22. *Douglass' Monthly*, May 1861.
23. FD, Rochester, New York, address, May 5, 1861.
24. *Douglass' Monthly*, May 1861.
25. *Douglass' Monthly*, May 1861.
26. Bland, *Life of Benjamin F. Butler* (1879), pp. 51–52.
27. *Douglass' Monthly*, September 1861.
28. Quoted in Robertson, James Jr., *Stonewall Jackson* (New York: Simon and Schuster Macmillan, 1997), p. 263.
29. Perret, *Lincoln's War* (2004), p. 67.

### CHAPTER 10: WAR IN THE WEST

1. Denton, *Passion and Principle* (2007), p. 293.
2. Frémont, *Memoirs of My Life* (2001), pp. 221–22.
3. Rebecca Harding Davis, quoted in Denton, *Passion and Principle* (2007), p. 309.
4. Frémont's Declaration, August 30, 1861.
5. *New York Evening Post,* September 1861.
6. Stowe, *The Independent*, September 21, 1861.
7. *Douglass' Monthly*, October 1861.
8. AL to John Frémont, September 2, 1861.
9. John Frémont to AL, September 8, 1861.
10. Hay, *Inside Lincoln's White House* (1997), p. 123.
11. *Douglass' Monthly*, October 1861.
12. *Douglass' Monthly*, September 1861.
13. Handbill reprinted in *Douglass' Monthly*, December 1861.

### CHAPTER 11: TO PROCLAIM OR NOT TO PROCLAIM

1. Donald, *Lincoln* (1995), p. 336.
2. Foner, *The Life and Writings of Frederick Douglass*, vol. 3 (1952), p. 20.
3. Nevins, *Diary of the Civil War: George Templeton Strong* (1952), p. 302.
4. Sumner, "The Barbarism of Slavery," June 4, 1860.
5. FD to Charles Sumner, April 8, 1862.

6. Douglass, "The War and How to End It," March 25, 1862.
7. Donald, *Charles Sumner and the Coming of the Civil War* (1960), p. 383.
8. Poore, "Lincoln and the Newspaper Correspondents," in Rice, *Reminiscences of Abraham Lincoln by Distinguished Men of His Time* (1888), p. 333.
9. Mary Lincoln to Mrs. Orne, November 28, 1869.
10. Randall, *Mary Lincoln* (1953), p. 356.
11. Donald, *Charles Sumner and the Coming of the Civil War* (1960), p. 388.
12. Mary Lincoln to Mrs. Orne, November 28, 1869.
13. Charles Sumner, letter, *The Independent*, June 19, 1862.
14. Nevins, *The War for the Union* (1960), p. 5.
15. Douglass, "What to the Slave Is the Fourth of July," Rochester, New York, July 4, 1852.
16. *The Liberator*, July 7, 1854.
17. AL to Orville Hickman Browning, September 22, 1861.
18. Starr, *Bohemian Brigade* (1954), p. 125; Donald, *Charles Sumner and the Rights of Man* (1970), p. 60. Italics added.
19. Here and after, the story comes from painter Francis B. Carpenter; see Fehrenbacher and Fehrenbacher, *Recollected Words of Abraham Lincoln* (1996), pp. 79–80.
20. Lyman Trumbull quoted in Foner, *Fiery Trial* (2010), p. 222.
21. AL, "Address on Colonization to a Deputation of Negroes," August 14, 1862.
22. *Douglass' Monthly*, September 1862.
23. FD to Montgomery Blair, September 16, 1862.
24. AL to Horace Greeley, August 22, 1862.
25. See Kendrick and Kendrick, *Douglas and Lincoln* (2008), p. 111; FD to Gerrit Smith, September 8, 1862.
26. George S. Boutwell to J. G. Holland, June 10, 1865.
27. AL to George McClellan, September 15, 1862.
28. Edwards Pierrepont, quoted in Fehrenbacher and Fehrenbacher, *Recollected Words of Abraham Lincoln* (1996), p. 360.
29. *Douglass' Monthly*, October 1862.
30. Douglass, *Life and Times* (1881), p. 356.
31. Stowe and Stowe, *Harriet Beecher Stowe: The Story of Her Life* (1911), p. 203. See also Quarles, *Lincoln and the Negro* (1962), p. 134.
32. Guelzo, *Lincoln's Emancipation Proclamation* (2004), pp. 182–83.
33. *The Liberator*, January 16, 1863; and Douglass, *Life and Times* (1881), pp. 358–60.

## CHAPTER 12: TURNING POINT AT GETTYSBURG

1. Emancipation Proclamation, January 1, 1863.
2. Emilio, *History of the Fifty-Fourth Regiment* (1894), p. 12. See also Charles Heller, *Portrait of an Abolitionist: A Biography of George Luther Stearns* (Westport, CT: Greenwood Press, 1996).

3. *Douglass' Monthly*, May 1861.
4. Charles Sumner to Carl Schurz, July 5, 1862.
5. Edwin Stanton, quoted in Foner, *Fiery Trial* (2010), p. 230.
6. *Douglass' Monthly*, January 1863.
7. *Douglass' Monthly*, March 1863.
8. Douglass, "Men of Color, to Arms," March 21, 1863.
9. James Shepherd Pike to William H. Seward, December 31, 1862.
10. *Die Presse*, October 12, 1862.
11. AL to Andrew Johnson, March 26, 1863.
12. William Henry Wadsworth to S. L. M. Barlow, December 18, 1863.
13. *Chicago Tribune*, June 1, 1863.
14. Brooks, *Washington in the Time of Lincoln* (1896), pp. 47–58.
15. Nathaniel Banks, quoted in Cornish, *The Sable Arm* (1956, 1987), p. 143.
16. Charles Dana quoted in *War of the Rebellion: The Official Records of the Union and Confederate Armies*. Series 1, vol. 24, pt. 1, War Department, p. 106.
17. George Meade to Henry Halleck, July 2, 1863.
18. Rusling, *Men and Things I Saw in Civil War Days* (1894), p. 15.
19. AL to Ulysses S. Grant, August 9, 1863.
20. *Douglass' Monthly*, August 1863.
21. Douglass, *Life and Times* (1881), p. 362.
22. Lewis Douglass to Helen Amelia Loguen, July 20, 1863.
23. FD to George Stearns, August 1, 1863.
24. FD to George Stearns, August 12, 1863.

### CHAPTER 13: A BLACK VISITOR TO THE WHITE HOUSE

1. Ottilie Assing, quoted in Blight, *Frederick Douglass* (2018), p. 292.
2. FD recounted this first visit to Lincoln almost immediately in a letter to George Stearns, dated August 12, 1863. He did so repeatedly over the years, including in a Philadelphia speech, delivered on December 4, 1863; in a Brooklyn, New York, speech delivered near the end of his life, on February 13, 1893; and in *Life and Times* (1881). The quotations here are drawn from those sources unless otherwise noted.
3. David Wills to Abraham Lincoln, November 2, 1863.
4. David Wills to Andrew Curtin, July 24, 1863.
5. *New-York Tribune*, July 8, 1863.
6. Brooks, *Washington in the Time of Lincoln* (1896), pp. 252–53.
7. AL, The Gettysburg Address, November 19, 1863.

### CHAPTER 14: THE MISSION OF THE WAR

1. Douglass, *Life and Times* (1881), pp. 354–55.
2. FD to anonymous, February 17, 1864.

3. Douglass, *Life and Times* (1881), p. 358.
4. Here and after: FD, "The Mission of War," Cooper Union, January 13, 1864. Italics added.
5. Blassingame and McKivigan, eds. *The Frederick Douglass Papers*, vol. 4 (1991), p. 3.
6. *New York Times*, January 14, 1864.
7. The details of Lincoln's visit to City Point here and after are based on the account in Lieutenant Colonel Horace Porter's *Campaigning with Grant* (1907), pp. 216ff.
8. Horace Porter in *Campaigning with Grant* (1907), p. 281.
9. Welles, *Diary of Gideon Welles* (1911), p. 58.
10. AL to Albert G. Hodges, April 4, 1864.
11. AL to Ulysses S. Grant, August 9, 1863.
12. Ulysses S. Grant to AL, August 23, 1863; Bunting, *Ulysses S. Grant* (2004), p. 49.
13. Ulysses Grant to H. W. Halleck, August 1, 1864.
14. Eaton, *Grant, Lincoln, and the Freedman* (1907), pp. 167–75.
15. Diary of Joseph T. Mills, in *Collected Works of Abraham Lincoln*, vol. 7 (1953), p. 508.
16. Here and after, the several key sources for the details of Douglass and Lincoln's August 19 meeting are Douglass's own writings, including his letter to Theodore Tilton, October 15, 1874; *Life and Times* (1881), pp. 363–365; and "Abraham Lincoln, the Great Man of Our Century," an address given in Brooklyn, New York, on February 13, 1893.
17. Douglass, *Life and Times* (1881), p. 364.
18. FD to AL, August 29, 1864.
19. William T. Sherman to Will Halleck, September 3, 1864.
20. Here and after, quotations are from FD, "A Friendly Word to Maryland," November 17, 1864.
21. *Cambridge Intelligencer*, undated clipping, cited in *Frederick Douglass Papers*, vol. 4 (1991), p. 38.

### CHAPTER 15: MY FRIEND DOUGLASS

1. William T. Sherman to AL, December 22, 1864. Because the message had to be carried by ship back to Union territory, Lincoln received it on Christmas Day.
2. Hugh Highland Grant, quoted in Quarles, *Lincoln and the Negro* (1962), p. 223.
3. Brooks, *Washington in the Time of Lincoln* (1896), p. 207.
4. Charles R. Douglass to FD, February 9, 1865.
5. AL, February 1, 1865.
6. The poetic words are those of attendee Noah Brooks, Lincoln's friend and sometime confidant.
7. Douglass, "Lincoln and the Colored Troops" (1888), p. 320.
8. Brooks, *Washington in the Time of Lincoln* (1896), p. 238.

9. Douglass recounted two versions of this moment: In one it is Lincoln who indicates Douglass; in another it is Chief Justice Salmon Chase. Douglass, "Lincoln and the Colored Troops" (1888), p. 321; Douglass, *Life and Times* (1881), p. 370.

10. Here and after, Lincoln's words are drawn from his Second Inaugural Speech, March 4, 1865.

11. This vignette was recounted by Douglass in his *Life and Times* (1881), pp. 371ff, and in his address, delivered in Brooklyn, "Abraham Lincoln, the Great Man of Our Century," on February 13, 1893. The diaries of Henry Clay Warmoth, a young Union officer who overheard their conversation, corroborate the Douglass-Lincoln encounter.

12. Warmoth, *The Diary of Henry Clay Warmoth* (1960), p. 126.

13. *New York World,* March 6, 1865; *New-York Tribune*, March 5, 1865; and the *Daily Ohio Statesman*, March 6, 1865.

14. AL to Thurlow Weed, quoted in Donald, *Lincoln* (1995), p. 568.

15. Carpenter, *Six Months at the White House* (1866), p. 234.


CHAPTER 16: APRIL IS THE CRUELEST MONTH

1. Porter, *Incidents and Anecdotes of the Civil War* (1885), p. 294.

2. Sources for Lincoln's April 4, 1865, visit to Richmond include Bruce, *The Capture and Occupation of Richmond* (1927), pp. 31–33; Patrick, *The Fall of Richmond* (1960), pp. 127–33; and Porter, *Incidents and Anecdotes of the Civil War* (1885), pp. 294–302. Porter's recollections seem, at times, a bit too richly remembered to be entirely accurate.

3. Porter, *Incidents and Anecdotes of the Civil War* (1885), p. 295.

4. FD, "The Fall of Richmond," April 4, 1865.

5. Booth, *Right or Wrong* (2001), p. 169.

6. Achorn, *Every Drop of Blood* (2020), pp. 113, 117.

7. James F. Moulton to his uncle, April 17, 1865.

8. Nicolay and Hay, *Abraham Lincoln*, vol. 10 (1890), pp. 285–86.

9. Donald, *Lincoln* (1995), p. 593.

10. Oates, *With Malice Toward None* (1977), p. 468.

11. Nicolay and Hay, "The Fourteenth of April," *Century Magazine*, vol. 40 (January 1890), p. 432.

12. Of the many, many versions of the assassination story, one of the most complete is Terry Alford's *Fortune's Fool* (2015).

13. Gideon Welles, quoted in Foner, *Fiery Trial* (2010), p. 332.

14. Nicolay and Hay, *Abraham Lincoln*, vol. 10 (1890), p. 302.

15. Douglass, *Life and Times* (1881), pp. 378–79.

16. Here and after, FD, "Our Martyred President," April 15, 1865.

17. Douglass, *Life and Times* (1881), p. 379.

## EPILOGUE: A BONE-HANDLED CANE

1. Keckley, *Behind the Scenes* (1868), p. 191.
2. *Rochester Democrat and Chronicle*, April 28, 1865.
3. Nicolay and Hay, *Abraham Lincoln*, vol. 10 (1890), p. 323.
4. FD, "Lincoln and the Colored Troops" (1909), p. 325.
5. FD to Mrs. Abraham Lincoln, August 17, 1865.
6. As reported in the *New York World*; see Blight, *Frederick Douglass* (2018), pp. 473–75.
7. Douglass, *Life and Times* (1881), p. 380.
8. *New National Era*, June 6 and 17, 1872.
9. Donald, *Charles Sumner and the Rights of Man* (1970), pp. 586–87.
10. The stories of Charlotte Scott, the Freedman's Memorial, and the events of April 14, 1876, have been recounted often. Minor details differ from one version to another, but the most reliable sources include Quarles, *Lincoln and the Negro* (1962), pp. 3–14; Stauffer, *Giants* (2008), pp. 302–6; and Blight, *Frederick Douglass* (2018), pp. 1–9.
11. Here and after, Douglass, "Oration in Memory of Abraham Lincoln," April 14, 1876.
12. Douglass, *Life and Times* (1881), p. 380.
13. Office of Record of Deeds, District of Columbia, folio 77.
14. Quarles, *Frederick Douglass* (1948), pp. 336, 339.
15. FD to anonymous, n.d. *The Life and Writings of Frederick Douglass*, vol. 4 (1955), p. 115.
16. Douglass, *Life and Times* (1881), p. 378.
17. FD, "In Law Free: In fact, A Slave," April 16, 1888.
18. Foner and Taylor, eds. *Frederick Douglass, Selected Speeches and Writings* (1999), p. xiii.
19. Quarles's *Frederick Douglass* (Washington, D.C.: Associated Publishers) appeared in 1948.
20. Lerone Bennett Jr., "Was Lincoln a White Supremacist?," *Ebony*, February 1968.
21. For a detailed dissection of secessionist conventions, see Charles B. Dew, *Apostles of Disunion* (Charlottesville: University Press of Virginia, 2001).
22. James Gillespie Blaine, *Twenty Years of Congress: From Lincoln to Garfield*, vol. 2. (Norwich, CT: Henry Bill, 1884), p. 49.
23. AL to A. G. Hodges, April 4, 1864.

## AFTERWORD: THE MAINTENANCE OF MEMORY

1. Michael Gold, "Who Tore Down This Frederick Douglass Statue?" *New York Times*, July 7, 2020, https://www.nytimes.com/2020/07/07/nyregion/frederick-douglass-statue-rochester.html.

2. Douglass, "Oration in Memory of Abraham Lincoln" (speech, Washington, D.C., April 14, 1876).

3. FD to editor of the *National Republican*, April 19, 1876.

4. Christopher R. Eliot, "The Lincoln Emancipation Statue," *Journal of Negro History* 29, no. 4 (October 1944), p. 472.

5. Eliot, "The Lincoln Emancipation Statue," p. 475.

6. "Emancipation Group," Boston.gov, July 13, 2020, https://www.boston.gov/departments/arts-and-culture/emancipation-group.

7. Hannah Natanson, Joe Heim, Michael E. Miller, and Peter Jamison, "Protesters Denounce Abraham Lincoln Statue in D.C., Urge Removal of Emancipation Memorial," *Washington Post,* June 26, 2020, https://www.washingtonpost.com/local/protesters-denounce-abraham-lincoln-statue-in-dc-urge-removal-of-emancipation-memorial/2020/06/25/02646910-b704-11ea-a510-55bf26485c93_story.

8. "Emancipation Group."

9. "Protesters Denounce Abraham Lincoln Statue in D.C., Urge Removal of Emancipation Memorial."

10. James Hohmann, "The Daily 202: Why a Freed Slave Is Kneeling in the Lincoln Statue in D.C. That Some Are Trying to Remove," *Washington Post,* July 2, 2020, https://www.washingtonpost.com/news/powerpost/paloma/daily-202/2020/07/01/daily-202-why-a-freed-slave-is-kneeling-in-the-lincoln-statue-in-d-c-that-some-are-trying-to-remove/5efc1671602ff10807192d1b.

11. David W. Blight, "Yes, the Freedmen's Memorial Uses Racist Imagery. But Don't Tear It Down," *Washington Post*, June 25, 2020, https://www.washingtonpost.com/opinions/2020/06/25/yes-freedmens-memorial-uses-racist-imagery-dont-tear-it-down.

# FOR FURTHER READING

Achorn, Edward. *Every Drop of Blood*. New York: Grove-Atlantic, 2020.

Adams, John Quincy. *Memoirs of John Quincy Adams: His Diary from 1795–1848*. Charles Francis Adams, ed. Philadelphia, PA: J. B. Lippincott and Co., 1876.

Alford, Terry. *Fortune's Fool: The Life of John Wilkes Booth*. New York: Oxford University Press, 2015.

Barnes, L. Diane. *Frederick Douglass: A Life in Documents*. Charlottesville: University of Virginia Press, 2013.

Basler, Roy P. "Did President Lincoln Give the Smallpox to William Johnson?" *Huntington Library Quarterly* 35, no. 3 (May 1972), pp. 279–84.

Berlin, Ira. *The Long Emancipation: The Demise of Slavery in the United States*. Cambridge, MA: Harvard University Press, 2015.

Beveridge, Albert J. *Abraham Lincoln: 1809–1858*. Boston: Houghton Mifflin Co., 1928.

Bingham, Caleb, ed. *The Columbian Orator*. Boston: Manning and Loring, 1797.

Bland, T. A. *Life of Benjamin F. Butler*. Boston: Lee and Shepard, 1879.

Blassingame, John W., and John McKivigan, eds. *The Frederick Douglass Papers*. 5 vols. New Haven: Yale University Press, 1979, 1982, 1985, 1991, 1992.

Blight, David. *Frederick Douglass' Civil War*. Baton Rouge: Louisiana State University Press, 1989.

———. *Frederick Douglass: Prophet of Freedom*. New York: Simon and Schuster, 2018.

Booth, John Wilkes. *Right or Wrong, God Judge Me: The Writing of John Wilkes Booth*. Urbana: University of Illinois Press, 2001.

Boteler, Alexander R. "Recollections of the John Brown Raid," *Century Magazine*, July 1883, pp. 399–411.

Breiseth, Christopher N. "Lincoln and Douglass: Another Debate." *Journal of the Illinois Historical Society* 68, no. 1 (February 1975), pp. 9–26.

Brooks, Noah. *Washington in the Time of Lincoln.* New York: The Century Company, 1896.

Browne, Robert H. *Lincoln and the Men of His Time.* 2 vols. Chicago: Blakely-Oswald Printing Co., 1907.

Bruce, George A. *The Capture and Occupation of Richmond.* Richmond, VA: 1927.

Bunting, Josiah, III. *Ulysses S. Grant.* New York: Times Books, 2004.

Burlingame, Michael. *The Inner World of Abraham Lincoln.* Urbana: University of Illinois Press, 1994.

Carpenter, Francis. *Six Months at the White House: The Story of a Picture.* New York: Hurd and Houghton, 1866.

Cornish, Dudley Taylor. *The Sable Arm: Black Troops in the Union Army, 1861–1865.* Lawrence: University of Kansas Press, 1987.

Davis, Cullom, et al., eds. *The Public and the Private Lincoln: Contemporary Perspectives.* Carbondale: Southern Illinois University Press, 1979.

Denton, Sally. *Passion and Principle: John and Jessie Frémont, the Couple Whose Power, Politics, and Love Shaped Nineteenth-Century America.* New York: Bloomsbury, 2007.

Detzer, David. *Allegiance: Fort Sumter, Charleston, and the Beginning of the Civil War.* New York: Harcourt, 2001.

Dew, Charles B. *Apostles of Disunion: Southern Secession Commissioners and the Causes of the Civil War.* Charlottesville: University of Virginia Press, 2001.

Donald, David [Herbert]. *Charles Sumner and the Coming of the Civil War.* New York: Alfred A. Knopf, 1960.

———. *Charles Sumner and the Rights of Man.* New York: Alfred A. Knopf, 1970.

Donald, David Herbert. *Lincoln.* New York: Simon and Schuster, 1995.

Douglass, Frederick. *Douglass' Monthly.* Available online at the Smithsonian Institution. See https://transcription.si.edu/project/13034.

———. *Narrative of the Life of Frederick Douglass, an American Slave.* Boston: Anti-Slavery Office, 1845.

———. *My Bondage and My Freedom.* New York: Miller, Orton and Mulligan, 1855.

———. *Life and Times of Frederick Douglass, Written by Himself, His Early Life as a Slave, His Escape from Bondage, and His Complete History to the Present Time.* Hartford, CT: Park Publishing Co., 1881.

———. "Lincoln and the Colored Troops" in *Reminiscences of Abraham Lincoln by Distinguished Men of His Time*, Allen Thorndike Rice, ed. New York: North American Review, 1888, pp. 315–25.

———. *The Frederick Douglass Papers.* Philip W. Foner, ed. 3 vols. New York: International Publishers, 1950, 1952.

———. *The Frederick Douglass Papers.* Blassingame, John W., and John McKivigan, eds. 5 vols. New Haven: Yale University Press, 1979, 1982, 1985, 1991, 1992.

————. *Autobiographies.* Henry Louis Gates Jr., ed. New York: Library of America, 1994.

Eaton, John. *Grant, Lincoln, and the Freedman: Reminiscences of the Civil War.* New York: Longmans, Green, and Company, 1907.

Emilio, Luis Fenolossa. *History of the Fifty-Fourth Regiment of Massachusetts Volunteer Infantry, 1862–1865.* Boston: Boston Book Company, 1894.

Fehrenbacher, Don E., and Virginia Fehrenbacher, eds. *Recollected Words of Abraham Lincoln.* Stanford, CA: Stanford University Press, 1996.

Findley, Paul. *A. Lincoln: The Crucible of Congress.* New York: Crown Publishers, 1979.

Foner, Eric. *The Fiery Trial: Abraham Lincoln and American Slavery.* New York: W. W. Norton and Co., 2010.

Foner, Philip, ed. *The Life and Writings of Frederick Douglass.* 3 vols. New York: International Publishers, 1950, 1952.

Foner, Philip S[heldon]. *Frederick Douglass: A Biography.* New York: Citadel Press, 1969.

Foner, Philip, and Yuval Taylor, eds. *Frederick Douglass, Selected Speeches and Writings.* Chicago: Lawrence Hill Books, 1999.

Freeman, Andrew A. *Abraham Lincoln Comes to New York.* New York: Coward, McCann, 1960.

Frémont, Jessie Benton. *Memoirs of My Life.* New York: Cooper Square Press, 2001.

Guelzo, Allen C. *Lincoln's Emancipation Proclamation: The End of Slavery in America.* Simon and Schuster, 2004.

Hay, John. *Inside Lincoln's White House: The Complete Civil War Diary of John Hay.* Michael Burlingame and John R. Turner Ettlinger, eds. Carbondale: South Illinois University Press, 1997.

Herndon, William H., and Jesse William Weik. *Herndon's Lincoln: The True Story of a Great Life.* Chicago: Bedford-Clarke, 1890.

Hochman, Barbara. "'Uncle Tom's Cabin' in the 'National Era.'" *Book History,* 2004, pp. 143–69.

Holzer, Harold. *Lincoln at Cooper Union: The Speech That Made Abraham Lincoln President.* New York: Simon and Schuster, 2004.

Horwitz, Tony. *Midnight Rising: John Brown and the Raid That Sparked the Civil War.* New York: Henry Holt and Company, 2011.

Huggins, Nathan Irvin. *Slave and Citizen: The Life of Frederick Douglass.* Boston: Little, Brown and Co., 1980.

Keckley, Elizabeth. *Behind the Scenes, or, Thirty Years a Slave, and Four Years at the White House.* New York: G. W. Carleton, 1868.

Kendrick, Paul, and Stephen Kendrick. *Douglas and Lincoln: How a Revolutionary Black Leader and a Reluctant Liberator Struggled to End Slavery and Save the Union.* New York: Walker, 2008.

Lamon, Ward H. *The Life of Lincoln, from His Birth to Inauguration as President.* Boston: James R. Osgood and Co., 1872.

Lampe, Gregory P. *Frederick Douglass: Freedom's Voice: 1818–1845.* East Lansing: Michigan State University Press, 1998.

Lehrman, Lewis F. *Lincoln at Peoria: The Turning Point.* Mechanicsburg, PA: Stackpole Books, 2008.

Lincoln, Abraham. *Collected Works of Abraham Lincoln.* Roy P. Basler, et al., eds. 9 vols. New Brunswick, NJ: Rutgers University Press, 1952–1955.

Lossing, Benson J. *The Pictorial History of the Civil War.* Vol. 1. Philadelphia, PA: G. W. Childs, 1868.

Mackey, Thomas C. "'That All Mankind Should Be Free': Lincoln and African Americans." *OAH Magazine of History* 21, no. 4 (October 2007), pp. 24–29.

May, Samuel J. *Some Reflections of Our Antislavery Conflict.* Boston: Fields, Osgood and Co., 1869.

McFeely, William S. *Frederick Douglass.* New York: Norton, 1990.

McPherson, James. *Battle Cry of Freedom.* New York: Oxford University Press, 1988.

———. *Lincoln and the Second American Revolution.* New York: Oxford University Press, 1991.

———. *This Mighty Scourge: Perspectives on the Civil War.* New York: Oxford University Press, 2007.

———. *Tried by War: Abraham Lincoln as Commander in Chief.* New York: Penguin, 2008.

———. *The Struggle for Equality: Abolitionists and the Negro in the Civil War and Reconstruction.* Princeton, NJ: Princeton University Press, 2014.

Meredith, Roy. *Mr. Lincoln's Camera Man: Mathew B. Brady.* 2nd ed. New York: Dover Publications, 1974.

Nevins, Allan, ed. *Diary of the Civil War: George Templeton Strong.* New York: Macmillan, 1952.

———. *The War for the Union: War Becomes Revolution.* New York: Charles Scribner's Sons, 1960.

Nicolay, John G., and John Hay. *Abraham Lincoln: A History.* 10 vols. New York: The Century Company, 1890.

Oakes, James. *The Radical and the Republican.* New York: W. W. Norton, 2007.

Oates, Stephen B. *To Purge This Land with Blood: A Biography of John Brown.* New York: Harper and Row, 1970.

———. *With Malice Toward None: The Life of Abraham Lincoln.* New York: Mentor, 1978.

Patrick, Rembert W. *The Fall of Richmond.* Baton Rouge: Louisiana State University Press, 1960.

Perret, Geoffrey. *Lincoln's War: The Untold Story of America's Greatest President as Commander in Chief.* New York: Random House, 2004.

Pierson, Michael D. "'All Southern Society Is Assailed by the Foulest Charges': Charles Sumner's 'The Crime against Kansas' and the Escalation of Republication Antislavery Rhetoric." *New England Quarterly* 68, no. 4 (December 1995), pp. 531–57.

Poore, Benjamin Pearly. "Lincoln and the Newspaper Correspondents," in *Reminiscences of Abraham Lincoln by Distinguished Men of His Time*, Allen Thorndike Rice, ed. New York: North American Review, 1888, pp. 327–42.

Porter, David D. *Incidents and Anecdotes of the Civil War.* New York: D. Appleton and Co., 1885.

Porter, Horace. *Campaigning with Grant.* New York: The Century Company, 1907.

Preston, Dickson J. *Young Frederick Douglass.* Baltimore, MD: Johns Hopkins University Press, 2018.

Quarles, Benjamin. *Frederick Douglass.* Washington, D.C.: Associated Publishers, 1948.

———. *Lincoln and the Negro.* Oxford University Press, 1962.

———, ed. *Frederick Douglass.* Englewood, NJ: Prentice-Hall, Inc., 1968.

Randall, Ruth Painter. *Mary Lincoln: A Biography of Marriage.* Boston: Little, Brown, 1953.

Reynolds, David S. *John Brown, Abolitionist: The Man Who Killed Slavery, Sparked the Civil War, and Seeded Civil Rights.* New York: Alfred A. Knopf, 2005.

Ruchames, Louis, ed. *John Brown: The Making of a Revolutionary.* New York: Grosset and Dunlap, 1969.

Rusling, James F. *Men and Things I Saw in Civil War Days.* New York: Eaton and Mains, 1899.

Savage, Kirk. *Standing Soldiers, Kneeling Slaves.* Princeton, NJ: Princeton University Press, 2018.

Searcher, Victor. *Lincoln's Journey to Greatness: A Factual Account of the Twelve-Day Inaugural Trip.* Philadelphia, PA: John C. Winston Co., 1960.

Simpson, Brooks D., ed. *The Civil War: The Third Year Told by Those Who Lived It.* New York: Library of America, 2013.

Speed, Joshua. *Reminiscences of Abraham Lincoln.* Louisville, KY: Bradley and Gilbert Co., 1896.

Starr, Louis M. *Bohemian Brigade: Civil War Newsmen in Action.* New York: Alfred A. Knopf, 1954.

Stauffer, John. *The Black Hearts of Men.* Cambridge, MA: Harvard University Press, 2002.

———. *Giants: The Parallel Lives of Frederick Douglass and Abraham Lincoln.* New York: Twelve, 2008.

Stauffer, John, Zoe Trodd, and Celeste-Marie Bernier. *Picturing Frederick Douglass: An Illustrated Biography of the Nineteenth Century's Most Photographed American.* New York: Liveright, 2015.

Stowe, Charles Edward, and Lyman Beecher Stowe. *Harriet Beecher Stowe: The Story of Her Life.* Boston: Houghton Mifflin Co., 1911.

Sundquist, Eric J., ed. *Frederick Douglass: New Literary and Historical Essays.* Cambridge, UK: Cambridge University Press, 1990.

Temple, Wayne C. "Lincoln's Fence Rails." *Journal of the Illinois State Historical Society* 47, no. 1 (spring 1954), pp. 20–34.

Thomas, John L. *The Liberator, William Lloyd Garrison: A Biography.* Boston: Little, Brown and Co., 1963.

Villard, Oswald Garrison. *John Brown, 1800–1859: A Biography Fifty Years After.* Boston: Houghton Mifflin Co., 1909.

Vorenberg, Michael. *Final Freedom: The Civil War, the Abolition of Slavery, and the Thirteenth Amendment.* Cambridge, UK: Cambridge University Press, 2001.

Waller, Douglas. *Lincoln's Spies: Their Secret War to Save a Nation.* New York: Simon and Schuster, 2019.

Warmoth, Henry Clay. *The Diary of Henry Clay Warmoth, 1861–1867.* Paul H. Hass. MS thesis. University of Wisconsin, 1961.

Welles, Gideon. *Diary of Gideon Welles, Secretary of the Navy under Lincoln and Johnson.* Boston: Houghton Mifflin Co., 1911.

Wickenden, Dorothy. "Lincoln and Douglas: Dismantling the Peculiar Institution." *The Wilson Quarterly* 14, no. 4 (Autumn 1990), pp. 102–12.

Wills, Garry. *Lincoln at Gettysburg: The Words That Remade America.* New York: Simon and Schuster, 1992.

Wilson, Douglas L. *Honor's Voice: The Transformation of Abraham Lincoln.* New York: Alfred A. Knopf, 1998.

Wilson, Douglas L., and Rodney O. Davis, eds. *Herndon's Informant: Letters, Interviews, and Statements About Abraham Lincoln.* Urbana: University of Illinois Press, 1997.

Wilson, Rufus Rockwell. *Intimate Memories of Lincoln.* Elmira, NY: Primavera Press, 1945.

# INDEX

Note: Page numbers in *italics* refer to photographs or illustrations.

Douglass's reservations about, 193
and Eaton, 199–200
education of, 4, 5, 16, 20
and emancipation message spread in
    South, 204–5, 206
emancipation of slaves in Washington,
    D.C., 146–47
Emancipation Proclamation, 151–52, *151*,
    157, 159–63, *162*, 243
emancipation uncoupled from peace
    (proposed), 203–4, 206
on equality, 90, 109, 185, 187, 189–90, 251
evolving views on Black people, 90, 109,
    153, 161, 184–85, 254
evolving views on slavery, 20, 37, 50–51,
    63, 64–65, 87, 149, 153, 198, 247, 254
exposure to plight of enslaved people,
    49–50, 51
flatboat run aground incident, 1–2
at Ford's Theatre, 231–32, 233–35, *324*
and Fort Sumter's fall, 123
Freedman's Memorial, 243–46, *245*
and Frémont's emancipation decree,
    137–40, 150
at the front, 194–98, *196*, *199*
and Fugitive Slave Act, 97, 121, 122
funeral train for, 239–40
Gettysburg Address, 187–88, 189–90, 193
and Grant, 195–98
as "Great Emancipator," 224, 224n, 253
and Harper's Ferry insurrection, 96–97
historical perspective on, 252–53
home of, 39
"House Divided" speech, 87
Illinois General Assembly campaign,
    17–18
inauguration and Inaugural Address,
    First, 115, 120–22
inauguration and Inaugural Address,
    Second, 210, 213–18, *215*, *221*, 240
and Kansas–Nebraska Act, 62–63, 64–65
law practice of, 19, 20, 36, 39
leaving Illinois for Washington, 113–14
*liberty for all* as benchmark of, 115
and literacy, 5
marriage to Mary Todd, 39
militia service of, 17
Peoria speech of, 63, 64–65, 89
photograph made by Brady, 93–95, *95*,
    105–6, *105*

presidential election (1840), 37
presidential election (1860), 101–3, 104–8
presidential election (1864), *194*, 195–96,
    197–98, 203, 206–7, 207n
and "Rail Splitter" moniker, 101–3,
    106, *107*
reading of, 5, 16
reason exercised by, 37
reputation for truthfulness, 62
in Richmond after capture of
    city, 222–26
in Richmond after fall of city, *225*
and secession crisis, 114, 116–17, 121–22
service in U.S. House, 49, 50, 87
service on Illinois legislature, 19, 20, 39
on slavery as cause of Civil War, 210, 213,
    217, 218, 253
sobriety of, 16
speaking/oratory skills of, 16–17
and Stowe, 160–61
and Sumner, 148–50
surveying work of, 18–19
and Thirteenth Amendment, 211, 213,
    213n, 243
Union preservation as priority of, 115,
    156, 190, 193, 247, 254–55
U.S. Senate campaign, 87–91
victory speech of, 230
on voting rights of Black citizens, 255
and wrestling match with Armstrong,
    13–15, *15*
youth of, 3–6, 3n
Lincoln, Eddie (son), 49, 62
Lincoln, Mary Todd (wife), *38*, *143*
abolitionism of, 147, 147n
background of, 38, 147
children of, 39, 62
and death of son, Willie, 143
early relationship with Lincoln, 37–39
head injury of, 173, 175
and Lincoln's assassination, *324*, *325*
and Lincoln's second inauguration, *221*
marriage to Lincoln, 39
in mourning for Lincoln, 239–40
move to Washington, D.C., 49
and postwar mood of Lincoln, 231
and presidential campaign (1860), 103
and Sumner, 147–48, 147n
and walking stick given to Douglass,
    240–41

# IMAGE CREDITS

p. 15   A young Lincoln wrestles Jack Armstrong: Historical Images Archive / Alamy Stock Photo.

p. 27   Anna Murray Douglass: Frederick Douglass National Historic Site / NPS

p. 32   William Lloyd Garrison: Library of Congress, Prints & Photographs Division [LC-USZ62-10320]

p. 35   First photo of Frederick Douglass: Collection of Greg French

p. 38   (Left) Abraham Lincoln, Congressman-elect from Illinois: Library of Congress, Prints & Photographs Division, photograph by Nicholas H. Shepherd [LC-DIG-ppmsca-53842]

p. 38   (Right) Mary Todd Lincoln, wife of Abraham Lincoln: Library of Congress, Prints & Photographs Division, photograph by Nicholas H. Shepherd [LC-USZ6-300]

p. 43   *Fighting the Mob in Indiana:* Frederick Douglass, *Life and Times of Frederick Douglass, Written by Himself, His Early Life as a Slave, His Escape from Bondage, and His Complete History to the Present Time,* by Frederick Douglass (Hartford, CT: Park Publishing Co., 1881), p. 235

p. 45   *The Fugitive's Song:* Library of Congress, Prints & Photographs Division [LC-DIG-ppmsca-07616]

p. 54   Portrait of Gerrit Smith: Boston Public Library

p. 59   Title page from volume 1, U.S. first edition of *Uncle Tom's Cabin: or, Life Among the Lowly* by Harriet Beecher Stowe (1811–1896) published in 1852: AF Fotografie / Alamy Stock Photo

p. 60   Author and abolitionist Harriet Beecher Stowe: Library of Congress, Prints & Photographs Division, Liljenquist Family collection [LC-DIG-ppmsca-49807]

p. 67   Charles Sumner: National Archives

p. 68   *Arguments of the Chivalry* print: Library of Congress, Prints & Photographs Division [LC-USZ62-38851]

p. 70   John Brown: Library of Congress, Prints & Photographs Division [LC-USZ62-106337]

p. 74   Dred Scott: Library of Congress, Prints & Photographs Division by Century Company [LC-USZ62-5092]

IMAGE CREDITS

p. 170 Robert E. Lee at Chancellorsville: Library of Congress, Prints & Photographs Division [LC-USZ62-51832]

p. 174 *The Battle of Gettysburg:* Library of Congress, Prints & Photographs Division [LC-DIG-pga-03266]

p. 176 *Storming Fort Wagner:* Library of Congress, Prints & Photographs Division by Kurz & Allison [LC-DIG-pga-01949]

p. 180 Secretary of War Edwin Stanton: Library of Congress, Prints & Photographs Division, Liljenquist Family Collection [LC-DIG-ppmsca-52235]

p. 184 Frederick Douglass, 1863: Edwin Burke Ives (1832–1906) and Reuben L. Andrews, January 21 1863, Howell Street, Hillsdale, MI, Carte-de-viste (2½ x 4 in), Hillsdale College. Photograph courtesy of Hillsdale College

p. 191 Lincoln portrait by Alexander Gardner: Library of Congress, Prints & Photographs Division by Alexander Gardner [LC-DIG-npcc-01932]

p. 194 *Long Abraham Lincoln a Little Longer* cartoon: *Harper's Weekly*, November 26, 1864

p. 196 *President Lincoln, General Grant, and Tad Lincoln at a Railway Station* sketch: Purchase from the J. H. Wade Fund, the Cleveland Museum of Art

p. 199 President Lincoln at Fort Stevens: Courtesy DC Public Library, The People's Archive

p. 208 Frederick Douglass at Lloyd family graveyard: From the New York Public Library

p. 212 Passage of the Thirteenth Amendment: *Harper's Weekly*, 18 February 1865

p. 215 President Abraham Lincoln delivering second inaugural address in front of the U.S. Capitol, March 4, 1865: Library of Congress, Prints & Photographs Division by Alexander Gardner [LC-USZ62-8122]

p. 221 *Abraham Lincoln's Last Reception*: Library of Congress, Prints & Photographs Division [LC-DIG-pga-01590]

p. 225 Lincoln shaking hands with a Black Union soldier (*City Point/65--"Good god, you goin to shake with me, Uncle Abe"*): Library of Congress, Miscellaneous Items in High Demand by Charles W. Reed [LC-USZ62-75182]

p. 228 *The Surrender of General Lee. And His Entire Army to Lieut General Grant, April 9th, 1865*: Library of Congress, Prints & Photographs Division by John Smith [LC-DIG-pga 08989]

p. 230 John Wilkes Booth: Library of Congress, Prints & Photographs Division [LC-USZ62-25166]

p. 234 *Assassination of Lincoln*: Library of Congress National Photo Company Collection [LC-F81-2117]

p. 236 Lincoln on his deathbed surrounded by mourners: Library of Congress, Prints & Photographs Division [LC-DIG-ppmsca-46775]

p. 244 Fred K. Douglas (i.e., Frederick Douglass): Library of Congress, Prints & Photographs Division by Mathew B. Brady [LC-DIG-ppmsca-70869]

p. 245 Emancipation statue, Washington, D.C.: Library of Congress, Prints & Photographs Division, Detroit Publishing Company [LC-DIG-det-4a05594]

p. 249 Frederick Douglass, Helen Pitts Douglass and Eva: National Park Service (FRDO 3912)

p. 250 Abraham Lincoln, portrait by William E. Marshall: Library of Congress, Prints & Photographs Division [LC-DIG-ppmsca-46791]

p. 252 Frederick Douglass in His Study at Cedar Hill: National Park Service (FRDO3886)